This book is dedicated to my son and daughter-in-law,
Joseph and Erin White.

Collected Plays
by Katheryn White

White Light Press

Direct performance inquiries to the playwright:
Sojournerkw@aol.com

© 2009 Katheryn White/ Literary Guild East
White Light Press
71 Mt. Tabor Way
Ocean Grove NJ 07756
(732) 897-1451

ISBN: 978-0-578-01934-5

First Edition

Table of Contents

Alien Doctor
A Play in One Act

SETTING: sparsely decorated New York City apartment, the present.

CHARACTERS

STANLEY: a physician

ANA: a psychiatrist with a foreign-sounding accent

Discordant modern synthesizer music playing. Ana is exercising on the floor. Stanley watches her lustfully. He turns off music and lures her to the couch.

STANLEY

We never go anywhere.

ANA

Where would you like to go?

STANLEY

Ana dear, we've known each other for over a year. Couldn't we at least go away for a weekend?

ANA

A whole weekend Stanley? (He nods.) Maybe next year. (He pours himself a drink.)

STANLEY

I hate scotch.

ANA

Then why do you drink it?

STANLEY

Because you are so cold.

ANA

You will ruin your liver.

STANLEY

Good, then you can take it out.

ANA

I don't do surgery. You do surgery.

STANLEY

I can't operate on myself. I don't trust any of my greedy colleagues. So I guess I'll die. (She pours herself a drink.)

ANA

If that's what you want. (She toasts him) I have no time for your self-indulgent whining.

STANLEY

Shrinks are supposed to be sympathetic

ANA

I provide sympathy to my patients, not my lovers.

STANLEY

Is that all I am to you, a lover?

ANA

Is that bad?

STANLEY

You know we are more than that. What about our common interests? We're both doctors.

ANA

Our specialties are very different.

STANLEY

Are you embarrassed to be involved with a proctologist?

ANA

Don't be silly. My work explores the scope of the mind while yours...

STANLEY

Up the behind! I'm tired of proctology jokes. I'm tired of your arrogant attitude. I'm tired of begging and pleading for your time and space.

ANA

Then why don't you stop?

STANLEY

It's not that simple. I think I'm in love with you.

ANA

Don't you know?

STANLEY

I must be in love with you. Women call me and chase me all day long. All I see and think of is you.

ANA

Sounds like obsessive compulsive disorder to me.

STANLEY

Don't analyze me. You're giving me a nervous breakdown.

ANA

I'm not giving you anything.

STANLEY

Alright I'm having a nervous breakdown.

ANA

Please have the good taste not to have it here.

STANLEY

(He scrutinizes messy room, reaches behind pillow and holds up a rather plain bra.) What do you know about good taste? This is about as feminine as a jockstrap.

ANA

Forgive me. I'm alien.

STANLEY

Most aliens are tidy-clean freaks. Even with a maid, your place is a mess.

ANA

I have priorities.

STANLEY

And I'm not one of them. (She pours them more scotch)

ANA

But you are. I think about you all the time.

STANLEY

Then why can't you make a commitment to me?

ANA

It's very complicated.

STANLEY

We have the whole night. Explain.

ANA

Alright. I will try. Sit close to me.

STANLEY

Don't think about seducing me and changing the subject. I want to talk about us.

ANA

Alright. I have something to show you.)She goes to the closet) It must be out secret.

STANLEY

I'd be amazed if you could find anything in that closet.

ANA

It's sort of buried in the back.

STANLEY

(Anxious) I hope it's not the corpse of your dead husband.

ANA

I have no husband. (She comes out of the closet wearing a globe-like bubble space helmet. She is very serious.)

STANLEY

What on Earth is that?

ANA

My hat. Do you like it?

STANLEY

Does it come in bronze?

ANA

No. Let's sit down and discuss our lives.

STANLEY

Are you nuts? Does dressing up turn you on? Is this why you
can't make a commitment.

ANA

Yes.

STANLEY

Yes to what? Being crazy? Space dressing?

ANA

Calm down. Sit and listen.

STANLEY

Are you going to take off that helmet? (She shakes her head.) Can
you hear well enough to tell me the truth? (She nods.)

ANA

I am alien.

STANLEY

Big news. I knew you didn't pick up that accent at Columbia.

ANA

I'm not of east European descent, as you speculated. I'm sorry if I
mislead you.

STANLEY

I was wondering why you don't drink vodka. Then where does
your accent come from?

ANA

Poor communication and antiquated interpretative devices.

STANLEY
So where are you from, New Jersey?

ANA
No, I'm from another solar system.

STANLEY
Give me a break!

ANA
I'm trying to. Let me explain.

STANLEY
What is the name of your planet?

ANA
The name doesn't translate to English well.

STANLEY
I hope it's not Uranus. (She shakes her head) Where is it?

ANA
It's very complicated. You need to travel through a black hole.

STANLEY
(Raises his hands in frustration) Figures. I have to fall in love
with a woman from an alternate universe.

ANA
It's a nice planet.

STANLEY
Do they wear those helmets all the time?

ANA
No. These are just for traveling.

STANLEY
Could I visit you there?

ANA
Of course. You know Stanley I love the feel of my helmet. It
makes me so homesick.

STANLEY
Could we get married there?

ANA
There's no marriage there.

STANLEY
Stay here.

ANA
I miss my home. It has been three years.

STANLEY
Are there many aliens like you here infiltrating innocent people's lives? (She nods) must be good for your practice.

ANA
I received all my degrees from American and German universities on my last trip.

STANLEY
Do you want to take back part of me as a souvenir from this visit?

ANA
It depends on which part you would like to offer.

STANLEY
Take off that helmet and talk to me.

ANA
No, I like it. I have one in my closet you can wear.

STANLEY
Did it belong to a former lover from outer space?

ANA
No, it's spare. I brought it in case I met someone special. (She goes to closet and brings out other helmet.) Do you like it?

STANLEY
I can't wear that. Are you making me the victim of some sort of role playing game?

ANA

Please try on the hat. It will look so nice on you. (He obeys.)
Looking at you like this makes me more homesick.

STANLEY

How do you get home from here?

ANA

(She goes back to her closet and retrieves her ray-gun.) You have
to shoot me.

STANLEY

I'm a pacifist. I can't even squash a cockroach.

ANA

Please. It's not a deadly weapon. It will evacuate me, not kill me.
(She places gun in his hands.)

STANLEY

I can't shoot a living being. You are living, aren't you?

ANA

Look, Stanley, I could shoot myself and disappear, but it would
mean so much to me if you would shoot me.

SAN

Ana, do you realize this is the closest to intimacy we've ever
gotten?

ANA

If you want to join me on my planet then after shooting me, you
simply shoot yourself.

STANLEY

Sounds like Romeo and Juliet.

ANA

You want romance.

STANLEY

I don't want resurrection.

ANA

We could live together forever in an alternate universe.

STANLEY

Could you bring me back home for the holidays?

ANA

Please shoot me Stanley. I want to go home.

STANLEY

This is so sudden. Do you love me?

ANA

Love has nothing to do with creating interplanetary connections.

STANLEY

Couldn't we just go to the Hamptons first?

ANA

Shoot!

STANLEY

Paris for a week?

ANA

I slept with your friend John.

STANLEY

(His whole body shakes nervously as he tries to steady the gun.)
Not my best friend John? (She nods, baiting him)
John and I went to Harvard together and he's a catholic.

ANA

Obviously, you boys learned many useful things there.

STANLEY

When did you and John do it?

ANA

Last week when you were at malpractice conference in L.A.

                    STANLEY
I'm shocked. I'm devastated. I'm...
(in a panic, he shoots her.)
... a killer!
(Lights flash in strobe as she disappears. Her bra is left behind.
He picks it up and addresses the audience.)

Is this the end or beginning of our relationship?

(He puts bra in his pocket and plays with his gun. Lights fade. In
darkness we hear another gunshot.)

End of Scene 1.

Setting: sparsely decorated room on Nexus, six months later.

*A variation of the discordant synthesizer music from scene 1 is playing. Ana and
Stanley are dressed in identical body-suits. Stanley is smoking a water pipe and
appears quite relaxed. Ana is reading a bloomingdale's catalog and appears
agitated. The room is sparse and monochromatic. Framed portraits of Stanley's
parents are on one side of the couch table and drawings of Ana's parents are on the
other. Stanley's parents are sophisticated eastsiders. Ana's parents have sort of light
bulb heads with no hair.*

                    ANA
We never go anywhere.

                    STANLEY
Where would you like to go?

                    ANA
(She slams down magazine and paces.) Shopping. I want to go
shopping.

                    STANLEY
Ana darling, there is no need to shop here. Everything is
provided.

                    ANA
Stanley you don't understand. I miss the process of shopping. I
miss all the cosmetic counters at Bloomingdales. I miss those
fabulous boutiques at Bendels. I miss the service at Saks. I miss
the smoked salmon at Zabars.

STANLEY

Try to relax. (He offers her a smoke. She turns away, angry.) We need nothing here.

ANA

I miss the challenge of being a consumer. I miss choosing colors, textures, spices. Stanley, it's more than the sales - oh the sales. Do you realize that this Bloomingdales catalog is more than a season old? I cant imagine what I'm missing.

STANLEY

I miss nothing. This is Utopia!

ANA

It's not Utopia. It's Nexus - my home planet, the center of the universe, nowhere.

STANLEY

(He embraces her from the back in sort of a bear hug. She fights it.)
I came here for you; to make you happy.

ANA

Well, I'm not happy.

STANLEY

(He releases her.) Well, I'm not sure I want to return to Earth.

ANA

Earth is your home.

STANLEY

Home is with you. I'm so glad you tricked me into this.

ANA

We can go back the same way. (She runs to closet and gets helmets and gun. He stretches out on couch relaxed. He beckons her. She sets helmets at foot of couch then sits at edge of couch and plays with gun. When he caresses her neck, she stiffens.)

STANLEY

Stop playing with that gun.

ANA

Stanley I think you are jealous of my gun. I let you play with it.
(He takes it from here and sets it behind the couch.)

STANLEY

I don't want any accidents. I may want to visit Earth sometime,
but not soon. I'm falling in love with this temperate climate, slow
pace, natural food, immaculate shelters and simple clothing.

ANA

You want to become like this atmosphere - Sterile.

STANLEY

There's nothing like life in a controlled germ free environment.

ANA

With the stimulation of running around the interior of a bell jar.

STANLEY

There's always the free library.

ANA

Everything is free here. Yet, all of the Earth's great literature is
not included here.

STANLEY

I guess there's a limit to what you can catch on microfilm.

ANA

The hybrids seem to favor Harold Robbins over Shakespeare.

STANLEY

They have a ton of poetry. We can spend the evening reading to
each other.

ANA

We did that last night. Canned Bach chamber music the night
before. I want to go to a disco. have you wondered why there
aren't any discos here?

STANLEY

Obvious. Discos are unsanitary- too much closeness and sweat.
You never wanted to go to a disco on Earth.

ANA

I have the choice on Earth. Here there are only elevated arts, high moral standards and the ripest fruit.

STANLEY

And clean air. It's amazing! No one smokes, pollutes or sweats here.

ANA

Sweat cleanses your pores.

STANLEY

Sweat smells. Kiss me. (She obeys then pulls back.) Why are you acting unhappy?

ANA

I'm not acting, I am unhappy. (She gets up. He lays on his back feeding himself grapes from the end table.)

STANLEY

Have some grapes. Perhaps your blood sugar is low.

ANA

Don't start talking like an Earth doctor.

STANLEY

God, I wish the hybrids would allow me to bring some of their medical knowledge back to Earth. No diseases, no pain. People just die of old age.

ANA

Old age and boredom.

STANLEY

You're bored because you are a mutant. Your Earth assimilation gave you a unique identity, a different value system and hair.

ANA

The hybrids here, with their light bulb heads, want so badly to look like you. It takes several generations of hybrids mixing with humans to create a humanoid mutant, like me.

STANLEY

(Embraces her affectionately) I'll testify that it's well worth the wait. All those pitiful Earth men, like me, don't have a clue to what's missing in their lives.

ANA

On Earth you said you wanted to marry me. Do you still want to?

STANLEY

There's no marriage here.

ANA

(She sits close to him, forcing him to reposition himself.) I know marriage is not practices here. What I'm asking you is do you still want to marry me?

STANLEY

Read my lips. No - marriage - here.

ANA

Do you love me?

STANLEY

I love everybody here.

ANA

(Becoming terribly agitated) That's what's wrong with this place. Everybody looks the same, sounds the same, feels the same. I can't stand it. It's too easy.

STANLEY

It's not easy. It's simple. Beauty in simplicity. Life as art.

ANA

On Earth you're a proctologist. Here you're a philosopher.

STANLEY

Maybe tomorrow night we should read Laotse.

ANA

I'd prefer Ayn Rand.

STANLEY

Let me massage you.

ANA

(She lets him massage her neck and back.) Stanley, I've been thinking a lot about Earth marriages and relationships. I miss the way you used to beg.

STANLEY

(Laughs.) I don't roll over and play dead anymore either.

ANA

Stanley you can't imagine how I long for those words.

STANLEY

Which words?

ANA

Will you marry me?

STANLEY

I can't believe you really want to get married.

ANA

Remember ow jealous you were of your friend John and me? What happened to those feelings?

STANLEY

I feel no anger towards John. I guess in a way, he's indirectly responsible for landing us here.

ANA

I want to marry you Stanley and I want to go back to Earth.

STANLEY

Not to live? Don't tell me you actually want to live on that extinct planet.

ANA

Part of the time.

STANLEY

If I go through this marriage ceremony on Earth do you promise
we'll come back here in a week?

ANA

I not only promise, but I'll make sure you get your own gun so you
can come back here whenever you wish.

STANLEY

Gee they don't allow aliens here their own gun. Do you really
think you can arrange it?

ANA

We know I've earned the best connections.

STANLEY

I just hoe you're not going to try and trick me when we get back to
Earth.

ANA

Why would I trick you? I love you. I want to marry you.

STANLEY

Do you think your family will make the wedding?

ANA

(Points to their photos) They won't fit in.
If we could find a way to disguise them, they might find the
ceremony amusing.

STANLEY

Amusing? What do you have in mind?

ANA

A church. A long white gown. "Here comes the bride."

STANLEY

The works.

ANA

(She stands and pulls him toward her.) The works.

STANLEY
Who's going to pay for this shindig?

ANA
You still have money on Earth. Actually I still have money there.
We'll have a blast.

STANLEY
Sure after we blow it all, we can shoot each other and land back
here.

ANA
Not such a bad deal.

STANLEY
My parents will never understand.

ANA
Oh, I'll finally get to meet them.

STANLEY
It won't be easy.

ANA
They'll love me.

STANLEY
My mother terrorized all my girlfriends. She'll scrutinize you,
test you, take you to Saks.

ANA
Saks. That's where we'll form our bond.

STANLEY
Where should I say you're from?

ANA
You won't tell them the truth?

STANLEY
They'd rather hear a nice lie. Nice lies, like good manners create
safe distances.

                    ANA
Oh Stanley, you are becoming a philosopher.

                    STANLEY
I like wallowing in the world of ideas.

                    ANA
I think, your family, like you, are well educated people. They'll
understand me.

                    STANLEY
Because they are well educated they will never understand you or
this state of affairs.

                    ANA
Your father is a psychiatrist, like me.

                    STANLEY
Not like you. He's a Freudian. It will take forever.

                    ANA
Alright, tell them I'm from Romania.

                    STANLEY
How do I explain your parents.

                    ANA
(Looks at her parents' portraits) I'll have to find them wigs, hats,
makeup and clothes. Say I'm adopted.

                    STANLEY
We'll rewrite history.

                    ANA
Everybody does.

                    STANLEY
But I do have to warn you that my mother can be very difficult.
She'll never stop asking you questions. She'll try to trick you.
She never forgets any details or facts.

                    ANA
Being a New York D.A. is a very hard job.

STANLEY

And she makes it harder. I wouldn't want to be up against her in court.

ANA

Maybe we better tell her the truth about me.

STANLEY

What if she freaks out?

ANA

Then we'll just have to shoot her.

STANLEY

(Taken a back) Shoot my mom?

ANA

With the ray gun Stanley. We could bring her here.

STANLEY

Oh no. Her metabolism couldn't stand all this tranquility. She'd paint everything hot pink.

ANA

I bet your mother will be great at planning our reception.

STANLEY

Reception? Where? Why? How?

ANA

(She nods and smiles) The Plaza Hotel. Because it is one of the most romantic places in New York. We'll charge everything.

STANLEY

(Takes her in his arms.) It will be out of this world.

ANA

Oh Stanley. We are the luckiest of beings. We will possess the best of both possible worlds.
(They start making love as lights dim.)

END SCENE II

SCENE III

Setting: suite in Plaza Hotel, a few weeks later.

A variation of synthesizer piece from previous parts. Stanley and Ana are in robes in living room section of their suite. They are drinking champagne in front of mute TV.

ANA

I love being alone with you Stanley.

STANLEY

Marriage means never having to be alone again.

ANA

We had the kind of wedding people only dream about. (She gets up and uses her wedding veil as a multi-purpose prop.) Everything was perfect. No one could believe my dress. Ecru really is my color. No one will ever know it's a Valentino sample. Your mother filled the chapel with white roses, calla lilies. And you said she wasn't sincere. When your friend sang "Because" I saw your father wipe a tear from his eye. Everyone had fun at the reception. We should have danced more. But there's never enough time.

STANLEY

You never looked more beautiful.

ANA

I wanted you to dance with me all night. I wanted to cry when the music stopped.

STANLEY

All celebrations end.

ANA

I want to hold this night. I want tonight's warm glowing images to crystallize in my imagination.

STANLEY

You've become a poet Ana.

ANA

It's all that reading we did to each other on Nexus. Something clicked.

STANLEY

A short circuit?

ANA

Maybe a bolt of lightning between hemispheres.

STANLEY

Are you serious?

ANA

Kiss me. Recharge my magnetic field (They kiss and laugh, playfully.)

STANLEY

What do you miss most about Nexus?

ANA

The politics.

STANLEY

There's no politics there.

ANA

Exactly. What do you miss?

STANLEY

The tranquility. And I miss the way that the stars appear so low you feel that you could almost touch them.

ANA

It is beautiful. But here we have TV.

STANLEY

You really did miss TV, didn't you? (She nods.) And I thought I was in love with this great intellectual.

ANA

I miss my work on Earth. There's no need for psychiatrists on Nexus. I would like to practice here 11 months a year and spend August in Nexus.

STANLEY

We agreed to divide the year half on Earth and half on Nexus.

ANA

I wish my parents came.

STANLEY

My parents understood your story. I had a hard time keeping a straight face; especially when you described how painstaking their experiments are with apes in Tanzania. Someday they'll have to come home and my mother will insist on meeting them.

ANA

By then they'll love me and I can take them to Nexus and show them incredible ape humanoid mutations.

STANLEY

You never cease to amaze me. Your brain power is like a computer, once you're fed information you can immediately process it.

ANA

It's not just me. It's everyone on Nexus. Our educational system is a millennium ahead of yours.

STANLEY

I really miss Nexus.

ANA

We are not scheduled to return until next month. I want to go to the theater, museums, discos and Bloomingdales.

STANLEY

At some point I am going to have to try to explain Nexus to my family. They don't understand me wanting to spend half the year in Africa when I have such a good practice here. And the other doctors in my group don't understand the concept of a freelance proctologist.

ANA

What about me? I can't be a part time therapist. Patients expect
to see a shrink at least once a week. The only thing I can do is
work part time at an emergency center where I can refer people.

STANLEY

Maybe you should learn a new profession. Only take you a couple
of weeks.

ANA

Do you think there's a market for freelance brain surgery?

STANLEY

I know. Study proctology.

ANA

Maybe. We are such a good team.

STANLEY

Oh no. That could evolve into a whole new set of proctology
jokes.

ANA

What do married alien proctologists do during a fight?

STANLEY

Turn the other cheek. (He winces.)

ANA

Alright, I know you hate proctology jokes. I'll find another
freelance profession.

STANLEY

How about wife and mother.

ANA

That's a full time job.

STANLEY

No time off, but great benefits. God what could our kid be like?

ANA

Humanoid. Probably born with your looks and my intelligence.

                    STANLEY
I'm not so dumb. I was in Mensa.

                     ANA
Primary education is best on Nexus. Once you learn the basics
you can live anywhere.

                    STANLEY
Will it take 9 months. Or do they speed that up on Nexus?

                     ANA
It will take 9 months. But I know how to avoid pain and have a
speedy delivery.

                    STANLEY
Maybe we should have a whole bunch of kids.

                     ANA
An interplanetary football team.

                    STANLEY
Oh, let's get started. (He leads her toward the bedroom.)

                     ANA
Let's watch a little TV first.

                    STANLEY
But darling, I'm in the mood.

                     ANA
Hold that thought. It's time for David Letterman.

                    STANLEY
Talk shows on our wedding night?

                     ANA
How about a movie? (She turns on TV with remote)

                    STANLEY
(He takes remote away from her. Tries leading her to bedroom.)
Let's create something special.
(She takes back remote.)

ANA

That's it! I'll infiltrate NYU and learn filmmaking, or maybe I'll become a great playwright in the manner of Neil Simon, and make a lot of money so we can buy a mansion in the Hamptons.

STANLEY

Ana darling. Try to be happy and content with what we have. Our lives are perfect.

ANA

Intellectual challenges are most important to me here.

STANLEY

When you have the power to be anything and do everything where's the challenge?

ANA

The challenge is in the process. The rewards are secondary.

STANLEY

The rewards are primary here. I wouldn't do proctology for free.

ANA

You mean you do it for the money?

STANLEY

What other satisfaction could one get in my field? There aren't too many perfect assholes.

ANA

I didn't realize you had such low job satisfaction.

STANLEY

It's not a problem if I know I will be able to spend half a year on Nexus.

ANA

I guess we are so lucky that we have the best of both worlds.

STANLEY

You are the best of all worlds.

                         ANA
I am so glad I can make you happy. You can make me happy by
watching a little TV. (He shirks.) Please. Just 30 minutes. (He
pouts, but sits beside her on couch.) I promise we will have at least
45 minutes of lovemaking later.

                       STANLEY
What about the morning?

                         ANA
You know I love the *TODAY* show.

                       STANLEY
Maybe we can get in some quickies during the commercials.

                         ANA
(She kisses him on the forehead.)
Whatever you say my darling.

Ana clicks on TV remote

                    TV NEWSMAN
This is your emergency broadcast network. This is not a test. We
are in a state of emergency. I repeat this is an emergency.

The national guard in on alert to assist people to subways and
shelters (Faint sirens heard from outside.) Astronomers from
Goddard Space Labs have spotted a meteorite through their
Hubble telescope. It weights about 1,000 tons, is streaking
through Earth's atmosphere and heading for New York City. If
we're lucky it will head back into space. If not... (static, picture on
screen goes)

                         ANA
That's about the same size as the meteorite reported to have
destroyed the atmosphere on Mars.

                       STANLEY
Fine time for an astronomy lesson. Where is your gun?

ANA

Should be in my suitcase. (She heads to bedroom) The helmets
may be at your folds place with the bulk of our luggage. (She
returns with gun)

STANLEY

How could you leave our helmets there? Oh God my folks. What
do we do? (Heads for the phone.) It's dead. Lines must be jammed.
How can we alert them?

ANA

Without our helmets it will be a rough trip - quite dangerous.

STANLEY

What do we do? Where do we go? (The lights go dim)

ANA

Stanley, I'm scared. This is supposed to be the happiest night of
our lives.

STANLEY

It may be our last night. Hold me.

ANA

We have to leave this room. We have to find shelter. Flee to safety
of the New York subways.

STANLEY

The gun Ana. Maybe we should risk the trip and go back.

ANA

Maybe the alert will pass. Maybe it's a false alarm.

STANLEY

Maybe this is the end of the world. It's frightening to look out the
window and see total darkness.

ANA

The sirens got fainter. What does that mean? Where can we go?

STANLEY

Let's go to Nexus.

                              ANA
What about this city? Our friends? Our family?

                           STANLEY
There is no choice, you have to shoot us. We can do nothing to
save them. Their lies are in the hands of fate. Our fate is within
your hands. Shoot!

                              ANA
I know. We can protect our heads with my bridal veil and your top
hat. They are not as sturdy as our helmets but can help diffuse the
turbulence.
(She fetches them and they put them on_

                           STANLEY
How fortunate we chose to get married today.

                              ANA
Oh how I'll miss that tiny plastic couple from atop our wedding
cake.

                           STANLEY
(He takes her in his arms.)
My darling, maybe someday we can return to Earth.

                              ANA
And excavate some of our sacred memories. (She puts plastic
bride and groom in her robe pocket.)

                           STANLEY
Anything you want. The future is yours my darling. For now,
will you please shoot!

*The lights go totally out. The sirens become louder. Two shots are heard. Lights
come up to show an empty room. A sign drops from the heaves "The End."*

                          END

Dream Street

CAST OF CHARACTERS

CONNIE: A playwright over 30; dresses simply, in black, complimented by a necklace of pearls.

CONSTANCE: An actress over 50; dresses with the elegance of another era, wears a long necklace of pearls.

JOHN: A lighting designer/technician, over 30.

SCENE: The stage of an empty theater, on Broadway, in New York City.

TIME: The Present

SETTING: The stage is set for a rehearsal of Connie's play "Encores." Furniture is covered with drop cloths. A covered mirror rests upstage. A small table is set with wine, two goblets, and a candle, down stage left. Connie's purse and script rest on a stool, down stage right.

AT RISE: It is around 10 p.m. Connie appears upstage center, shielding her eyes from the sudden intense glare of stage lights. She is holding a note and flashlight while focusing on John, the lighting technician, opposite her above the rear of the house in the lighting booth.

> CONNIE
> (She is anxious, testy. He is calm, obsequious.) I want just enough light to see the stage. (Lights dim) Give me one spot, stage right, on the stool. (Spot appears on stool) Can you set the timer to turn the lights off at midnight?

> JOHN
> What if the lights go out and your meeting isn't over?

> CONNIE
> I have my flashlight.

> JOHN
> The flashlight is awfully small. The darkness can play strange tricks on your imagination. I can set it for later.

CONNIE

No. I'm not afraid of the dark. Besides, I have my candle. I'll be fine. Trust me.

JOHN

Do you want me to stay until he gets here? I'm worried about your safety. He could be some kind of nut.

CONNIE

No, John, go on home. I'll be fine. Believe me. Though I do wish you had gotten a look at him. I wonder what you could have been doing when he was in your booth.

JOHN

It's a mystery how he got into my lighting booth, taped that note for you onto my follow spot. I always lock this booth. I'm really sorry I missed him.

CONNIE

It is puzzling. Unless my secret admirer is connected with the show.

JOHN

Who? Your cast includes femme fatales of the geriatric stage and a young gay guy.

CONNIE

Then it has to be someone from the outside or some shadow from my past.

JOHN

An old beau is better than an axe murderer.

CONNIE

You haven't met some of my old beaus.

JOHN

I'm worried.

CONNIE

My only worry is that he won't show up. (She looks at her note hopefully).

JOHN

Think positive.

CONNIE

It's getting late. You should leave. Go home.

JOHN

Alright, alright, I'm going. Take care of yourself, okay?

CONNIE

Okay, 'nite.

(She waves goodbye and watches him leave. When alone she pours herself wine and addresses the empty audience. She looks at her watch, picks up her script, and focuses stage left, fretting to herself. We hear Maurice Ravel's "Pavane for a Dead Princess" (piano version) faintly grow in the background.)

CONNIE

I'm not even sure that this is a happy ending; it's largo and I want adagio. If I make any more last-minute changes the actors will kill me.

(Constance, unnoticed, moves quietly through the house towards the stage)

CONNIE-CONT

That music...my dream.

(Constance appears stage right, carrying a loaf of bread)

CONNIE

(Startled, breathless) Oh! I...I...

(Music becomes very low)

CONSTANCE

Didn't expect to see me.

CONNIE
The note said a secret admirer.

CONSTANCE
And you expected a man.

CONNIE
(Embarrassed, nods) I am happy to see you.

CONSTANCE
Especially now.

CONNIE
Yes, especially now. (Pours wine for the both of them)

CONSTANCE
(Sniffs wine) Heavenly bouquet.

CONNIE
It's not Cote Rotie.

CONSTANCE
(Music fades) Our secret.

CONNIE
I've missed you so much.

CONSTANCE
I'm always with you.

CONNIE
I talk to you a lot when I'm alone.

CONSTANCE
I hear you.

CONNIE
Why am I always so scared; afraid of making the wrong choices?

CONSTANCE
We're born scared. The light is blinding.

CONNIE

Then comes the rain.

CONSTANCE

Rain is absorbed with sunshine.

Connie I've always been intrigued by the movement of the clouds.
After Aunt Anna died, I lay on my back in the grass, looking at
the sky and tracing the patters of her life.

CONSTANCE

You never shared that with me before.

CONNIE

I forgot. I guess I buried that memory. I was five.

CONSTANCE

Anna was 35 when she died.

CONNIE

She had a heavy laugh.

CONSTANCE

She had tuberculosis.

CONNIE

She liked making people laugh. I remember her doing some
dance with long white gloves at parties.

CONSTANCE

She did a lot of impersonations. She was a wonderful
comedienne. The dance you remember was one an actress named
Joan Davis did in vaudeville...way before your time.

CONNIE

I remember when I was about 10 years old and going through a
trunk in our attic and finding Aunt Anna's gown and gloves. I
put them on and felt her energy. Her willowy spirit moved me...I
danced and danced to the silent music of my imagination.

CONSTANCE

Music was on of your gifts. You were an excellent pianist.

CONNIE

I worked very hard. I was never good enough.

CONSTANCE

Oh, I loved your playing.

CONNIE

It brought me stress. I started too late. My technique was weak. I couldn't get into Julliard.

CONSTANCE

You always wanted the best.

CONNIE

I was taught never to accept anything less.

CONSTANCE

With that lesson the struggle begins.

CONNIE

I wanted to be like you.

CONSTANCE

A starving actress.

CONNIE

You were wonderful, hardly starving. That reminds me. I had a dream about you the other night. It was strange because it included you, my family, and my horrid ex-husband Sam. That haunting melody I heard when you appeared tonight, Ravel's "Pavane for a Dead Princess", played in the background in my dream.

CONSTANCE

A dream set to music; how lovely. You haven't lost your gift, you've exchanged music for another legacy. That reminds me. Connie, look at yourself. You're putting on weight.

CONNIE

(She looks at herself at covered mirror, as if she can see) You were lucky; never had to worry about your weight.

CONSTANCE

I wasn't lucky, I watched what I ate. I enjoyed chocolates, champagne, but always in moderation.

CONNIE

I eat everything chocolate when I'm under pressure or depressed. Why do I get so depressed?

CONSTANCE

Mood swings are the burden of people who allow themselves to feel too much. It's how you spend the time between the highs and lows that can make you an artist. The suffering to balance.

CONNIE

I feel safe here. The theater is my home.

CONSTANCE

You know where the boundaries are.

CONNIE

I like feeling in control, like a puppeteer. Maybe that's why I became a playwright instead of an actress.

CONSTANCE

You must be pleased. "Encores" is a success.

CONNIE

How do you know? It doesn't open until tomorrow night. Why do you think I'm such a wreck?

CONSTANCE

I know. I'm here for you. Trust me.

CONNIE

I do trust you. But I still can't find the right make-up.

CONSTANCE

Stop trying. Step back and look at yourself.

CONNIE

(Studies herself in covered mirror) Too tall. Funny nose, chipped tooth. My forehead is getting wrinkled and those bags under my eyes and..

CONSTANCE
Celebrate who you are. You are all you have.

CONNIE
What about my children? My work?

CONSTANCE
Icing on the cake.

CONNIE
I want you to look me in the eyes and tell me everything is going
to be alright.

CONSTANCE
In the best of all possible worlds.

CONNIE
In this one.

CONSTANCE
I can't lie to you.

CONNIE
Is something awful going to happen?

CONSTANCE
Something awful is always happening.

CONNIE
(Anxious)
My children?

CONSTANCE
How are your children?

CONNIE
They were well when I left today. Jesse had a cold, but there was
no fever. So I sent him to school.

CONSTANCE
How's Dina?

CONNIE

Dina's fine. She's having trouble with her reading – dyslexia. No real problems.

CONSTANCE

No real problems.

CONNIE

What are you trying to say?

CONSTANCE

I'm not trying to say anything. You're a playwright. I'm an actress. Arm me with the keys to unlock your dreams.

CONNIE

You remain the most insightful person I've ever known. You explained the circle of people around me and defined my place. You gave me the strength to follow my dreams.

CONSTANCE

Strength is not a gift. Our common history makes us strong. It's the bond that unites us. There are no barriers between women, only physical differences and geography.

CONNIE

You once said I swam through the safe zones.

CONSTANCE

You were taught to swim well. We were born risk takers.

CONNIE

I took some risks in my play.

CONSTANCE

I'm proud of you.

CONNIE

You loved me unconditionally.

CONSTANCE

Is there any other way?

                    CONNIE
Your acting inspired me.

                    CONSTANCE
You can't imagine how I miss the magic of being on stage.

                    CONNIE
You're on a stage, You have an audience. Perform.

                    CONSTANCE
Oh. The mortal headache of decision. I loved playing
"Pygmalion", "Medea", "Major Barbara", "The Ivory Door", "The
Wisteria Trees"...

                    CONNIE
That was Helen Hayes.

                    CONSTANCE
Oh, yes. She played it in New York. I played it in Philadelphia.
You know what they say about Philadelphia?

                    CONNIE
The city of brotherly love?

                    CONSTANCE
Forget it. You're too young. Anyway, I was perfect for that part
in "The Wisteria Trees". I was so close to it that I could feel those
damn trees. Alright, alright, which character of mine did you like
the best?

                    CONNIE
I always had fun at the operettas and the comedies, but I think my
fondest memory was my first. The first time I saw you on stage. I
think I was six or seven.

                    CONSTANCE
(Interrupts) seven. The play was Shaw's "Saint Joan".

                    CONNIE
Ah, "Saint Joan". Would you?

                    CONSTANCE
A votre servici.

CONNIE

I remember how I cried when they sentenced you to be burned at
the stake and how you tore up the write of execution and stared
down your accusers.

CONSTANCE

(She moves to spotlight by stool and sets her stage). Rouen, 30th
of May, 1431.

(Joan addresses her accusers)

Yes they told me you were fools, and that I was not to listen to
your fine words nor to trust to your charity. You promised me my
life; but you lied. You think that life is nothing but not being stone
dead...I could let the banners and the trumpets and the knights
and soldiers pass me and leave me behind as they leave the other
women, if only I could still hear the wind in the trees, the larks in
the sunshine, the young lambs crying through the healthy frost,
and the blessed, blessed church bells that send my angel voices
floating to me on the wind. But without these things I cannot live;
and by your wanting to take them away from me, or from any
human creature, I know that your counsel is of the devil, and mine
is of God. (The spotlight leaves her. Connie applauds.)

CONSTANCE-CONT

(To herself) pity the wings of memory. I have forgotten so much.

CONNIE

I should have used that scene to display your craft in "Encores". I
don't know why I chose "Three Sisters".

CONSTANCE

Your play is about three actresses. I am only one part of your
blessed trinity.

CONNIE

You know the character I created from your life was the most
compelling of the three. All of the actresses in our company vied
to play you.

CONSTANCE

It's a wonderful part. But, why did you have to draw me so old?

CONNIE

The play is about three mature actresses; their histories, relationships.

CONSTANCE

At least you could have made me the youngest of the three.

CONNIE

I gave you a boyfriend.

CONSTANCE

I appreciated that. I loved the competition between the ladies. And I liked winning.

CONNIE

I gave you the best part. So why are you complaining?

CONSTANCE

(Ravel's "Pavane" is faintly heard.) I would have liked my mirror to reflect me in my prime. Not an old woman talking about the past. It would have been more fun reliving or re-seeing the past; squeezing into thin dresses.

CONNIE

What is there now?

CONSTANCE

(Music grows)
Take my hands.

(Connie obeys and their touching becomes a dance. Their distance becomes smaller. They swirl faster, clinging to each other's arms in counterpoint to the gentle music. When the music fades they drop to the floor. Their tears turn to laughter.)

CONSTANCE-CONT

Let me help you (she brings Connie to her feet).

CONNIE

The music again. It reminds me of that dream, hazy memories. Do you think I have the talent to be a good writer?

CONSTANCE
Don't drown your spirit with doubts. We know you have talent.
Listen to your muse, not your critic.

CONNIE
Do you think I'll ever find the man of my dreams?

CONSTANCE
You found him thrice, maybe you'll find him again.

CONNIE
I don't want to grow old alone.

CONSTANCE
We all grow old alone.

CONNIE
I get very lonely.

CONSTANCE
Look in the mirror.

CONNIE
My reflection can't hold me at night.

CONSTANCE
You can find someone to hold you, but we all travel alone. Keep
working on your plays. Enjoy your theater, your children, your
friends, your sunshine.

CONNIE
There's never enough time.

CONSTANCE
We're dancing in the shadows of time.

CONNIE
There are no clocks in our hearts.

CONSTANCE
My clock has stopped. My life is defined. Yours is still a
metaphor.

CONNIE

(Anxious) Please don't leave yet. We have to look at my dream
once more. I have to understand why you came.

CONSTANCE

You understand. I want you to remember me.

CONNIE

Will you visit again?

CONSTANCE

We've traveled together before. We may meet again.

CONNIE

How? When?

CONSTANCE

I can't make you any promises. The answers lie with the stars, not
my lips of your imagination.

*(Connie moves down stage to look into the audience for her dream. Constance moves
alongside her. They share the vision, though Constance slightly upstages Connie).*

CONNIE

My dream is vivid now.

(She looks out at the audience as if a film of her dream is facing her).

I see a long, narrow table made of oak. It is so long that my
parents, sister, and Sam are facing me. They are eating bread and
I am standing, pouring them wine. They are talking to each other,
not noticing me. You appear with the music. I'm the only one
who sees you or hears the music.

(Constance stands behind her, touches her, and looks with her at the vision.)

I talk to my family. They don't respond. I am invisible. Now you are pointing to me and saying "You can do it, Connie. You can." I am saying, "I can do it. I can." Our rhythms unite, resonate and pound, like a chant, an invocation.

CONSTANCE
Let the words settle, like rain from your mind to your heart. (Whisper) You can do it! You can!

CONNIE
(She Turns her back on the dream and embraces Constance.) I can do it! I can! (She turns her back to the audience.) The dream is gone, but I can feel it's energy.

CONSTANCE
The dream is yours.

CONNIE
(Catching her breath) I feel so strong, cleanses, empowered.

CONSTANCE
Your future is now.

CONNIE
Thank you. I don't know what else to say. We've hardly touched the wine. Could I offer you some more?

CONSTANCE
You were always the perfect hostess.

CONNIE
I was taught well. (She starts to pour Constance more wine, and she stops her.) More bread? I ate a lot of it, my nerves. (Connie breaks the last piece of bread and hands half of it to Constance.) Where did you get this bread?

CONSTANCE
We have our ways.

CONNIE
Next time could you get a loaf of whole wheat or rye? This was so dry.

CONSTANCE
Try dipping it in the wine.

CONNIE
That's messy.

CONSTANCE
Still don't like getting your hands dirty. But your posture has improved.

CONNIE
I plan on not slouching anymore.

CONSTANCE
Yes. Stand tall. It's good for your spine. (Slowly backs away).

CONNIE
Where are you going?

CONSTANCE
I have to leave.

CONNIE
Where? Why? It's not enough to say goodbye.

CONSTANCE
There's no need to ever say goodbye. Good-bye is a gesture, a convention, a symbol of peace.

CONNIE
Then what should we say?

CONSTANCE
You're the playwright. Think of appropriate exit lines. Words to explicate our journey. (Connie becomes sullen.) Make the words sound joyful. Play them in a major key. You are wearing the mask of tragedy. Put on the other mask and enjoy your composition.

CONNIE
(As Constance starts to exit stage. Connie tries to hold onto her.) This was such a short visit. Please stay just a little longer.

CONSTANCE

I'm sorry, my dear. Our lives are too short. All visits need end. (Breaks her hold with Connie and runs into the audience.) I must go.

CONNIE

(Angry) Come back! Don't leave me! (Ravel's "Pavane" faintly rises.) Say you'll come again...can I expect you again?

CONSTANCE

My darling...have no expectations.

CONNIE

(Thoughtfully echoes Constance's words; toasts crowd). Have no expectations.

(A door is slammed and a rustling of keys is heard. Connie, in confusion, peers into the audience, attempting to recognize the intruder whom she realizes is John).

JOHN

Didn't he ever show? (John walks on stage. Connie seems startled, but pleased).

CONNIE

Well I seem to be alone now.

JOHN

It doesn't look like anyone has been here. You've hardly touched the wine. There's no mud from anyone's shoes or nothing.

CONNIE

I guess I've just been here talking to myself.

JOHN

Still worried about the ending of your play? (She shakes her head). Oh! You figured it out? Great! Any light changes? (She shakes her head). Great! Look, don't be embarrassed to admit that you got stood up. Happens all the time.

CONNIE

I'm nervous about tomorrow night. I spent time working on my dialogue. I made some last minute line changes.

JOHN

Yeah, I heard some of it. That's why after I let myself in I went back and slammed the door so you would know someone was here and stop talkin'.

CONNIE

What did you hear?

JOHN

Somethin' about having no expectations. Sounded pretty good to me!

CONNIE

God, I'm so embarrassed.

JOHN

No, don't be. I know you didn't expect to see me.

CONNIE

I don't know what to expect anymore.

JOHN

You seem alright for someone who just got stood up.

CONNIE

I'm fine, really. Look, John, why don't you have some of this wine? We can't let it go to waste.

JOHN

Thanks. (He takes a glass of wine and examines the bottle in his hand.) Not bad. Looks pretty fancy. (Takes a sip). Better than I'm used to. Probably cost more than five bucks, too.

CONNIE

Yeah, a little more. I'm sorry I have nothing to offer you to go with it.

JOHN

It's okay, we'll just pick up a slice of pizza when I walk you home.

CONNIE

You came all the way back just to walk me home?

JOHN

Or put you in a cab. Whatever you want.

CONNIE

What if you came back and my "secret admirer" was here?

JOHN

Then I would have split. That's why I was trying to be so quiet. I don't know, I guess I just didn't trust this character. He just left his note, didn't show his face or anything.

CONNIE

Thanks, John. You might not think that I appreciate you, but I do. I really do. I know I can be a bitch sometimes during rehearsal.

JOHN

No, I understand. You're an artist. You have every right to be temperamental.

CONNIE

No, being an "artist" doesn't give anyone license to be abusive or unkind.

JOHN

What's with you? I thought you artist types got a kick outta pushing people 'round?

CONNIE

Not anymore. (Lights go out).

JOHN

Shit! I forgot about the timer.

CONNIE

I can't see a thing. Where on earth did I put my flashlight?

JOHN

Glad I brought mine. (He turns it on and points the beam at her.)

CONNIE

I can't see where I left the damn thing. It's a good thing you cane,
Id be lost without you. Literally. (They laugh).

JOHN

My light should be enough to get us out of here. Let me just down
my wine and we'll go.

CONNIE

Take your time. Hey, why don't we walk home? It's only twenty
blocks.

JOHN

And it's beautiful out. It's a nice bright Manhattan night.

CONNIE

A bright night, eh? Are there a lot of stars out?

JOHN

Stars? I don't know, we'll have to take a look. When I said bright,
I mean the bright lights of Broadway, you know. Dream street.

CONNIE

Of course. Sometimes it's hard to see the stars in this city when
you're blinded by so many bright lights.

JOHN

Hey you're talking to the lighting man. I know all about these
things. You wanna go get a bite and talk?

CONNIE

Sure. I'm starving. That pizza you mentioned before sounds
good.

JOHN

My treat. How about a little opening night celebration?

*(They exit the stage and walk down the steps into the house. He shines the light for
them on the steps and notices something.)*

JOHN-CONT

Hey, what's this?

CONNIE

(Confused) What?

JOHN

There are bread crumbs all over these steps. Some actor could trip on them and it would be all over. I'll have to talk to the stage manager first thing tomorrow about that lousy cleaning service.

CONNIE

I'd better stay close to you. It's so hard to see.

JOHN

I thought you said you weren't afraid of the dark?

CONNIE

I need just enough light to see the stage.

(John guides them out. They share a laugh. The theater exit door slams and locks.)

Total Blackout.

END

Hourglass Shrines: A Conversation with Hrosvitha of Gandersheim

CHARACTERS:

ROSWITHA (aka ROZ/HROSVITHA): a nun and playwright from circa 1000. She is dressed in a black robe with a white wimple, a black veil, a rope around her waist that holds a large key and black rosary beads.

EVE: a theatrical director circa 2000. She is dressed in shorts, a tee shirt (imprinted saying), sandals, a wristwatch and a necklace with a large dangling crystal.

SETTING: Summertime in a medieval garden adjacent to a very old Gothic style church. Upstage is a small raised bower framed with an arbor under which is set weathered benches and a table. There is a patio in the center with a podium. The garden is composed of four sections that include herbs for cooking, medicine, and drying and small vegetables. The pathways that separate the gardens form a cross.

AT RISE: Medieval music is heard in the distance (early Gregorian chant.) Eve is seated on a bench in the upper right corner of the garden. She is practicing yoga and chants "OM." There are a few books at her feet. Roswitha enters from the chapel (stage right) and walks to the center of the cross and pauses to remove a large book from her habit. As she walks downstage to address the audience a bright light engulfs her and the chant stops.

ROSWITHA

I come to thee, bowing low like a reed to submit my little work to
thy most knowledgeable judgment. Though my plays are written
to touch your minds, they are created with a humble heart. I hope
to glorify God in my quests with a strong voice that will offer
women the power to vow an uncompromising fidelity to Chastity
and Truth. I feel like a soul in a strange universe searching,
wandering, foraging through an enchanted forest whose path is
concealed by dense snow. I am constantly trying to find my way
seeking the footprints of one who has gone before I proceed with
guidance to my glorious destiny with God. I hope to be inspired
by the eloquent works of learned folk now or in the future.
With God's help I might perhaps find a means of improving my
uncouth, unschooled workmanship. I am defenseless because I
do not speak with authority. I fear my uncultured way may be
altered with great knowledge yet to come. I pardon the time I take
of yours to listen to my humble offerings (she gets louder). I offer
thee thanks to share thy humble unworthy words. (Louder) I vow.

EVE

(Annoyed) Will you stop apologizing! (Embarrassed when she realizes a nun is speaking) Oh, I'm sorry. Are you rehearsing something?

ROSWITHA

(Startled) I am most sorry for disturbing thy sleep.

EVE

I wasn't sleeping. I was doing some reading and writing.

ROSWITHA

I will precede with a more quiet tone. I must practice the speech to proceed the performance of my play DULCITIUS for part of a celebration of the visit of his most holiness.

EVE

(Cuts in) I can't believe this!

ROSWITHA

I too fee so honored also that we will be graced by a visit from Emperor Otho at our blessed Abbey of Gandersheim.

EVE

I don't know who this Otto guy is. I was referring to the play you mentioned, DULCITIUS. That's what I was reading when you entered. I have some notes. I'm working on translating it from Latin.

ROSWITHA

I am indeed most flattered that thou would consider my work worthy of noble consideration.

EVE

It's a strange play, a lot of weird stuff going on. Are you directing it at your convent or something?

ROSWITHA

I direct the flow of language and action of movement to the best of my limited knowledge.

EVE

I bet you're from the Society for Creative Anachronism?

ROSWITHA
Pray what society is that?

EVE
(Shakes her head) They're an organization that celebrates life in the Middle Ages.

ROSWITHA
I celebrate life in all ages.

EVE
Are you for real? (Roz is confused) Where are you performing?

ROSWITHA
I am performing now.

EVE
Where?

ROSWITHA
Everywhere. I perform at God's will.

EVE
The play! Where are you doing DULCITIUS?

ROSWITHA
My play will be presented on these sacred grounds at this Abbey Gandersheim.

EVE
We are not in Gandersheim, Dorothy. We're in Hoboken.

ROSWITHA
(Confused) Ho-Bo-Kin?

EVE
That's the Hudson River, not the Rhine.

ROSWITHA
I beg your pardon. I just left mass. Did you not hear our Holy Chants?

EVE

One of us is lost.

ROSWITHA

We may both be lost sheep of my Lord.

EVE

I speak of venues; you speak of illusions.

ROSWITHA

Does it matter much from which stage we address our audience?

EVE

Who are you anyway and what are you doing here?

ROSWITHA

I am the humble vowed Roswitha of Gandersheim.

EVE

What's going on here? Are you saying you are the writer who I am translating, the nun who lived one thousand years ago?

ROSWITHA

My words are heard now, so I must live.

EVE

It must be the Echinacea. This garden is an antibiotic field.

ROSWITHA

I tend to tonic herbs to heal the Knights we care for after battle. Who art thou? What is thy Christina name?

EVE

What makes you think I'm Christian?

ROSWITHA

Then thou be a Pagan in search of redemption?

EVE

My name is Eve. What should I call you?

ROSWITHA

I am called Roswitha of Gandersheim.

EVE
Can I just call you Roz?

ROSWITHA
If it pleaseth thou. Roz. I like it.

EVE
I don't know if I'm dreaming or awake, but I believe that you and I want to know more. Why are you here today with me?

ROSWITHA
Moments ago I found myself drowsy after noon - not too uncommon I dare say. The chants were piercing my heart, so intense they were that my breath had stopped and I felt like the trance of exiting a dream. The garden called my spirit and my mind directed me to the podium at the center of the garden wherein thou heard my loud discourse. The air felt, and still does feel, like Gandersheim. I inhale the aroma of rosemary, lavender, and the roses shrinking in your corner from the chilled wind. Where does the illusion begin? Where in time am I lost? The breeze carries my memories of life in the convent; a convent I don't see. Why dost thou say we are in Hoboken?

EVE
I live in the city - New York City.

ROZ
(Confused) I know of no such place near Gandersheim, so you must be correct. I must be lost. Yet this garden is quite a comfortable and familiar place to be lost in. Perhaps we've found a labyrinth in time.

EVE
Or a maze in space, a spiritual plane?

ROZ
If we are traveling in spiritual planes, are we traveling outward or inward?

EVE
I'm so confused.

ROZ

Does it matter where we are when a storm arises? The thunder is growing louder and quite strange.

EVE

That's not thunder. It's Newark Airport - plane engines roaring.

ROZ

It sounds like a storm to me.

EVE

Never mind. It's only air traffic.

ROZ

Air traffic sounds unhealthy, ominous.

EVE

If something isn't done soon we'll all start exhaling gray smoke, like dragons.

ROZ

So you are saying there might be dragons near Hoboken? Hoboken must be a mystical place.

EVE

It might just be that. (She takes out her pocket calendar) My organizer says 1999.

ROZ

I only have my play book. To my knowledge when I entered the chapel it was midday in fourth day of the seventh month 999.

EVE

Looks like a lot has happened since breakfast.

ROZ

One thousand years, if my calculations are correct. Thou art to me in time as I am to Queen Cleopatra.

EVE

Precisely, if you are who you claim to be. How do I know you are not an actress playing a Saxon nun of the tenth century?

ROZ

I guess thou cannot be assured of who I am as I cannot be assured
of whom thou be.

EVE

Maybe it's not one of us that's confused, it's both of us, sort of in a
time warp.

ROZ

Confusion is the mind's labyrinth. Dost thou believe in miracles?

EVE

I haven't thought about them till now.

ROZ

One must be prepared and seize the moment when a miracle might
occur.

EVE

Maybe we should seize this moment and just relax and try to get
to know each other in spite of our age differences.

ROZ

Indeed, thou art a most intriguing soul.

EVE

I'm a director. I'm in Hoboken to work on a production of plays
by women from the Middle Ages for a festival of Medieval Drama
here at Saint Peter's. We have big plans for your plays. After this
church production we hope to take it to the Cloisters and maybe
Rome.

ROZ

Oh, Rome. I would like to go to Rome with thee. May I join thee
on thy noble journey?

EVE

If it works out. If you're free.

ROZ

I am most honored thou wishes to present my small plays. For the
texts' limitations I am most sorry.

EVE

Stop apologizing. If you are who you say you are, you can give me some insight into your work. How can I make your plays accessible to a modern audience?

ROZ

Perhaps your audience would prefer PAPHNUTIUS or SAPIENTIA. DULCITIUS upset my abbess, the noble Gerberga.

EVE

The premise is weak. The plot is unbelievable. How could a general mistake pots and pans for women?

ROZ

Oh, let me explain. The general was lusting after the three virgins in question. When he was told he would find them in the kitchen at nightfall, he was filled with lust. His delusions from the body's passion drove him to embrace the pots and pans, believing they were the objects of his desire.

EVE

Pots and pans? Give me a break.

ROZ

Dulcitius dented many pans and kitchen tools in his lust for the virgins. He represented the misguided rag of the Pagans. The comedy of the situation evoked laughter in the convent which truly upset my noble Abbess Gerberga, whose piety and decorum are of the highest inspiration.

EVE

You were criticized for evoking laughter? (Roz nods) My audience appreciates levity. I'd like to play it for laughs.

ROZ

If that will please your audience, then so be it. SAPIENTIA is the favorite of many because it tells of the martyrdom of the three virgins. Faith, Hope, and Charity. It was received with the highest acclaim.

EVE

SAPIENTIA may be your most accessible work. I'll do the three plays together. Let's see, I could do SAPIENTIA first,

then DULCITIUS for laughs before intermission, then end with
PAPHNUTIUS, which has the most expressive dialogue.

ROZ

I am very excited. I cannot wait to see thy vision of my work.

EVE

Let's look at your texts. I'm not worried about SAPIENTIA. I'd
like to try and stage DULCITIUS in commedia del arte style.

ROZ

O, comedy, as in the work of my inspiration, Terence.

EVE

I suppose by inspiration you mean that you read him as part
of your literary education, because your work is so different.
Terence's plays speak of the frailty of women; your work speaks of
the heroic sacrifices of Christian women.

ROZ

It is true that I was most fortunate to have been of gentile birth
and privileged to receive a classical education strictly observing
the rule of St. Benedict, under the direction of the Abbess
Gerberga, a niece of the Emperor Otho I.

EVE

I went to NYU. I teach acting and yoga. This is my first paid
directing job.

ROZ

We are both indeed learned creatures of God.

EVE

While I have you here, let's look at your texts to see if I can direct
and produce your plays in a state that will be the most true to your
vision and meaningful to a modern audience.

ROZ

I put myself at your service.

EVE

I don't think we need to work on SAPIENTA. Let's start with the
infamous scene from DULCITIUS.

ROZ
(Embarrassed, she opens her portfolio as Eve opens her small text)
That scene would be the fourth.

EVE
The three holy virgins, Agape, Chionia, and Irena are watching
Dulcitius, Governor of Thessalonica, enter their kitchen through a
crack in the door. I will improvise his part downstage as you read
the text.

*(She positions herself downstage and assumes the posture of the foolish Governor,
taking off one shoe in a commedia de arte position.)*

ROZ
(Reading, as Eve acts out in mime)

AGAPE
What noise is that outside our door?

IRENA
It is that wretch, Dulcitius.

CHIONIA
Now may God protect us!

AGAPE
Amen.

CHIONIA
There is more noise! It sounds like the clashing of pots and pans
and fire-irons.

IRENA
I will go and look. Come quick and peep through the crack of the
door!

AGAPE
What is it?

IRENA

Oh, look! He must be out of his senses! I believe he thinks he is kissing us.

AGAPE

What is he doing?

IRENA

Now he presses the saucepans tenderly to his breast, now the kettles and frying pans! He is kissing them hard!

CHIONIA

How absurd!

IRENA

His face, his hands, his clothes! They are as black as soot. He looks like the Ethiope.

AGAPE

I am glad. His body should turn black - to match his soul, which is possessed of a devil.

IRENA

Look! He is going now. Let us watch the soldiers and see what they do when he goes out.

EVE

End of scene. Then a few short scenes later he is feeling insecure about his appearance. He envisions himself a handsome brute. He feels the women should not have insulted him with such deception.

(She addresses the audience in his posture)
He says: "Ye gods, what has happened to me? Am I not dressed to my best? Am I not clean and fine in my person? And yet Everyone who meets me expresses disgust at the sight of me and will tell me the truth. But here she comes. Her looks are wild, her hair unbound, and all her household follow her weeps.

(She moves out of character)
This guy is in trouble big time.

ROZ

Dulcitius is possessed with feverish desire that controls his senses and misshapes his soul. His madness has soiled his spirit.

EVE

In other words, he's nuts? Lost it. Bonkers. Not operating with a full deck?
(Roz looks confused)
In modern terms we would call it paranoia, a form of mental delusion and persecution.

ROZ

He is possessed by the devil. It is too late for his soul to be saved, but the virgins are redeemed through sacrifice.

EVE

Martyrs?

ROZ

In the end the holy virgins become martyrs as Agape and Chionia are burnt, and Irena shot to death with arrows.

EVE

How do we play that for laughs? How can we advertise it as a human comedy with such as ending?

ROZ

All comedy is human. Shall we proceed to PAPHNUTIUS? I don't have much time. I must attend vespers soon.

EVE

The last scene is very poetic.

ROZ

PAPHNUTIUS concerns the conversion of the beautiful Thais by the hermit Paphnutius. She repents, renounces her evil ways and does penance for three years in a narrow cell. Paphnutius learns from a vision that her humility has won her a place in paradise. Thais is brought out of her cell to die. Paphnutius stays by her side until her soul has left her body.

EVE

Let's use the upstage bench as the death-bed.
(Roz follows Eve's direction and reclines on the bench)
Your read Thais and I'll read Paphnutius (Paph.).

ROZ

Scene thirteen. (Pause to set the mood)

THAIS

Holy father, do not leave me. Stay near to comfort me in this hour
of my death.

PAPH

I will not leave you, Thais, until your soul has taken flight to the
stars, and I have buried your body.

THAIS

I feel the end is near. Brother, do not leave me.

PAPH

Now is the time to pray.

THAIS

Oh, God, who made me, take pity on me. Grant the soul which
thou didst breathe into me may now happily return to thee. Oh,
God, who made me, pity me.

PAPH

Thais! Thais! Oh, loving humble spirit, pass to thy glory! May
angels lead her into Paradise! Oh, uncreated beauty, existing in
truth without material form, grant that the divers parts of this
human body now to be dissolved, may return to their original
elements! Grant that the soul, given from on high, may soar into
light and joy, and that the body may be cherished peacefully in the
soft lap of the earth until that day when, the ashes being brought
together again, and the life-giving sap restored to the veins, this
same Thais may rise again, a perfect human being as before, and
take her place among the glorious white flock who shall be led
into the joy of eternity. Grant this, Oh Thou Who alone art what
Thou art; Who livest and reignest and art glorious in the Unity
and perfect Trinity through infinite ages!

(Eve helps Roz off the bench and they return to center stage)

EVE
Reminds me a little of the end of HAMLET.

ROZ
What be Harriet?

EVE
Hamlet is the name of a play written by Shakespeare, the world's
most famous playwright who lived about 500 years after you.

ROZ
And you live 500 years after him. How are our plays similar?

EVE
The plays themselves are dissimilar in content, but at the end,
after Hamlet's death, his friend Horatio says, "Now cracks a noble
heart. Good night, sweet prince. And flights of angels sing thee to
thy rest." And you said in PAPHNUTIUS, "Angels lead her into
Paradise!"

ROZ
The sentiments sound clearly similar. All writers of plays share a
common desire to replicate the human condition.

EVE
In other words, all playwrights are kleptomaniacs.

ROZ
(Confused by the term)
I do not always understand thy words, but thy sentiments are
clear. I believe all writers of plays continue the human dialogue.
Though tongues and stories might differ, feelings remain the
same.

EVE
In other words, humans give form to definition.

ROZ
Indeed. Human life is one of many miracles that inspire us.

EVE

Life is simple; humans more complex.

ROZ

Life is a war between the flesh and the spirit and the spirit wins.

EVE

Aren't our bodies preserved through our genes, passed on
biologically to our descendants? Our flesh lives through others.

ROZ

You mean the way our gardens re-seed and grow?

EVE

We're humans, not herbs or flowers.

ROZ

We have souls and spirits. Do you believe in miracles?

EVE

Why do you keep asking me that?

ROZ

It is our gift as spirits to believe in higher powers, gifts from God
that we can not explain.

EVE

Like your visit?

ROZ

Perhaps thy journey is the miracle.

EVE

Is our meeting a time warp, a miracle, or a dream?

ROZ

Great visions occur in dreams. In sleep our eyes can see messages
from our souls, buried signs, timeless images - some with voices
that speak truths that sometime frighten us.

EVE

Is all this a dream?

ROZ

The garden is real.
(She picks some lavender and crushes it in her hand)
Smell this sweet lavender and tell me if is real.

EVE

(Eve inhales the lavender and takes some into her hands.)
I'll pick us some rosemary and sage.

(She picks some rosemary and sage and shares it with Roz. They inhale it and smile. Roz takes Eve's hands and holds them to her lips.)

ROZ

Let us pray.

EVE

I don't know how.

ROZ

You must pray, give thanks to our Lord.

EVE

I never have time. I don't think about it. I don't know how.

ROZ

Will thou try to pray with me?

EVE

I don't know any prayers, except maybe the "Our Father."

ROZ

Let us chant the word "alleluia."

EVE

You mean "hallelujah."

ROZ

It means praise to God. Eve, can I come and chant my OM? (Roz nods) Take my hands and close thine eyes. When thou art ready to chant your OM, I will sing my "alleluia."

(After a moment of concentration they chant, creating a chant that lasts for about two minutes. Their concentration is broken by the chime of church bells.)

How dost thou feel?

                    EVE
I can feel my heart beat.

                    ROZ
Let thy heart's beat guide thee.

                    EVE
I feel wonderful, charged, empowered.

                    ROZ
Yes, prayer can do great things, sometimes miracles.

                    EVE
I'm trying to follow you, but you seem so far ahead of me.

                    ROZ
Only a millennium, but thou art a good learner and seeker of truth.

                    EVE
Thank you for our time together.

                    ROZ
It's our Lord's time; we only encase a small part of it.

                    EVE
Like little hourglasses.

                    ROZ
Precisely. The bells are calling for vespers and I am growing weary.

                    EVE
This garden needs tending. There are so many weeds I haven't notices till today.

                    ROZ

Maybe thou did not care to see. Caring and listening will help
thou to see more.

                    EVE

Maybe a miracle?

                    ROZ

One never knows when a miracle will appear, but one must be
open to the possibility.

                    EVE

I will remember and practice our chant.

                    ROZ

Thou may share it with others. Now I must go to vespers. Would
thou care to accompany me?

                    EVE

I'm not ready. I want to spend more time in the garden.

                    ROZ

Life is a most precious gift from our Lord. Enjoy thy precious
life, my child. Adieu.

(Roz heads upstage to exit as Eve goes downstage and starts
pulling weeds out of the garden. Roz addresses the audience)

May God bless thee and keep thee in peace.

                    END

Selling Venus

Setting: Interior of an artist's loft. There is little furniture. There are three canvases upstage that depict modern versions of Botticelli's "Venus." At Rise Byron is painting on a fourth canvas. Upbeat Classical music is playing from his CD player. He cheerfully hums to the music when there's a knock on the door. He turns off music and answers the door. It is Victoria who appears stressed and exhausted. He calmly goes to kiss her and she heads for the open bottle of wine on the table.

BYRON

Slay any dragons at work today?

VICTORIA

Oh Byron, you have the good life. You paint all day, do a little tai chi, teach a couple of classes at the college. You are always so calm. I really wish I could bottle your serenity and wear it as perfume.

BYRON

Sounds like an interesting marketing concept. Sell it to one of your clients.

VICTORIA

I have too much work. I don't have time to market brilliant ideas. I only have time for you, my good friend.

BYRON

Would my good friend like to join me for dinner this evening?

VICTORIA

Love to. What are you fixing?

BYRON

Let me check the fridge, my dear.

Setting: Interior of an artist's loft. There is little furniture. There are three canvases upstage that depict modern versions of Botticelli's "Venus." At Rise Byron is painting on a fourth canvas. Upbeat Classical music is playing from his CD player. He cheerfully hums to the music when there's a knock on the door. He turns off music and answers the door. It is Victoria who appears stressed and exhausted. He calmly goes to kiss her and she heads for the open bottle of wine on the table.

BYRON

Slay any dragons at work today?

VICTORIA

Oh Byron, you have the good life. You paint all day, do a little tai chi, teach a couple of classes at the college. You are always so calm. I really wish I could bottle your serenity and wear it as perfume.

BYRON

Sounds like an interesting marketing concept. Sell it to one of your clients.

VICTORIA

I have too much work. I don't have time to market brilliant ideas. I only have time for you, my good friend.

BYRON

Would my good friend like to join me for dinner this evening?

VICTORIA

Love to. What are you fixing?

BYRON

Let me check the fridge, my dear.

He opens his fridge and looks.

VICTORIA

All I have in my fridge is opened flat champagne, olives and condoms.

He takes out some salad and chicken breasts and fixes dinner as they chat.

BYRON
Why do you keep your condoms there?

VICTORIA
I don't want them to melt.

BYRON
Melt? Victoria, you amaze me. Do any of your gentleman friends
ever complain?

VICTORIA
Oh no. They warm up pretty fast. You should try it.

BYRON
No dear. I'm afraid I'd confuse the condoms with my wonton
wraps.

VICTORIA
You need to play safe Byron. There are too many diseases around.

She pours herself more wine.

BYRON
I don't play at all nowadays. (He pauses to watch her drink). I wish
you could find other ways than alcohol to calm yourself down.

VICTORIA
So do I. Some days I feel my heart is racing so fast that I will
never catch it. I seem to only relax when I'm here.

BYRON
So I guess I don't make your heart throb.

VICTORIA
You're my confessor, my closest friend.

BYRON
All right Vicky, what's on your mind today?

VICTORIA
Benjamin said he's going to recommend me for partner.

BYRON

Aren't you too young? From what you've told me most of the partners at Silver and Miser are over forty and married.

VICTORIA

You know I'm very smart, graduated top in my class in law school and...

BYRON

Sexy. Perhaps Benjamin Silver lusts for more than your mind.

VICTORIA

Oh he does. He wants to have an affair with me. He told me over lunch.

BYRON

Oh, so you had a hot lunch. That's why you're so anxious. (She nods.) How much time do you have to consider his proposition?

VICTORIA

It all depends on where we find ourselves after your opening tomorrow night, if you get my drift.

BYRON

Like an avalanche. Be careful. At least I can check him out tomorrow night.

VICTORIA

He's so cute.

BYRON

Babies are cute. Men are handsome or rich.

VICTORIA

You're handsome. Benjamin is sort of short and pudgy.

BYRON

Short and pudgy sounds like a bulldog.

VICTORIA

Well, he has the kind of looks that grow on you, like a lot of great, brilliant men. He's like Henry Kissinger. You fall in love with the mind and then the man.

BYRON

Academic analysis is good for a classroom. What's important is if he turns you on and makes you happy.

VICTORIA

I sound shallow, don't I?

BYRON

Not shallow; clinical. You don't really know him well.

VICTORIA

I know you well. I'll say clever things about you tomorrow night.

BYRON

(Charmed)
Like what?

VICTORIA

I like the way you make me feel about myself. I appreciate all the gracious meals you make for me. You are fun to shop with. When I'm sad you make me laugh or give me too much wine. You anticipate my every wish. You sometimes finish my sentences. You..

BYRON

Enough! Enough. You are making me sound like a saint.

VICTORIA

Close. I should call you Lord Byron. Your poetry is your painting.

BYRON

Doing things with you gives me great pleasure.

VICTORIA

Will you have any kind of a date tomorrow night?

BYRON

How many kinds of dates are there? (Laughing) No. I'm going alone. Any advice on what I should wear?

VICTORIA

I'm wearing a black silk sheath.

> BYRON

Your Calvin Klein? (She nods) With your violet pashmina? (She nods)

> VICTORIA

You read my mind.

> BYRON

I helped you choose your wardrobe. I'm thinking of wearing black pants with a black shirt and tie.

> VICTORIA

Oh, we'd look perfect together.

> BYRON

But you're going with an Italian designer suit.

> VICTORIA

Do you think you could take a picture of me tomorrow night in front of one of your paintings at the Gallery?

> BYRON

Done. But please don't explain my work to people. I hate it when they ask me questions about Botticelli. I'm not an art historian. I'm a painter and his work inspired this idea, but I know nothing of the man. The artist and the man are separate issues.

> VICTORIA

Most people will just associate Venus with love. I'll just read the titles "Venus 1, Venus 2 , 3 and 4" and ask them what they think.

> BYRON

That's fine. That's all they need to think about, Venus and love. And now we can think about eating. Would you please light the candles?

She lights candles as he sets food on the table, then turns off the light and heads to the CD player to put on some music.

VICTORIA
What did I do to deserve someone like you?

BYRON
Just being you.

Scene 2. The Following night around midnight. Byron's paintings are gone. An empty easel rests near the wall. Byron and Victoria loudly enter. She is in tears; he tries to comfort her.

VICTORIA
Tonight was supposed to be magical. Instead it was tragic. I was so looking forward to tonight. You were looking forward to tonight. And I spoiled it for you.

BYRON
(Tries to comfort her)
Stop that. I had a very successful evening. I may have sold my whole "Venus" series. (Pause) I'm sorry you were hurt.

VICTORIA
This evening shouldn't be about me. Why do I do that?

BYRON
You were disappointed. You were hurt. I'm sorry.

VICTORIA
Byron, my dear, You are always so calm. Don't you ever feel pain? (He nods) How do you deal with it? How do you deal with pain?

BYRON
I transfer my pain into my art work. If I'm lucky I sell it.

VICTORIA
Like tonight. I am happy for you and I hope they pay you a lot of money.

BYRON
The money isn't as important as the sale. I get by on my teaching and remember I get my apartment pretty cheap because of a working artist subsidy.

                              VICTORIA

I wish I could be more like you. Money is so important to me
because I didn't have much growing up.

                              BYRON

Stop with the Scarlet O'Hara routine. You'll never go hungry
because of your marketable skills. You seem to love being a
lawyer. If you do what you are committed to and love you should
be happy.

                              VICTORIA

I should be happy, but I'm not. I'm always frustrated, anxious,
exhausted...

                              BYRON

Then try something else.

                              VICTORIA

I don't know anything else. I Can't even draw a straight line, so I
can't be an artist. I have no voice, so I can't sing. (Pause) Maybe I
should just go to the office tomorrow and bury myself in contracts
and depositions.

                              BYRON

Maybe. But I'm not sure if it is wise to spend your Sunday buried
in the shadow of the man who caused you so much pain tonight.
Will he be there tomorrow?

                              VICTORIA

Probably. He's a workaholic. He works about fifty to sixty
hours a week. He didn't go in today, so he'll probably be in his
office tomorrow. I have to go to work tomorrow. I need to face
Benjamin.

                              BYRON

Yes, and he has to face you.

                              VICTORIA

He is two faced. He was so nice to me Friday. He said we'd go out
dancing after your opening. I believed him. Then he changes his
mind and leaves with someone else. Look how I got all dolled up
for him?

BYRON

I know. You looked gorgeous.

VICTORIA

Did I look better than that floozy he left with? (He nods) She's only a secretary. I'm almost a partner. I've learned never to trust a woman with red hair.

BYRON

It was obviously dyed. She wasn't a natural redhead.

VICTORIA

How can you tell?

BYRON

X-ray vision. Besides her skirt was so short that every time she sat on a stool you could see up her dress.

VICTORIA

And you looked?

BYRON

(He nods and smiles)
Look Victoria, you know I'm an artist. I'm used to seeing naked bodies all the time. I studied anatomy. At one time I even thought about medical school.

VICTORIA

I can't believe you looked. I hope you're not planning on calling her and asking her to model for you.

BYRON

Not a chance. She's not my type. She had such fat ankles. And did you get a load at her ass? Yuk.

VICTORIA

You know if this wasn't happening to me I'd find this situation funny.

BYRON

Vicky, my dear, it is happening to you. You need to live through your feelings.

VICTORIA

I know it will make be stronger. I don't care about being stronger. I want to be happy. What should I do?

BYRON

In my opinion you have two choices. One, quit Silver and Miser. Two, confront him and put your feeling out on the table.

VICTORIA

It would only be my feelings on the table. I'll be the main course.

BYRON

I don't know. You asked for my opinion. I'm no Dr. Phil. Maybe you need a shrink.

VICTORIA

Done that. No time to do it again. If my Lord Byron were straight, I'd have three choices.

BYRON

(Stands up defensively)
What are you talking about? I am straight.

VICTORIA

But, you never talk about women, except that stupid model who posed for you, Carla, and your mother.

BYRON

And that makes me gay? (She shrugs her shoulders defensively) You have known me for almost three years. Have I ever discussed any of my relationships with you?

VICTORIA

Not really. I guess we just discussed my relationships. I just assumed because...

BYRON

Because I didn't come on to you? You assumed because I wasn't salivating at your feet that I must be gay.

VICTORIA

Well, you never made a pass at me and there were plenty of opportunities.

BYRON

The next thing you'll bring up is my sense of style, gourmet recipes and my flair for interior decoration.

VICTORIA

You did a great job with my apartment.

BYRON

Why don't you have some more wine and put your feelings on my table.

VICTORIA

I'm confused. I don't know what to say. I can't find the right words.

BYRON

A lawyer short on words. Isn't that another stereotype? Aren't you suppose to know how to manipulate words? You really do compartmentalize things.

VICTORIA

I'm sorry.

BYRON

Sorry isn't enough. A lot of my artistic and non-artistic friends are gay. If I were gay I'd be proud of it. But you've made me into a stereotype, a cliche.

VICTORIA

I'm sorry.

BYRON

Stop apologizing. You are who you are. You need to get out into the world more, the real world. Maybe you should quit that S and M law firm and work for legal aid. You need to experience how people with real problems live.

VICTORIA

Maybe I should.

BYRON

You'd make a lot less money.

VICTORIA
I don't know, maybe less is more.

BYRON
Please leave the world of cliches.

VICTORIA
If you want to discuss reality, I have a few questions for you.

BYRON
Fine, I'll open some wine.

He gets a bottle of wine and she follows him, trying to maintain
eye contact.

VICTORIA
Do you find me attractive? (He nods) What's wrong with me?

BYRON
I guess all these questions will be about you.

VICTORIA
Indulge me just a little more. You've indulged me so much for so
long.

BYRON
Fine. What's another day in purgatory?

VICTORIA
I feel if I had a third choice I could wind up in heaven.

BYRON
What do you mean?

VICTORIA
You said I had two choices. (He nods) What if my third choice
were you?

BYRON
Are you going to try and seduce me tonight?

VICTORIA
Would you consider taking a shot at it?

BYRON

Shot is not the right word. I've been in love with you for a long time.

VICTORIA

I've had feelings for you too, but I always repressed them.

BYRON

Because you believed I was gay. (She nods) The reason I never expressed my true feelings to you before was because I didn't think I could afford you.

VICTORIA

Really? That's silly.

BYRON

Admit it Victoria, you do like money. (She nods) Remember I'm the guy who always went shopping with you to impress other guys.

VICTORIA

I know, but like therapy, I've been there done that. I like money, but I don't need it.

BYRON

Thinking about Legal Aid?

VICTORIA

It's an option. I certainly wouldn't have to worry about running into the likes of Benjamin there.

BYRON

We may have another crisis if I sell my paintings to that sheik.

VICTORIA

What's that?

BYRON

He's thinking about paying the asking price.

VICTORIA

Wow! That was...

> BYRON

Five hundred K.

> VICTORIA

That's more than I make in two years.

> BYRON

I could keep you in Calvin Klein.

> VICTORIA

Could a relationship hurt our friendship?

> BYRON

It could or it could make it stronger. Try to avoid having expectations. Let some of my free spirit genes rub off on you.

> VICTORIA

Have you ever really imagined or thought of us as more than friends?

> BYRON

There is nothing more than a friend. Who knows with a little luck we could become best friends.

> VICTORIA

How about going to my place for a change?

> BYRON

Thought you'd never ask.

They exit with wine.

END

© 2001 Katheryn White

Number Our Days
A Play in One Act

CAST:

LOU FORMAN: Attorney, 70s

KITTY MACCHIO: Dress Shop Owner, 70s

WAITER

TIME: 1976

SETTING: A small, elegant restaurant in New York City. Evening.

AT RISE, Lou is seated alone at a corner table sipping a martini.

Soft music is being played in the background. He appears distracted and nervous as his eyes keep watch at the entrance door. Kitty, dressed stylishly, wearing dark glasses, enters with confidence and grace. Lou stands, puts down his drink and greets her. Music fades.

LOU

Good evening, Kitty. You look beautiful.

KITTY

Nit dos iz sheyn, vos iz sheyn, nor dos, vos es gefelt. (Beautiful is not what beautiful is, but what one likes)

LOU

You remembered. (She nods). My mother taught you well. I'd add to that phrase that what is beautiful is also whom one loves.

KITTY

I'm surprised you even recognized me after all these years.

LOU

What are years to old friends? (He kisses her cheek, takes her hand as he helps her to be seated)

I will always recognize that smile. You are still a stylish lady.

Waiter brings champagne to table.

KITTY

You look well, Lou. Time has been kind to you. Ah, you remembered how much I love champagne!

LOU

I remember everything about you. Years ago, I memorized every feature of your lovely face. Your light is always with me. (He takes off her glasses.) Your eyes still laugh at me.

KITTY

Those are prescription. I need them to see. They are dark because glare impairs my judgement. (She takes them back, but doesn't put them on.) I was happy to hear from you, as always. I've treasured your letters through all these years. You have always been there when I needed you.

LOU

Isn't that what friends are for? (He pours them champagne, then raises his glasses to toast. She raises hers to his.) L'Chiam!

KITTY

To Friends! We were the best; so young and so much in love..

LOU

I never stopped loving you Kitty. I saw you every day of my life. At every cornerstone I turned you stood in the shadows. I did everything for you...waited. My whole life has prepared me for this moment.

KITTY

(Nervous)
This is too much. I don't know what to say. (She looks away for a moment) I am happy to see you. (He takes her hand.)

Lou, I love champagne, but I'm diabetic and need to eat something. (She pulls her hand back.)

Lou motions to the waiter for bread and menus.

LOU

In mother's last years she regretted her decision and wanted to see you. You were married then. It wouldn't have been appropriate to ask you to see her.

KITTY

I still remember some of the Yiddish your mother taught me when I'd hang out on your stoop. I really missed my time with her. I can still see her standing erect at the open mouth of her long grand piano tapping time on its top. I was so afraid that if I got the rhythm wrong the top would crash down and devour me.

LOU

You were such a quick learner. I'll never forget when you were about ten and sat down at our piano and just played Bach after hearing my mother play it. Music flowed through your fingertips. You had perfect pitch … an open heart.

KITTY

You know what I liked most about your mother?

LOU

I hope it was her son.

KITTY

(Ignoring his remark)

Her love for learning… and her music. I could have listened to her play for hours.

LOU

Me too. That was her greatest love.

KITTY

Second greatest. You were her real treasure. I'll never forget the look on her face when you were delivering your valedictory speech. I didn't think her face was big enough to hold her smile.

LOU

You should have seen her when I finished law school. She held my arm tight afterward and kept telling everybody she met, "This is my son; the lawyer."

KITTY

Too bad your father missed that.

LOU

Yeah. He died too young. So she leaned on me.

KITTY

If I had been Jewish, she would have leaned on me a little. Maybe she'd have accepted me as her daughter.

LOU

Maybe. (Beat) Do you know that I never brought anyone home after she broke us up.

KITTY

Was the religious thing really the only reason? Or did she just use that as an excuse?

LOU

That was all of it. I don't know how many times I heard her say how much she liked you... and she always followed it up with, "If only she were Jewish."

KITTY

I can't help it if my parents were Christian.

LOU

I think you were the only Dutch Lutheran she ever met. Come to think of it you're the only one I ever met.

KITTY

My parents weren't even the same denomination.

LOU

I didn't know that.

KITTY

Mom was raised a Presbyterian, went to that old church on Fifth Ave. She changed when she married my Dad.

LOU

I remember your family going to St. Mark's. (Pause) Now it all makes sense.

KITTY

What makes sense?

LOU

That a girl with a Presbyterian mother and Dutch Lutheran father
would fall in love with a Jewish guy and end up married to an
Italian Catholic.

KITTY

What never made sense to me was being stuck with a name like
Kitty Van Schoonhoven

LOU

I loved that name… it had character. Your whole family was so
different from mine. Every time I came to your house I felt like
Alice must have felt when she stepped through the looking glass.

KITTY

Is that supposed to be a compliment?

LOU

You know what I liked most about your family?

KITTY

I hope it was their daughter.

LOU

I loved those pretty hats you and your sister's wore at Easter. And
I liked your father's stories about his family and ancestors when
New York was called something else? You know.

KITTY

New Amsterdam.

LOU

Right. New Amsterdam. And his family was Puritan or something

KITTY

His family went back more than three hundred years in this
country.

LOU

So you could join the DAR if you want to.

                    KITTY
I suppose so. I think there's even some old Dutch society I could
join, but I have enough to do.

                    LOU
What would make you happy?

                    KITTY
I am happy. I would have been happier joining you, converting to
Judaism, being your wife.

                    LOU
That would have made me happy.

                    KITTY
But life didn't work out that way, did it?

                    LOU
True, but, you did well. You married a wealthy contractor. He
bought you a new fur every time he found a new mistress.

                    KITTY
I did have a lot of furs. They're out of style now. He also gave
me two wonderful children that I love .And, I have seven
grandchildren .

                    LOU
And I never married. I would have loved children and
grandchildren.

                    KITTY
I think we better order, Lou. The waiter looks anxious. (She puts
on glasses long enough to read menu then takes them off again.)
The sea bass sounds great.

                    LOU
Excellent choice. (To waiter) Two sea bass please. (Waiter nods
and heads to kitchen.)

                    KITTY
You should have married.

LOU

Should have, could have, would have. Tsoriss (woes, suffering). What does that all mean?

KITTY

Remember after my divorce when I wrote you about it?

LOU

Yes, I wrote you back and said I was thinking of moving to Israel and would you go with me. You said no.

KITTY

Then you went to Israel, anyway.

LOU

I thought only of you. I stayed there one year. I came back to New York and had to start all over again.

KITTY

You don't look the worst for wear.

LOU

I had a partner, but we lost business when I was away. We split . My clients lost confidence in me.

KITTY

Did you sell the brownstone on East Ninth street?

LOU

My mother died there. I lived there for awhile. Then I sold it and moved to Forrest Hills. I have a beautiful home there. I can't wait to show it to you.

KITTY

I have a beautiful apartment behind my dress shop in north Jersey.

LOU

I'm sorry Kitty, but I can't see you in the Jersey suburbs. You were a wonderful child actress in your Aunt's company. You could play piano by ear. You had such potential.

KITTY

I traded my stage aspirations for a comfortable home in
Westchester and a summer home on a lake. After the divorce I
decided I liked the lake town and started my shop there.

LOU

All that talent. (Shakes his head) What a waste… what a waste.

KITTY

Not wasted. I used ,or you might say I channeled my gifts
differently. I did community theatre all around Morris County.
One of my granddaughters studied acting and is a successful
playwright .She also plays piano. I bought her a baby grand when
she turned thirteen. She even bears my name. If she's lucky she
may marry a mensch like you.

LOU

May I meet her?

KITTY

(Cautious)

She's too young for you.

LOU

I didn't mean that. I just want to see if she's like you.

KITTY

She's taller. Kitty's face looks a lot like mine when I was young,
except her complexion is darker. We have the same nose and
profile. She knows I'm meeting you.

LOU

What does she think of that?

KITTY

She's a romantic; thinks it's a good idea.

LOU

Please let me meet her. She could be the granddaughter I never
had.

KITTY

I don't know, Lou. My life is carved in stone; yours is still putty.

LOU

More like sand. With sand you can make cement. Look, this could be our last chance.

KITTY

Kitty, lives on the Upper Westside and loves to meet me along Canal street when I buy for my store. She says, "How could you have ever left New York?" I say, "New York left me." I had to make a life and I did.

LOU

You broke my heart.

KITTY

Two broken hearts. That's the past. We can't change that.

LOU

We still like the same things.

KITTY

We'll always be soul mates.

LOU

I hate that term ,soul mates. It reminds me of all those personals in New York Magazine. We'll be soul mates when we're dead. I want a life mate.

KITTY

I think it's a nice term; souls are souls dead or alive. Souls are eternal.

LOU

I don't want to get into a discussion of Jewish verses Christian. I want to know what your life is like. Can I add to the quality of your life? Can I help you in any way?

KITTY

Actually, the quality of my life is fine, aside from the occasional robbery.

LOU

Robbery? What do you mean?

KITTY

(She leans towards him)
I'm alone in my store and about once a month this guy comes in
with a gun and cleans out my cash register. He must feel a little
guilty because he says someday he'll pay me back.

LOU

What, when he wins the lottery? Oy Vey! (Oh no) Now I'm
worried about you.

KITTY

Don't worry. I don't think he'll ever use his gun.

LOU

A gun! Oy Vey. (He puts his hands on his head and shakes his
head)

KITTY

He's a young, scared drug addict or something. Anyway he's
troubled and a little dangerous. I'm an easy mark.

LOU

Please don't talk like that. There is no such thing as being a little
dangerous. If he's a drug addict he may get stressed and hurt you.
This is so upsetting. I can't think about it.

KITTY

Then Don't think about it. I'm not giving up the store. My
daughter is always after me to sell. What would I do sit in some
condo in Miami Beach and play cards all day? I have to be busy;
keep my mind and body active. I value my independence. I have
a great life. I take a cruise every winter after the holidays. I go
down the shore with my kids for a couple of weeks in the summer.

LOU

It's December. When is your next cruise?

KITTY

February.

                    LOU
May I take you?

                    KITTY
I can take myself. I already booked with a friend .

                    LOU
Male or female?

                    KITTY
Does it matter? (He nods.) Female. How can you get jealous after
all these years?

                    LOU
"Age cannot wither her, nor custom stale

Her infinite variety. Other women cloy

The appetites they feed, but she makes hungry

Where most she satisfies."

                    KITTY
"Antony and Cleopatra."

                    LOU
Remember when we read Shakespeare's plays in the park?

                    KITTY
It took us four summers to read them all.

                    LOU
We didn't just read them, we lived through them. We fought ever
battle, won every war and died for love.

                    KITTY
We also laughed a lot. Don't forget the comedies.

                    LOU
You were destined to be a great actress.

                    KITTY
Then I guess I proved destiny wrong.

LOU

Fate has been against us, but we can change it now.

KITTY

Fate is fate. Our lives grew in different directions.

LOU

Maybe our true fate was to connect for our twilight years.

KITTY

Twilight is dim. It's hard to see what's ahead of us. The light
shines on the past.

LOU

The light is in your heart.

KITTY

We made our choices long ago. We knew we couldn't marry
because it would destroy Your family.

LOU

That was your decision Kitty. I would have married you in spite of
my mother's beliefs. She would have gotten over it.

KITTY

No. She loved me as a stepdaughter, but never a daughter- in- law,
never as your wife!

LOU

Believe me, she regretted that night. She regretted what she said to
you. She regretted never having any grandchildren. She regretted
losing you and hurting me.

KITTY

Isn't that nice! It only took her a lifetime to add up those regrets.
My last memory of her was Her words, "I will go into mourning
if you wed. "She would consider her only child dead. I couldn't
do that to her. I couldn't do that to you. You should have married,
Lou. You should have created a good life for yourself. You should
never had carried my memory in your pocket like a dollar bill.
Our time was spent.

LOU

Please don't say that. That dollar bill you talk about is worth a
million now. I treasure you and value you more now than ever. I
beg you, please to give me another chance.

KITTY

I don't think I know how, Lou. I don't know how to change my life
now.

LOU

Please forgive my mother for hurting you. I know she loved you.

KITTY

I forgave your mother years ago. I knew she had beliefs that she
held dear.

I understood her feelings, I couldn't break her heart. Have you
forgiven her?

LOU

Yes, but it was hard. It took me longer than you. I was angry for
so many years. I bottled it up; drank too much. When I came back
from Israel my mother was very ill and frail. I took care of her
until she died. She suffered so. It was hard.

She takes his hand.

KITTY

I'm sorry, Lou. I wish I could have seen her before she died. She
was a great lady.

LOU

You are a great lady. I wish you would consider growing old with
me.

KITTY

We are old. We're not growing. I'm shrinking. With my
osteoporosis I'm getting smaller all the time. Pretty soon I'll be
invisible.

LOU

Our time, life itself is precious. The Bible says, " We have to learn to number our days, so that we may gain a heart of wisdom."

KITTY

Imagine you quoting the Bible to me. You're an enigma. I don't think about the future. I live for the contentment of today. You seem to be still searching.

LOU

My journey is over. I have found you again. Please let me walk in your shadow, before the darkness falls.

KITTY

That's very sweet, Lou. I'm moved, but I can't... (He puts his finger to her lips.)

LOU

Please don't decide now. Let me book a room on your cruise ship. Let me be the third wheel on your vacation.

KITTY

My eyesight is bad. The candlelight creates funny shadows. Without my glasses, you look like a blurry spirit with a glowing aura, like a saint.

LOU

Have I just been canonized, or are you having blood sugar problems?

KITTY

I better eat something.

He butters her some bread and hands it it to her. She takes a small bite and plays with it.

LOU

Do you ever feel lonely?

KITTY

Sometimes, but when that happens I make myself busy. I take a walk, knit, buy myself a new hat or take the bus to Atlantic City.

LOU

I'll drive us down to Atlantic City.

KITTY

Tonight?

LOU

Sure. If you like.

KITTY

Not tonight, I have an early doctor's appointment tomorrow.

LOU

Will you let me take you to Atlantic City one night next week? (She smiles)

I could take your friend too, if you think I'd try to take advantage of you.

KITTY

I know I can trust that you'll try and take advantage of me. (They laugh)

Sure. Why not?

LOU

Then we have another date? (She nods) Just you and me?

KITTY

Sure. That will be lovely.

LOU

You know I'm going to work on getting you to fall in love with me again.

KITTY

You know I'm afraid of falling.

LOU

I'm not talking bone loss; I'm talking romance. If you fall I'll pick you up and carry you home.

KITTY

That's sweet. Maybe I'll fall for you. I think I might enjoy you picking me up.

I haven't been held in a long time.

LOU

Give me a hug.

They hug as the food arrives.

KITTY

What a glorious evening. It's like a dream.

LOU

Remember, those who don't pursue their dreams are haunted by them.

He pours them more champagne and toasts.

LOU

L'Chiam. (To others in restaurant.) To Life!

KITTY

L'Chiam!

Background music rises. They eat dinner and continue their talk.

THE END.

© 2004 Katheryn White

Last Rights
A Play in One Act

SETTING: A viewing room in a funeral home. There is a public entrance -way and a private exit door on the other side. An open casket reveals an attractive middle aged man.

CAST:

JOHN AIELLO: attorney laid- out in casket.

TOM: attractive funeral director, wears black suit.

KIT BROWN: beautiful actress, elegantly dressed.

JOANIE WEISS: cute school teacher, wears long black dress and floppy hat.

MARIE WINSTON : Sophisticated lawyer, wears tailored suit.

ANA AIELLO: older wealthy woman, wears black ensemble and a hat with a veil.

JORGE CORTEZ: handsome young Hispanic professional singer.

TIME: The present.

At rise, Tom, the funeral director enters, from the private door to tidy things up and make sure the flowers look their best. When he is satisfied he goes to the public door and leads in the first visitor, Kit, then stands, like a guard at the public entrance where a guest book rests on a podium. This is his stance for most of the play. Kit struts in dramatically then rests at the head of the coffin.

TOM

(Mechanical)
Welcome. Please sign the guest book before you leave.

KIT

(Ignores Tom; focuses only on John)
Why? Why? Why? I can't believe I will never hear your excuses again.

Kit kisses John's forehead as Joanie freezes at the doorway. Tom escorts her in.

TOM
Welcome. Please sign the guest book before you leave.

Joanie can't bring herself to go near the coffin. She retreats to the corner of the room near the foot of the casket and sobs. Kit strokes John's hair and tries to look into his eyes. Marie enters with a briefcase and a strident air.

MARIE
(Looks at her watch and then at Tom)
It's just 3 PM. Why were these people let in early? The announcement said 3.

TOM
Welcome. Please sign the guest book before you leave.

Marie shakes her head, struts about the room reading the cards on the flowers until she finds the one she sent. She moves her arrangement to the front, adjusts the card then moves to the head of the casket and eyes Kit.

KIT
(To Marie)
You look like you might be a colleague of John's.

MARIE
I'm Marie Winston (extends her hand) You look like a client or a former girlfriend.

Joanie suddenly seems interested, though she doesn't move from her corner.

KIT
My name is Kit Brown. I guess I am a former girlfriend. We're all former some things to him now. The obituary didn't say how he died. I was shocked that no one called me. I had to read the tragic announcement in the local newspaper.

MARIE
He and I were partners in the same firm. One of the senior partners called me to say that when John didn't show up for work they sent someone to check on him and discovered he had died in his sleep. By the time I arrived the funeral home was removing the body.

KIT

Was he alone?

MARIE

I don't know. We all die alone.

KIT

Poor John was a mess. He didn't take care of himself or his house.

MARIE

He was planning on selling his house. We were going to leave the firm and open our own in another town and buy a house together.

KIT

He never mentioned that to me.

MARIE

Why should he?

KIT

Because we were involved.

MARIE

That's nonsense. If you were involved I would know about it.

JOANIE

(Takes a step out of her corner)
I should have been the first to know. I'm Joanie Weiss. John and I were engaged.

The others look at her, surprised. Joanie extends her hand displaying a diamond ring. Kit takes off her gloves and displays her diamond. Marie puts her hands in her pockets and walks towards Joanie.

MARIE

(To Joanie)
Just when did you and that corpse get engaged?

JOANIE

(Sobs)
Don't call him that.

MARIE
What should I call him?

KIT
Be kind. The poor girl is really upset.

MARIE
OK then, when did the two of you become engaged to that John?

KIT
He gave me this ring just last week.

JOANIE
Our betrothal took place on my birthday two weeks ago.

MARIE
Well, two nights ago that stiff and I worked late in the office.

(Looks the others in the eyes)
We did that a lot. We decided to leave the firm and start our own in Morristown. We made a plan to look at properties this week. He suggested making the partnership complete both personally and professionally. He gave me this. (She reveals an emerald ring. The others look hurt.)

JOANIE
(Moves closer to the casket)
Two nights ago he did say he had to work late.

KIT
He worked late a lot, canceled dates at the last minute, sometimes worked weekends.

MARIE
That's our John. He was a whiz at alibis. Marie moves Joanie to the edge of the casket. All three women are at the casket staring at John.

JOANIE
John was a good man.

KIT
Good at a lot of things, master of none.

MARIE
Seems he was a master of deceit. Look at his face. He looks better dead than alive.

KIT
It's the make-up. (She touches his face and some of the make-up comes off on her fingers.) Yuk. They certainly put a lot of grease paint on him.

JOANIE
You destroyed his look. Now it looks like he has a hole in his face.

KIT
If it bothers you fix it.

JOANIE
I can't touch him.

Marie takes a compact out of her purse and fixes his face.

MARIE
What are you afraid of? He can't hurt you now.

JOANIE
He is hurting me now. The sight of the two of you hurts me because I want to believe he would have married me.

KIT
Believe what you want. We'll never know. John has gone to "the undiscovered country."

MARIE
This is no time for Shakespeare. We aren't mourning a poet; we're grieving for a bastard; an insatiable womanizer; a thief.

JOANIE
He wasn't a thief.

MARIE
Oh no? Have you ever seen his tax returns?

JOANIE
I would never interfere with his business.

MARIE
You should know what you're getting into. A wife should know
about her husband's affairs.

KIT
Now she knows about us. Why would he show her his tax returns?

MARIE
(To Kit)
Did he show them to you?

KIT
Why would he? I never showed him mine. What are you trying to
tell us?

MARIE
Don't expect any big inheritance after the IRS finishes with his
earthly remains.

*Joanie goes to the flower arrangement she sent and takes out a long stemmed red
rose. She places it at John's hands.*

JOANIE
I never cared about his money. I only cared about his love.

KIT
Knowledge is power and love is blind.

MARIE
Good use of cliches Kit. I think the three of us suffered from acute
myopia.

KIT
Just who was this man who proposed to us? Why had he never
married and why now propose to the three of us?

MARIE
Did you check to see if he was ever married before?

JOANIE

He said he never married before because he was waiting for the right woman; his soul mate.

KIT

And now there are/were three candidates.

MARIE

I've known him for ten years. I've seen women come and go. I supported and counseled him more times than I can count. Until recently we acted like brother and sister and then one day things changed.

JOANIE

What happened?

MARIE

Obviously nothing special. He proposed.

Kit sniffs at something in the casket.

KIT

Do you smell something funny?

MARIE

There aren't a lot of laughs here. (Sniffs)

JOANIE

Is there a smell of death?

MARIE

There shouldn't be if the body was preserved properly.

KIT

It smells like after-shave.

JOANIE

Maybe they shaved him as part of the cosmetic work on his face.

Marie moves the rose from John's hands and puts it in his mouth.

                    MARIE
Perhaps the flower will help. Now he looks like the pig he was;
waiting to be roasted.

                    JOANIE
That's vulgar. (She places another rose in his hands.)
Kit takes some perfume out of her purse and sprays John's face.

                    KIT
Now that's better. I wonder how an embalmed body feels.

                    MARIE
Touch him.

*Kit reaches into the coffin, feels his arms, chest etc. (Curiously exploring the corpse)
The others are repelled.*

                    KIT
He doesn't feel cold. I guess the clothes make the embalming feel
natural. It's sort of like playing with play-dough except you can't
create only knead. That's sort of like it was when I was with him.
He couldn't change or alter his ways, but I didn't care because I
felt I needed him.

                    JOANIE
He made me feel like I wanted to take care of him. He treated me
well.

                    MARIE
How?

                    JOANIE
He took me to nice places; you know the kind of places with
views, crystal and real china. He paid for everything; made me
feel special.

                    MARIE
With John, it was all about money. I didn't need his money. I have
plenty of my own. You needed him financially. Life couldn't be
too fancy on a teacher's salary.

JOANIE
I make a good salary and I have great benefits.

MARIE
Do you go to four star restaurants on your own?

JOANIE
No, but...

MARIE
You proved my point. (To Kit) When will you stop fondling that carcass? Are you a necrophiliac?

KIT
No, I'm a Methodist.

MARIE
Is your IQ over 100?

KIT
I don't know. Is yours?

At that moment Ana enters, her veil is down. She struts past Tom and ignores him

TOM
Welcome. Please sign the guest book before you leave.

Ana waves Tom off and runs towards the body.

MARIE
Can Lurch say anything else?

Ana pulls Kit away from the body.

ANA
(To Kit)
Get out of that casket! What do you think you're doing?

KIT

Feeling him up a bit for the last time. I miss his body.

ANA

How can the funeral director allow such behavior?

MARIE

He's a robot. He only cares about decorum and the flower arrangements. People are collateral to him.

Kit steps back from the body as Ana removes her veil. Marie recognizes her.

ANA

(To Marie)
I'm surprised you're here. Don't you have work at the office?

MARIE

Work can wait; death can't. Some of our colleagues will join us at the internment. Where's your entourage?

ANA

This funeral is a private matter.

JOANIE

Are you his mother?

ANA

(Taken back)
I'm his wife.

MARIE

Ex-wife. She calls herself Ana Aiello.

ANA

We were soul mates. I saw him only three days ago.

KIT

I don't understand.

MARIE

Just sit down, rest and look pretty.

JOANIE
Did he divorce you because you got old?

ANA
I divorced him because he was a philanderer. After the divorce
I became the other woman in all of his relationships. He always
came back to me.

MARIE
Ana was a professor of his in law school.

ANA
I helped him get through. He really wasn't that smart, but very
charming and he looked good in a tux, (Points to corpse) as you
can see.

KIT
How long ago did you get divorced?

ANA
I can't remember exactly. It was about ten years ago. I've dated so
many oppressively dull men. That's why I always kept the door
open for John. He was so full of life and now he's gone.

JOANIE
Did he tell you about me?

ANA
Who are you? What's your story?

Joanie retreats to a chair in the corner and sobs. Tom hands her a tissue.

MARIE
You know my story. I know yours. We have both catered to John
for too many years. You probably didn't know our plan about
leaving the firm, getting our own place.

ANA
In Morristown. Yes, he told me. I'm sure the version I got was
different from yours. He told me it was a professional move.

MARIE

He told me it would be a total partnership. We had a contract.

ANA

Sure. What does it matter now?

MARIE

We both put up money. Our funds are in a trust account.

ANA

His executor will handle matters.

MARIE

In other words, I'm screwed.

ANA

Probably. From what I understand you liked getting screwed, so you should be happy.

MARIE

I don't believe he discussed our sex life.

ANA

I lost my sex drive years ago. It turned him on to tell me about his escapades. I'm writing a book based on his stories; a prurient smorgasbord. Fiction of course.

Joanie puts her hands on her ears.

JOANIE

I can't listen to this. He was wonderful to me. Can we discuss his good points? Can we say some good things about the poor man?

KIT

He wasn't a poor man.

MARIE

He had good taste in wine.

ANA

I taught him well.

JOANIE

He had a good heart.

KIT

Obviously not. He had a heart attack. He had a lousy heart.

ANA

I know about Marie. I may know the stories of you other ladies, just not your names. (To Kit) How did you know John?

KIT

He came back stage after I played Billie in "Born Yesterday."

He loved my performance and bought me two dozen roses, not the usual "on sale" grocery store dozen, but two royal red dozen.

ANA

I'm impressed. Red means love. Did you get engaged the next day?

KIT

We spent a lot of evenings together after my shows. He took me on a business trip to Chicago. That's where we fell in love.

Joanie gets up, sighs and falls back into her chair.

JOANIE

I remember that trip. He was gone a week. He called me every day, during the day.

MARIE

He nailed me on a business trip to Boston when we had rooms next to each other. We made out well for the firm and even better for ourselves.

JOANIE

He never took me on a business trip, though he promised. He said once we were married he'd take me everywhere.

I'd never be alone again.

MARIE

Sure. I bet he promised you a European honeymoon.

JOANIE

Paris, Rome, London…

KIT

And Vienna. I was really looking forward to Vienna.

"Vienna my city of dreams." (She hums the melody and sways to the tune.)

ANA

(Laughs)
Been there, done that.

JOANIE

Did he take you there?

ANA

I've been to those places with him and without him. It didn't matter. Trips lack dimension when you're traveling with a narcissist.

MARIE

You certainly are cynical.

ANA

And clinical. I measure my means.

JOANIE

(To Ana)
You must care about him if you're here.

ANA

It's sort of like the first Chanel suit I bought. It no longer fits, but I can't bear to throw it away.

JOANIE

I will never forget him.

ANA

How did you meet?

JOANIE

It was love at first sight on match.com.

KIT

When did he find time for online dating?

MARIE

Probably while he was pretending to work. His office door was almost always closed. God knows what he did in there.

KIT

He did have a back door, so he could sneak in and out.

MARIE

And he could sneak people like you in and out undiscovered, like musical chairs.

KIT

It was fun. He even had a hidden bar and a big bathroom.

JOANIE

A hidden bar?

ANA

Just how well did you know John?

JOANIE

Well enough to get engaged. I think before we leave we should all share a nice story about John, so that we leave with positive feelings.

Marie's cell phone rings. She runs out into the entrance hall to speak. Ana rearranges the flowers and put hers in front of the casket.

KIT

That is a sweet idea Joanie. You are such a good person.

You would have been good for him. You're like one of those Biblical women.

ANA

Yes, Joanie is a Proverb 31 woman.

Marie returns with her cell phone at her ear, half listening.

MARIE

(Laughs)
A wife of noble character.

ANA

"She is worth more than precious rubies. Her husband can trust
her and she will greatly enrich <u>His</u> life."

JOANIE

That sounds good. I have to read that.

MARIE

I'll fax you a copy.

JOANIE

And Kit, you are such a glamorous actress. I always wanted to
be like you. You have such a fabulous figure and style. You could
probably get any man you want.

KIT

I must admit I have had a lot of offers, but John seemed so sincere.
He really admired my acting ability. He was very supportive and
he maintained good personal hygiene.

ANA

I know I'm older than the three of you, but I knew him better, not
only because I knew him longer. I had no expectations. Sometimes
I wouldn't see him for months then he would appear at my door
with flowers and sweet tidings of comfort and joy.

JOANIE

What do you think he intended to do? Do you think he would have
married one of us?

ANA

He was mercurial, hedonistic. I don't think he intended to go
ahead with any of his offers. He did and acted on what would give
him pleasure for the moment. Hedonists respond to what's given
to them; not what they have to give to others. They're instruments
of pleasure, not fountains of joy.

JOANIE

Did you ever think of remarrying?

ANA

What for? I couldn't have children. If I could have had a child I
might have been able to hold onto him more, but never completely.

KIT

He told me he didn't want children.

JOANIE

He told me he wanted two, a boy and a girl.

ANA

He probably told Marie he wanted the excitement of building a
legal empire. His dreams never considered the consequences of
his actions.

JOANIE

We made some elaborate and beautiful plans together. He
was going to buy us a Victorian house by the sea. I could stop
teaching, stay home with the children, do volunteer work, care for
an herb garden with a border of tea roses on a wooden fence.

KIT

Sounds lovely. He was going to semi-retire so that he could be
with me when I was on tour doing plays. He even considered
being my agent. He loved the theatre.

ANA

Yes, he was a frustrated actor. We both did amateur theatre when
we were young.

KIT

He told me he played Macbeth off Broadway.

> ANA

It was off off Broadway in New Jersey. Guess who played Lady Macbeth?

> KIT

You didn't.

> ANA

I did.

> JOANIE

He certainly had good taste in women.

Marie hears something on her phone that sets her into a rage. She throws her cell phone into the casket and starts punching John. She picks up his upper body and punches his face so hard that his make-up is disturbed and starts to run.

> MARIE

(To John)
You son of a bitch! How could you do this to me?

The other women restrain her and pull her away from the body as she kicks and screams.

> JOANIE

Does anyone have a compact to fix his face?

> ANA

(She fetches a compact from her purse and hands it to Joanie.)
Here, make him beautiful. With all that smeared heavy make-up he looks like Frankenstein.

> MARIE

He is a monster!

> JOANIE

(She fixes John's face.)
What's wrong Marie? What happened?

MARIE

I was on the phone with my bank. That double- edged prick drained our trust account the day he died. He took five hundred thousand dollars, most of which was mine. That was the money intended for our future.

KIT

What can you do?

ANA

Find out who the executor is. One of the lawyers in your firm must have written the will.

MARIE

Don't think I haven't thought about that. I have a call into him. If John took out the money in cash and didn't deposit it anywhere we can't trace it?

JOANIE

(Puts her arm around Marie to comfort her)
We are sharing positive memories of John. I'm sure you have something to say before we leave.

MARIE

What I have to say is that I feel like getting a knife and cutting off his masculinity and hanging it up on the flagpole outside this place.

KIT

That would be messy and nobody would know what it is.

MARIE

There's nothing I can do; he's dead. He's probably looking down at us, or up at us and laughing at our show.

(They laugh and move close to each other).

JOANIE

You know we really are an interesting bunch of gals. I'd like to see you all again. Maybe we can get together for dinner sometime.

ANA

We could go out to celebrate after his will is read.

KIT

Do you think we'll all be in the will?

ANA

We should be. With all his debts I doubt there will be much cash, but maybe we'll each get a painting or some trinket.

MARIE

Screw that. I want my money. (Her phone rings and she leaves the room).

JOANIE

I feel sorry for Marie. She invested so much.

ANA

I invested more. Who do you think helped to support him through law school? When we met he was my student, then my lover, then my project until we got married. We would still be married except I got tired of giving and getting nothing back. He had a strong sense of entitlement.

KIT

I thought he came from a rich family.

ANA

(Laughs)

I came from a rich family. He had a football scholarship in college and then loans and work in law school until I helped him out. His father left home when he was young and his mother was a teacher.

JOANIE

Like me.

ANA

Are you a single mom raising three kids?

JOANIE

I want children.

ANA

Yes, but you don't have them. You just have yourself to worry about.

JOANIE
What happened to his mother?

ANA
She died of cancer about ten years ago. She was a sweet modest woman who was very proud of her son's success.

KIT
Did John help his mother when she was sick?

ANA
Yes, he was very good to his mother. His siblings are teachers and he didn't see them very much. I'm surprised they're not here.

KIT
Everything happened so fast. He only died yesterday.

JOANIE
Maybe they'll still come. It's sad that there aren't too many people here.

Marie enters in a controlled state of anger.

MARIE
Seems like the schmuck screwed me over more dead than alive. His attorney has no record of any cash. Being John and I had the trust account together either one of us could have withdrawn whatever we wanted. He won't be able to process the will until next week. My money is gone.

JOANIE
You said you had a lot of money so does what you lost matter that much?

MARIE
It matters a lot. I took out equity on my house. I planned on paying that off when I sold my house and we bought one together. Now instead of a bright future I see a dark cloud of debt.

ANA
I'm sorry. You know he couldn't help himself.

                              MARIE
Where could the money be?

They all shake their heads and embrace her. A handsome young
man enters with a guitar hanging by a strap around his neck. He is
playing "Cielito Lindo."

                               TOM
Welcome. Don't forget to sign the guest book.

                              MARIE
If he says that once more I swear I'll shove the book up his ass.

Jorge struts around the room playing the guitar and singing. He is joyful and upbeat.
The women look confused even though they find him quite attractive.

                             JOANIE
(To Jorge)
Are you a relative?

                             JORGE
"Ay, ay, ay, ay,

 Canta y no llores,

Porque cantando se alegran,

Cielito lindo, bien merecido.."

                               KIT
Maybe he doesn't understand English.

                               ANA
Maybe he doesn't want to.

                             JOANIE
He seems likable. Maybe he has a story to share about John.

KIT
(Speaks slowly and loudly to Jorge as if that would help communicate)
How do you know John?

JORGE
John, he is my partner.

MARIE
You're not one of our firm's partners.

JORGE
Juan is mi espouse.

JOANIE
Spouse?

ANA
What's going on here?

MARIE
I thought you knew everything.

ANA
I'm thrown by this. (To Jorge) Who the Hell are you?

JORGE
Mi llamo Jorge Cortez. (He bows and takes off his hat.)

KIT
I don't understand. Are you really a woman?

JORGE
(He laughs)
Juan he is my partner. We plan go to Brazil.

KIT
Well, you can't go now.

JOANIE
(To Jorge)
He was my fiancé. We were engaged.

> JORGE
>
> That nice. You like to dance?

> JOANIE
>
> I do like to dance, but I don't think this is the time or the place.

> JORGE
>
> Why? Juan he like to dance.

> KIT
>
> There will be a gathering after the funeral maybe we can dance then?

> JORGE
>
> No, we dance now. I go to Brazil tonight.

Jorge resumes playing "Cielito Lindo." He dances around the room while singing, places his hat on Tom in the hope of getting a smile. Finally the women dance with him. Tom carefully closes the casket. They dance to the door, sign the book and leave. Jorge is the last to leave. After they all leave Tom locks the door behind them, then goes to the casket and opens it. He goes to the exit door, opens it and takes out a leather satchel, and two backpacks.

John slowly comes back to life and looks out into the audience with confusion. He moves in pain from all the abuse his body took. Tom helps him sit up in the casket.

When John sits up the fingers in his right hand appear bent as if he is holding a skull. He contemplates the image.

> JOHN
>
> Alas, poor Yorick! Are our lives anything more than a home movie?

Tom helps John out of the casket and helps him to stand.

JOHN
(To Tom)
That drug was powerful. I'm confused. My past is gone, written, buried. How should I compose my future?

(To audience)
Is there a bright side to the dark side? Are we all guided by the moon? Where do we go from here?

John puts on a backpack, picks up the satchel and heads towards the exit.

TOM
(To audience)
Welcome, don't forget to sign the guest book.

They leave together.

End

The Play's the Thing
A Play in One Act

SETTING: A Beach, around 6 PM

TIME: Summer

CHARACTERS

KIM: Attractive middle-aged woman

PAUL: Attractive middle-aged man

AT RISE: Kim is seated in her beach chair writing in a notebook. Paul walks by her, then retreats to face her. She smiles at him. He stoops down.

PAUL

Do you have a smoke?

KIM

I don't smoke.

PAUL

I saw you smoking here the other day.

KIM

I'm trying to stop. Left them home. How about a Snapple? (He nods. She takes one out of the cooler for him and one for herself)

PAUL

I always come down the beach after the lifeguards leave, when it's free.

KIM

I've noticed you. You're always alone, strutting along the water with your head cocked, like a poet in trance.

PAUL

(Under his breathe) More of a transient. (Perks up) And I've noticed you; thought you were pretty, but you always look busy, like you don't want to be disturbed. You always seem so involved with your writing. Workin' on a novel or somethin?

KIM

Something. I'm working on the first draft of a play.

He stretches out on the sand beside her.

PAUL

Wow! Goin to Broadway?

KIM

Doubtful. More off off Broadway; maybe Women's project. It's about a nasty break-up I had with a philandering boyfriend named John, a crooked lawyer.

PAUL

Hot and steamy? (She nods.) So this John was someone you knew? (She nods.)

KIM

I knew it was over when putting him in a play was more interesting than keeping him in my life.

PAUL

I have a story.

KIM

We all have stories. My story is burning to be written. I think John is the cruelest man I've ever known. He deserves a slow painful death.

PAUL

Are you torturing him in your play?

KIM

Not enough. I'm running out of ideas. I think Medieval torture is the best.

Ironically, last summer John and I went on a vacation to Italy and went to the Medieval Torture Museum in San Gimingnano, Italy.

PAUL

That must have been fun.

KIM

Better than an amusement park. Everybody knows about the
guillotine, but have you ever heard of the rectal, oral and vaginal
pear? (He shakes his head) The Inquisitional chair? (He shakes his
head) The mask of infamy or the cat's paw?

PAUL

(Laughs)
Are you serious? (Pause) I've heard of the cat's paw. I think there
was a short story about that. I like reading mysteries and horror
stories. Did you find your favorite brand of torture for this man
who screwed you?

KIM

Yes. My favorite was the wake of Juda's cradle. The victim was
suspended in the air and hung at the waist by an iron belt. His
hands and feet were bound, his legs were kept open by a stick so
that they could only move together. He was hoisted over a pointed
pyramid, then lowered so that its point penetrated the anus. The
accused with all his muscles contracted couldn't relax and fall
asleep.

PAUL

I can see why justice is blind.

KIM

Today they just inject the accused or pull a switch; neat and clean.

PAUL

A lot of innocent people have been executed.

KIM

I'm innocent. Why did that man torture me?

PAUL

Crime is in the eyes of the beholder.

KIM

I'm a victim. John has victimized several women. You'll have to
read my play.

PAUL

Love to read it. Do you want to read me some of it now?

КIM

No, this is a first draft I never share first drafts. I need to do more research.

PAUL

I like research too. I spend a lot of time in the library.

КIM

I used to live in the library, now I use the Internet.

PAUL

I 'd love to live in a library. I have spent occasional nights in Bradley Park Library.

КIM

Oh that's one of my favorites. It was the mansion of one of the founders of this town.

PAUL

I didn't know that. It's sort of like the Addams family with widows that are so warped that they can't close properly and a staircase with a hidden closet full of old broken furniture and pillows.

КIM

Just like home. My school's library is modern and quite good.

PAUL

Where do you teach?

КIM

Rutgers.

PAUL

Really? That's where I went to college. We're about the same age so you couldn't have been teachin there when I went.

КIM

What did you major in?

PAUL

Education. I went to State for my Masters, but never finished.

KIM

Do you teach?

PAUL

I did once a long time ago. I taught junior high.

KIM

Just like teaching college except our chairs are bigger.

PAUL

What do you teach at Rutgers?

KIM

English.

PAUL

Is this your first play?

KIM

No, I've been doing it for years. Can't make a living at it.

PAUL

I understand. It's hard to make a living these days.

KIM

What do you do?

PAUL

Not much, mostly night work.

KIM

I do most of my writing at night. Last night I was struggling
with this play; didn't know how to end it. I woke up this morning
remembering a nightmare I had . I've been juggling the images all
day. It's funny how our minds work.

PAUL

I have a story.

KIM

Why don't you write it?

PAUL

If I write it will you read it?

KIM

Sure. You can bring it by here. I'm usually here from late afternoon till dark.

PAUL

I know when you're here. We've noticed each other. Remember? (Pause) I sense there might even be a little attraction goin on. (They smile at each other and make brief eye contact.) I really do like this Snapple.

KIM

I buy a case of it every week. This is their new white tea. I love it.

PAUL

Boy, you're really up on these things.

KIM

Just read the Press everyday.

He notices the newspaper sticking out of her beach bag.

PAUL

Are you finished with your paper?

KIM

Sure, would you like it?

PAUL

Yes, thank you. (He takes paper and reads the first page.)

Do they ever write about anything but murder and crooked politicians?

KIM

The sleepy towns around here are finally waking up to the wheeling and dealing that has caused their taxes to rise. If my taxes go any higher I may have to move.

PAUL

Politicians know the right people so they can swindle, steal and rob the public blind everyday of the week.

KIM

I can remember when I didn't have to lock my door when I went out or close my windows at night.

PAUL

Those politicians are sneaky. I'm sure they can break any lock.

KIM

They don't need to; they have easy access to our purse strings, bank accounts, salaries. There's no right to privacy anymore.

PAUL

Their power is criminal.

KIM

They get away with murder.

PAUL

Who's not a criminal?

KIM

I'm innocent.

PAUL

I'm innocent too. Are we the only two people around who aren't criminals?

KIM

You're taking my definition too literally.

PAUL

I have a question for you that's been buggin me.

KIM

Shoot!

PAUL

Can someone be pro life and pro war?

KIM

Back to politics. I can't answer that. Talking politics makes me
crazy. You can't win. Personally I'm against war and feel a woman
has a right to choose.

PAUL

So, you believe in killing babies, but not soldiers?

KIM

I don't want to kill anybody.

PAUL

What about John, the villain in your play?

KIM

I don't want to kill him; just torture him.

PAUL

Medieval torture caused death. Wouldn't he die from the wake of
Juda's cradle?

KIM

I'm talking about irony, not reality. Like "A Modest Proposal"
wasn't really about eating babies to solve Ireland's economic
problems.

PAUL

Jonathan Swift.

KIM

Yes, you are well read.

PAUL

I told you I spend a lot of time in the library, especially in winter.

KIM

You're too young to be retired. Just what do you do?

PAUL

I have a story.

KIM

Yes, I know you have a story. Do you have a job?

PAUL

Don't need one.

KIM

Where do you live?

PAUL

Up the street at the Whitfield.

KIM

The Whitfield? Isn't that an S R O?

PAUL

Single room occupancy. That's correct.

KIM

That old hotel takes in a lot of criminals when they get out of jail.

PAUL

They aren't criminals when they get out. They served their time. .

KIM

 Are you an ex-con?

PAUL

I'm what they call a section eight. I was the victim of too many drugs.

KIM

You seem pretty normal to me.

PAUL

Things may not always be what they seem. Shakespeare. (Pause)

Could I have another Snapple, for later?

KIM

(Pause) Sure. (She takes hold of her purse)

PAUL

Well, it's almost dinnertime. I'm allowed back in my room after that. Residents can't stay in their rooms during the day. That's why there are so many residents on the streets.

                              KIM
That place should be closed down.

                              PAUL
Then we'll be on the streets all the time.

                              KIM
My house was robbed last year.

                              PAUL
Wasn't me. I was probably in the library. I better get goin. Good
talkin to you.

                              KIM
Yes. I'm sorry for your situation.

                              PAUL
Why, you didn't cause it. You're innocent.

                              KIM
Well you appear just like me.

                              PAUL
I have a story. You probably wouldn't have given me your time if
you knew I lived in the Whitfield.

                              KIM
Probably not.

                              PAUL
Don't worry. I won't bother you anymore.

                              KIM
Let me give you a few dollars. (She opens her purse)

                              PAUL
Lady, don't you know you shouldn't open your purse in front of
someone who lives in the Whitfield?

She hands him a five dollar bill and he takes it.

                              KIM
Thanks for listening to my story.

PAUL

Thank you for listening to mine. (He starts to walk away) Have a great day!

KIM

I know. By the way what's your name?

PAUL

Paul. Like in the Bible, Paul. I know you're name is Kim. I saw it on your driver's license when you opened your purse. I saw your address too.

KIM

You are clever, very observant.

PAUL

That's how I survive. Take care.

He leaves and she goes back to her notebook starts to write then looks back over her shoulder at Paul. Their eyes meet for a moment, then he turns back and leaves the beach.

END

Shadows of a Queen
A Play in One Act

Setting: Bare stage using rear projection images.

Time: Present in Egypt.

Characters: (Three characters and two voices.)

VOICE ONE (Samantha): Female Patient

VOICE TWO (Dr. Roemer): Psychologist

HATSHEPSUT: Queen/Pharaoh, dressed in a simple long tunic.

SAM: Male traveler dressed in jeans and white shirt.

SAMANTHA: Female traveler dressed in jeans and white shirt

SCENE ONE: At rise we see a slide projection of Hatshepsut's temple Deir El-Bahari and hear the voices of a female Patient and her Psychologist. (These could be pre-recorded.)

VOICE ONE
I had the dream again, the night after I booked my trip to Egypt.

VOICE TWO
I think you really need to go, confront what's haunting you.

VOICE ONE
In my dream I was left to die alone in a cold dark abyss. I lost everything; my wealth, power, beauty. The deepest pain remains the loss of my children. Sometimes in my dreams I hear their tiny voices calling for their mother; sobbing. Then I wake up in a cold sweat and tears…Dr. Roemer, I'm scared.

VOICE TWO
Of course you are, Sammantha. You need to feel the energy near the temple of Deir El-Bahari. You need to walk in the footsteps of Hatshepsut.

SPEAKER: **VOICE ONE**

I wonder. Can I go back that far? When you regressed me I went back three thousand years, but my message was not clear.

SPEAKER: **VOICE TWO**

There's no Rosetta stone for psychoanalysis; only language.

SPEAKER: **VOICE ONE**

From what I read about her much of her life was a mystery.

SPEAKER: **VOICE TWO**

All lives are mysteries whose codes are hidden in ancient spirits.

SPEAKER: **VOICE ONE**

How can I be sure I am seeking the right spirit?

SPEAKER: **VOICE TWO**

You can't be sure. Be open. Follow the Light.

SCENE TWO: Go to dark. Drums create a hypnotic transition to the next scene. At rise a spot light shows two travelers moving a large rock that admits them into a cave downstage. The travelers are similar in height and build. Sam has longish hair and Samantha's is short. In the dim light they could be identical twins.

SPEAKER: **SAMANTHA**

Sam, you could have pushed harder. That boulder weighed twice as much as me. You know I have a bad back.

SPEAKER: **SAM**

I did divert the boulder so it didn't kill us. Give me some credit. You were too anxious. We need to be careful. We're not supposed to be in these hills. We're too close to the temple. We could wind up in an Egyptian jail.

SPEAKER: **SAMANTHA**

It's after hours. The guards went home. We are tourists, hikers. We can say we're lost.

SPEAKER: **SAM**

Lost in thought. We need to be careful Samantha ... I need some water. (Takes two bottles of water out of his backpack and hands one to her). Where are the flashlights?

SAMANTHA

Sam, give me a minute. (She has a hard time getting her backpack off . Then squats down to fish through it. She unwinds to stand up holding her back) Oh my back hurts too much! We took too much stuff with us. I'm a very weak woman.

SAM

Sam, stop whining. Don't play the gender card with me. Having a penis doesn't give me a strong back. If you want to have a contest, my back probably hurts more than yours right now. Don't ask me to lift, push or carry anymore. This journey was your idea.

SAMANTHA

Fine. Can you handle a flashlight? (She hands him a large flashlight. He drops it.) Klutz!

SAM

Bitch!

SAMANTHA

This bickering isn't getting us anywhere.

SAM

I agree. Let's go!

Samantha turns on her flashlight. A large (Projected) shadow image of a statue of Hatshepsut appears on the upstage cave wall. Samantha grabs onto Sam who trips and they fall into each other's arms on the ground staring up at the figure. She uses her flashlight to explore the rest of the cave from her reclined position. At the far end of the cave they see a woman sitting on a rock. She is wearing a long frayed tunic.

HATSHEPSUT

(Sarcastic)
It is about Time ...I have waited so long.

SAMANTHA

(Clutches onto Sam)
She speaks English.

HATSHEPSUT

I possess the knowledge of all tongues.

SAMANTHA

Wow! Who are you?

HATSHEPSUT

(Laughs)
You do not know what path you traveled?

SAMANTHA

You can't be the Queen Hatshepsut?

HATSHEPSUT

I prefer Pharaoh.

SAM

This is too weird. Let's go. (Clings onto Samantha as he pulls her up.)

SAMANTHA

Don't be afraid. She won't harm us.

HATSHEPSUT

I have never harmed anyone.

SAMANTHA

Why are you here?

HATSHEPSUT

This is my final resting place. The gods told me you would come as others have before. The others were in search of treasure. The gods tell me you seek knowledge. You are scholars.

SAMANTHA

Yes! We are both college professors. I teach English and Sam teaches History.

HATSHEPSUT

You are old souls.

SAM

(To Samantha)
Maybe we're dead; killed by that boulder that nearly hit us.

Maybe it did hit us and we're goners.

HATSHEPSUT

I have been waiting here for you both for a long time.

SAM

Are we dead or alive?

HATSHEPSUT

We live many lives.

SAM

Lady, can you focus? Were we killed by that boulder or not?

HATSHEPSUT

It killed me as it trapped me here about three thousand years ago.

SAM

You look pretty good for being so old.

HATSHEPSUT

The two of you dress like slaves?

SAMANTHA

We're Americans.

HATSHEPSUT

Do all Americans dress like you?

SAMANTHA

We're dressed for exploring the hills and caves near Deir El-Bahari.

HATSHEPSUT

My temple. I hear it has been desecrated.

SAM

Who told you that?

HATSHEPSUT

My guides. They travel around me all the time. Some are here now.

SAMANTHA

I don't see anyone else.

HATSHEPSUT

They are my guides.

SAM

Would they let you leave with us?

HATSHEPSUT

I have nowhere to go. My assassin destroyed all memory of
me. He was a warrior. I was a lover of peace and order. Hathor,
goddess of beauty and love, inspired me. She is saddened at the
state of my temple now. It is no longer a sacred place. Thousands
of people come each day to stare at pictures on walls that they will
never understand and buy trinkets to validate their journey. Hathor
watches the masses and is only happy when the foreign artists
work at preserving its integrity.

SAMMANTHA

You actually talk to Hathor?

HATSHEPSUT

(Shrugs her shoulders)
What else do I have to do?

SAM

You could go out into the world and tell your story.

HATSHEPSUT

The gods will not allow it. They did not come to me until I passed
from mortal form. Amen Re gave special permission for your
visit. Soon Nut will absorb him and you will need to go.

SAMANTHA

Are you saying this visit was predestined?

HATSHEPSUT

All visits are destined from a higher power.

SAM

Are we the first mortals to find this cave?

HATSHEPSUT

Others have tried, like Howard Carter. The gods were not happy
with him as he disturbed the tomb of Tutankhamen. The gods

were pleased with your request. You are seekers of truth. A
powerful seer sent you.

SAMANTHA

You mean they heard me talking with my therapist, Dr. Roemer?

HATSHEPSUT

Your therapist was once a high priest in Karnak. Your return was
Your destiny.

SAMANTHA

I was here before?

HATSHEPSUT

That knowledge is held in your spirit. You need to listen to the
language of your heart.

SAMANTHA

Do I have special powers?

HATSHEPSUT

Everyone does. You need to learn how to listen and give thanks.

SAM

Can you tell us why us and why today?

HATSHEPSUT

Why not you, why not today?

SAMANTHA

Do you have a message for us to carry out of here into the
universe?

HATSHEPSUT

The universe is too large for my message. I will tell you the truth
about me, but I am not sure anyone will listen.

SAM

Do you want to leave with us?

HATSHEPSUT

Are you touched by the lunacy of the moon?

SAM

She thinks we're crazy!

HATSHEPSUT

I can not leave. What I want does not matter to your world.

SAMANTHA

Maybe it's lunacy; there's a full moon tonight… Sam, she's the ghost of Queen Hatshepsut, a spirit, the pharaoh I dreamed about.

HATSHEPSUT

Thank you for honoring my title, Pharaoh. My stepbrother/stepson Tuthmosis III destroyed most of my statues and put his name on the temples I built, like the one in Karnak where he also claimed the great obelisk that my grand Steward of Estates Senenmut built for me.

SAMANTHA

Rumor has it you had something going on with Senenmut.

HATSHEPSUT

Senenmut remains my secret, my sacred friend.

SAM

I sense you're still very angry at Tuthmosis?

HATSHEPSUT

His spirit has not died. He walks the earth today. He is a warrior capable of the worst cruelty. No one can stop him.

SAM

In history books Tuthmosis III was known as "the Napoleon of Ancient Egypt." What's his name today?

HATSHEPSUT

I do not know of names today. In my world he was Tuthmosis the Third, son of my husband who is also my half brother, Tuthmosis the second, by a different mother, a secondary wife, Aset. (She spits)

SAM

I'm so confused. You guys married brothers, sisters, children. How could you ever be normal?

HATSHEPSUT
What does normal mean?

SAM
Normalcy is relative to specific social orders.

SAMANTHA
Sam, you sound like a textbook. (To Hatshepsut) How did
Tuthmosis the third kill you?

HATSHEPSUT
Tuthmosis had his guards carry me here in the night, my throat
blocked by a gag of grape leaves wrapped in linen. He never
touched me, kept his hands clean of my blood. They tied my hands
behind my back in this very spot. Tuthmosis third removed a sheet
of papyrus from his sack and asked me to sign away my power
giving him total rule over upper and lower Egypt. I refused. He
waited. His guards released scorpions around me. I would not
submit. They left me here to die, closing the entrance to this cave
with the large boulder that brought you here.

SAMANTHA
Did the boulder kill us?

HATSHEPSUT
No, the two of you are free to go with my memory.

SAM
Can we share your story?

HATSHEPSUT
You may try, but few men will believe you.

SAMANTHA
I'll try. I'll write something about you.

HATSHEPSUT
I would like the truth written even though most will scorn it.

SAM
(To Samantha)
Sam, it sounds like your dream.

> SAMANTHA
>
> (Holds her head)
> Maybe I'm dreaming now?

> HATSHEPSUT
>
> All I have left are my dreams of glory, my good memories and the longing for my daughter the princess Neferure, whom I have not seen since that day.

> SAM
>
> Is there any physical evidence we can take with us to prove your existence?

> HATSHEPSUT
>
> They only left me a simple ring, no jewels. It is a small ring I planned to give to my daughter.

> SAMANTHA
>
> Could I have it?

> HATSHEPSUT
>
> (As in a trance)
> The gods tell me to toss it into the light.

Samantha stands in front of the cave downstage where the light seems to shine in stronger than before. Hatshepsut tosses the ring past her into the audience.

> SAMANTHA
>
> It's gone! We'll never find it out there.

> HATSHEPSUT
>
> The ring will remain in your heart with my memory.

> SAMANTHA
>
> Can I ask you a question about my dream?

> HATSHEPSUT
>
> It needs to be in haste as Nut is starting to consume the sun.

> SAM
>
> It is getting dark outside. We need to go.

SAMANTHA

I need to ask my question of the Pharaoh Queen Hatshepsut. (She reaches out to Hatshepsut.) Could I be the reincarnation of you?

HATSHEPSUT

I regret that I cannot answer that question. I know of only those who have come before me. I am not told who or how I may reappear. If you are me I wish you would learn how to dress better. A queen or pharaoh wears silk and jewels, not ugly, long, frayed pants.

SAMANTHA

They're called jeans. Mine are classic Levi Strauss.

Hatshepsut shakes her head and smiles.

SAM

When we get back to the ship we'll buy beautiful outfits for the Galabaya party tonight.

HATSHEPSUT

Go in peace, joy, music and love. Spread beauty in the world.

SAMANTHA

(To Sam)
We need to find that ring.

HATSHEPSUT

The ring will find its way in the world. Go with the light my children.

Where there is light there is life. Our minds are the channels of our souls.

If you allow your heart to nurture your mind you will understand the truth.

SCENE THREE: Hatshepsut disappears. The cave turns dark except for the light which appears at its exit. Sam and Samantha leave the cave as the backdrop of the temple returns.

SAM

Where did she go?

SAMANTHA

Her spirit appeared and now she's gone, like a dream.

SAM

Like the twinkle of one of those stars. What a beautiful night.

SAMANTHA

Magical...the Egyptian sky is like no other.

SAM

Never a cloud.

SAMANTHA

Do you remember something about a ring?

SAM

We'll never find it now.

SAMANTHA

It's not lost forever. We'll return.

SAM

(He kisses her.)
I believe we will. For now, let's get back to the ship. There's a party tonight!

THE END

Sentimental Journey
A Drama in Three Acts

CAST OF CHARACTERS

ALLEGRA WHILDE: A glamorous actress/dancer, over 60.

LIZ WHITE: An intellectual actress, over 60.

VIOLET SIMMS: A religious actress, over 70.

SAM SHAW: A writer/bartender, son of the Hotel owner, 20's.

DR. TED EASTMAN: A retired cardiologist/businessman, over 60.

SCENE: A grand old Victorian Hotel in a seaside resort.

TIME: 1985

ACT I. Scene 1

SETTING: Porch and adjacent Bar at a Victorian style seaside Hotel . The French doors leading to the Bar are open.

AT RISE: VIOLET is seated on rocking chair on porch softly humming "Sentimental Journey" (Green/Brown/Homer 1945). ALLEGRA, seated at bar sings.

ALLEGRA

Gonna take a Sentimental Journey.

Gonna set my heart at ease

Gonna make a Sentimental Journey

To renew old memories..."

(At the Bar Sam serves Allegra a drink that she savors with delight.)

ALLEGRA

Sam honey, you are a true artist.

(She holds up her drink as if to toast him.)

This is a perfect Sidecar.

                    SAM (BLUSHING)
Thank you Allegra.

                    ALLEGRA
Don't thank me honey. Let me thank you.

(She puts down her drink, reaches across the bar, clenches his head between her hands and kisses him loudly on the forehead.)

You inherited your father's knack for making your guests feel like royalty.

                    SAM
You are Royalty.

                    ALLEGRA
The Theatre provides few thrones and many hollow crowns.

                    SAM
Every summer I so look forward to your visits and your stories of the USO shows, Broadway musicals, serious drama.

                    ALLEGRA
Your father told me you are writing stories of your own.

                    SAM
Well, actually I'm half-way through my first novel.

                    ALLEGRA
A novel. How wonderful! What's it about?

                    SAM
It's called Tidal waves. It's a romantic fishing novel.

                    ALLEGRA
Fishing and romance, a new genre. I'm afraid I've always associated fishing with worms and worms with serpents and serpents with ex-husbands.

SAM

My novel has to do more with self-discovery, first love and fly fishing.

ALLEGRA

Sounds very intellectual like "Moby Dick" meets "Field and Stream." You must show it to me this week.

(Violet enters Bar. She sits at a table. Sam goes to her for her order.)

ALLEGRA (CONT.)

Violet dear, did you know Sam is writing his first novel?

VIOLET

I would have sworn my son told me Sam took up painting. Jimmy said that Sam sent him sketches.

ALLEGRA

Don't talk about Sam like he's not here. What about these sketches Sam?

SAM

I sent Jimmy a few short sketches of my characters, plot locations. That kind of stuff, not pictures.

VIOLET

I must confess I'm disappointed. I was hoping to buy an original painting by Sam for the living room of my new condo. What would I do with a novel? My eyes are so weak I can hardly read anymore.

ALLEGRA

Maybe we can persuade Sam to write a play about us.

VIOLET

Oh sure! Sure. Great idea. Who will he get to produce it? How will they cast it? Imagine having to audition to play yourself.

ALLEGRA

Imagine what it would be like to see yourself played by another actress.

                    VIOLET
I'm getting too old to imagine anything anymore. (motioning to
Allegra) Come sit by me.

(Allegra obeys almost falling off her bar stool.)

                 VIOLET (CONT.)
You know how much I dislike sitting at bars. We must maintain
our images as ladies.

                    ALLEGRA
My image is intact. At my age I don't have to worry.

                    VIOLET
At Sam's age you didn't worry. You never worry; that's one of
your flaws.

                ALLEGRA (TO SAM)
I'm ready for another honey..

                    VIOLET
I'll have a seltzer plain with a twist of lime (to Allegra) How
many sidecars have you had?

                    ALLEGRA
Enough to keep me on track. No lectures.

                    VIOLET
I pray for you all the time. Alcohol distorts judgement, kills brain
cells. You could fall, loose your memory, break your hip. It's too
much to think about.

                    ALLEGRA
Then don't think about it. I'm not ready to join the geriatric set.

                    VIOLET
We don't have to join. We're lifetime members. Remember dear,
I retired.

ALLEGRA

I'll never retire. I'll audition until I'm dead. Even then I'll offer my remains if a show needs a corpse.

(Liz appears at doorway, exhausted.)

LIZ

Hi Glory Girls. We're all together for one more year!

ALLEGRA

Lizzy, skip the Glory Girls, this isn't the Stage Door canteen. This is the House by the Sea. This isn't 1943; it's 1985.

LIZ

I'm not in the mood for your humor. I'm tired.

VIOLET (TO LIZ)

Darling, sit here by me and have some tea to revive you.

LIZ

I'd like to go upstairs and freshen up a bit. (She heads to the stairs.)

ALLEGRA (TEASING)

Are you sure you wouldn't like a little nip first?

LIZ

I don't need a nip. I need a nap. See you girls later. (She exits upstairs.)

ALLEGRA

Lizzy really let herself go.

VIOLET

I think she's depressed and she wears too much black.

ALLEGRA

Lizzy is still playing Masha in The Sea Gull. I can hear her moaning "I'm in mourning for my life. I'm unhappy."

VIOLET
Liz never recovered from the terrible tragedy of her life.

ALLEGRA
It's about time she comes out of mourning. Who hasn't experienced tragedy?

VIOLET
We all deal with pain differently. You turn every tragedy in your life into a romantic comedy.

ALLEGRA
I always like to leave them laughing.

VIOLET
This summer, try to be more patient with Liz.

ALLEGRA
I do try. She could have at least sat with us and had a drink before running upstairs.

VIOLET
Not everyone needs a drink to relax. This holiday may prove stressful.

SAM
It can't be the same without Lillian.

ALLEGRA
It won't be the same without Lillian. I felt her presence the minute I walked into the hotel today. Her perfume, Arpege, haunts this room. How many women wear Arpege today?

VIOLET
Lillian lives in my prayers. I talk to her every day.

SAM
My dad said he read in the papers Lillian had a stroke.

ALLEGRA
Lillian suffered her final stroke on stage during a performance of The Royal Family. She collapsed in the arms of the actress who played her daughter.

VIOLET

Lillian will be missed. She wouldn't want us to be sad. Let's try to raise our spirits before Liz comes downstairs.

ALLEGRA

(She raises her empty glass and gestures to Sam for a refill.)

I'll drink to that.

SAM

This one's on the house and I'll fix Liz her Jack Rose.

VIOLET (TO ALLEGRA)

Will you try to be nicer to Liz this year?

ALLEGRA

Stop repeating yourself. I already told you I'm as nice to her as I can be.

VIOLET

Liz is taking Lillian's death very hard.

ALLEGRA

Are you saying I'm not? Are you saying I'm insensitive?

VIOLET

I would never say that dear. You know...

(Liz enters and sits opposite Violet placing Allegra in center. Sam places drink in front of Liz. When he is not fixing drinks, he sits behind the bar reading or taking notes in his journal notebook.)

LIZ

(She nervously picks through her handbag for money.)

Sam, you remembered. How kind.

ALLEGRA

Stop fishing Lizzy. It's on me.

LIZ

Thank you. Please don't call me Lizzy. You know how I hate it.

VIOLET

Girls, let's try to get along. We don't have much time together.

LIZ

Any good news ladies?

ALLEGRA

I have an audition when I get back to New York.

LIZ

So do I.

ALLEGRA

Mine is a comic mystery featuring married society sleuths. Sort of like Nick and Nora Charles on social security.

LIZ

No Time for Crime.

ALLEGRA

That's it. Is that the one you're up for too? (Liz nods.) So, we compete again.

LIZ

I know the playwright.

ALLEGRA

I've worked with the director before. I think he had a little crush on me.

LIZ

They all do, but if it was only a little crush I suppose I have a chance. It's been years since we've been up for the same part.

ALLEGRA

Scared? (Liz shakes her head, smugly) We'll always be best friends. It's just like when we were up against Jane Cowl for Old Acquaintance. Remember?

LIZ

That time we lost. This time one of us will win and we'll celebrate her victory.

VIOLET

As long as it is not a Dark Victory.

LIZ

It will be a bright day if it's one of us. We should coax Violet into auditioning too.

ALLEGRA

Strengthen the odds.

VIOLET

Coax away. I'm firm about retiring. I'm happy gardening in Connecticut.

LIZ

I really haven't been happy since Stan died.

ALLEGRA

I don't need a man to make me happy.

LIZ

It helps.

ALLEGRA

For me companionship means the difference between eating at the Four Seasons and the Terminal Diner.

LIZ

I don't believe money can make one happy.

ALLEGRA

I It helps.

LIZ (TO ALLEGRA)

Were you ever really happy?

ALLEGRA

I can't say that I'm unhappy. If by really happy you mean moments of ecstasy, I can only think of .opening nights in the theatre and first night with lovers.

LIZ

You equate happiness with applause.

ALLEGRA

Applause and reverence.

VIOLET (SHAKEY)

I hate to break your witty chain of thought, but there's something on my mind.

LIZ (TO VIOLET)

Are you all right? You look a little pale.

ALLEGRA

You said your diabetes was under control. A shot of scotch may add a little color to your cheeks.

VIOLET

No no no. I can't drink alcohol. Besides the diabetes, remember all those years I spent in AA.

ALLEGRA

When were you in AA?

VIOLET

Allegra, you never listen.

(Allegra shakes her head and gestures an apology.)

VIOLET (CONT.)

I'm not talking about the past; I'm concerned with the future. I'm finding these August rituals too tiring. It's not that I don't love the two of you. It's just that this is a long trip and...

LIZ

You can't mean that. You can't. This is all I have to look forward to.

ALLEGRA

Violet may be right. It is a long trip. We're not working as much. It cost a lot of money.

(Liz gets noticeably more anxious.)

ALLEGRA (CONT.)

Don't get hysterical Lizzy. You've always been prone to hysteria. You'd make the perfect Lucia, if you had a voice.

LIZ

I can't bear the prospect of ending this. I hope it's not the money. I could contribute to your expenses. I have a little savings.

VIOLET

It's not the money dear. We all have a little savings.

ALLEGRA

I have nothing.

LIZ

I can't bear this discussion. Where would I go next August? My family's gone. You're the only friends I have left. I would die, simply die.

ALLEGRA

More hysterics. You'll die anyway.

VIOLET

Allegra, that's cruel. You don't mean that.

LIZ

She means it. She likes to torment me. She'll be happy to dance on my grave, if I don't dance on hers first.

VIOLET

Let's step back and see where our anxiety is coming from.

ALLEGRA

Let's get Violet a t-shirt (demonstrates across her chest) that says
METHOD ACTRESS.

VIOLET

Instead of attacking each other, let's remember Lillian. We're
upset because she's passed on.

LIZ

We're missing Lillian's mirror; her reflection on our lives.

ALLEGRA

And her ashes.

LIZ

Allegra must you bring that up now? I can't bear to think of
Lillian's remains.

ALLEGRA

We must think of it and get ready to face the charred remains of
our dear friend.

VIOLET

Back off Allegra.

ALLEGRA

Remember her sister is sending a container filled with her ashes
here. It was Lillian's wish that we dispose of them while on our
holiday.

VIOLET

Death Takes a Holiday. How ironical.

LIZ

How morbid. Stop it! Stop it!

ALLEGRA

We have to face it. It's part of the mourning process.

LIZ

I'm going to faint.

(Allegra helps her hold her drink and head up.)

VIOLET
I don't believe in cremation. Lillian's family should have had a viewing, a proper funeral mass, internment, a memorial service and a tombstone.

ALLEGRA
I believe in shrines.

LIZ
I feel deprived that I will not be able to visit her grave.

VIOLET
I feel the same way. I always visit the graves of my friends and relatives on their birthdays and Easter.

ALLEGRA
That sounds like a full time job. I thought you retired.

LIZ
I don't understand why Lillian didn't discuss this with us before she died.

ALLEGRA
Why don't you send her a telegram. See if she cares.

VIOLET (CONFUSED)
Are you talking about Lillian or her sister?

ALLEGRA (FRUSTRATED)
I give up. If it will make you girls happy, when the ashes arrive I will put them into three baggies and we can do with them what we wish.

VIOLET
That doesn't solve anything.

ALLEGRA
Maybe we can't solve this. Maybe it's already solved

                    LIZ
We have to accept Lillian's last request whether we agree with it
or not.

                  ALLEGRA
After all, it was her life.

                   VIOLET
We have to change the subject. I feel my blood sugar rising and I
don't want to faint.

                    LIZ
Please don't faint. Relax.

                  ALLEGRA
(Points to empty chair at table)

There's Lillian's chair. Should we talk to her or about her?

                   VIOLET
Remember how the four of us met?

                    LIZ
Of course. We met in New York City in the spring of 1941 at an
audition for a USO show going to Hawaii.

                   VIOLET
The Glory Girls.

                  ALLEGRA
Hope and Glory. Those were the days.

                    LIZ
Now that we're all in a sentimental mood, this may be a good time
to look at my photos from last summer.

(She takes photos from her purse and evokes no interest.)

              ALLEGRA (ANNOYED)
Later Lizzy.

VIOLET

After dinner, dear.

ALLEGRA

I'm not in the mood to reflect on my wrinkles.

LIZ

I had the photos processed with matte finish, not glossy. Wrinkles are less pronounced in matte.

VIOLET

Is that so? How clever dear.

ALLEGRA

Lizzy, will you put those photos away till later. You're annoying us.

LIZ

(Hurt she puts photos back in her handbag)

Us?

ALLEGRA

Let's go to the beach!

VIOLET

The sun is going down. It will be chilly and I'm fighting a cold. Summer colds are the worst they never leave you.

LIZ

I know. I'm recovering from one too. We could get pneumonia.

ALLEGRA

Come on girls. Lighten up! It's a warm, clear, beautiful afternoon. Let's think sunshine.

VIOLET

Has anyone thought about this evening? Do we want to eat here or go out?

                    SAM
Cook's special is Seafood Newburg.

                    LIZ
Forget newburg with my gallbladder.

                    VIOLET
What about cholesterol? I vote for fresh broiled fish at the Lobster
House.

(They all nod in agreement.)

                    LIZ
What about the rest of the evening? Are we going to the theater?

                    ALLEGRA
Sam honey, do you have the scoop on your local theaters?

                    SAM
Dial M for Murder at the Bayside and The King and I at the
Arena.

                    LIZ
What about the Mercury?

                    SAM
They're having a lot of problems there. They were supposed to do
Arsenic and Old Lace, but they had to postpone it.

                    ALLEGRA
I'm so sick of that relic of a play.

                    VIOLET
I've played Martha so many times I see her in my sleep.

                    SAM
Maybe you should run down there because I heard the reason they
postponed the show was because the actress playing that part had
a stroke.

(All three ladies perk up with interest.)

VIOLET

Poor thing, but strokes are not always fatal.

LIZ

Didn't she have an understudy?

ALLEGRA

Honey, this isn't New York. How many equity actresses over sixty
do you think live in this sleepy town?

LIZ

Sam, where did you get your information?

SAM

A guy named Joe, the producer, was in here the other day. He was
very upset, put down 3 shots of scotch before he could speak.

ALLEGRA

Sounds pretty desperate to me. The Straw Hat circuit is far from
Broadway, but I'm sure the show cost money. One of us could step
in and help him out.

LIZ

Um. Maybe we should give him a call tomorrow.

ALLEGRA

Call nothing. We'll sashay down to the Mercury after breakfast
and offer our services.

VIOLET

It could be my swan song.

ALLEGRA

I thought you already sang that song. You've been preaching
retirement since you arrived here.

LIZ

It would be a cinch for Violet.

                    VIOLET
The fairest thing for us to do is to approach him as a team and let
him decide.

                    LIZ
He may not want any of us.

                    ALLEGRA
How could he not want any of us? We're fantastic! Glory Girls.

                    LIZ
The three Graces.

                    VIOLET
I'm Faith. Liz is Hope. That makes Allegra.

                    ALLEGRA
Charity. Fine. Now that our roles are decided, let's go to the
beach.

                    VIOLET
I need to go upstairs and change. I haven't even unpacked yet.

                    ALLEGRA
Fine, let's go change.

(Allegra and Violet get up to leave. Liz stays put.)

                    LIZ
Please go without me girls. I'd like to rest here for a few more
minutes. Then I want to take a nap and shower before dinner, if
you don't mind.

                    ALLEGRA
We mind, but we'll excuse you this time because you look so pale.
Get some rest or we'll send you out to audition for Dracula.

(Allegra and Violet kiss Liz on the forehead and exit.)

                    SAM (SITS WITH LIZ)
Ya know I need a break. Would you mind some company?

LIZ
Please join me. Tell me about that book I hear you're writing.

SAM
Ah, we can talk about that some other time. I'd like to see your photos from last summer.

LIZ (LIGHTS UP AND TAKES PHOTOS FROM HER BAG)
I'd like you to have this one with you and Lillian.

SAM
Oh thank you so much.

(She spreads photos on table.)

LIZ
Let's get on with My Last Picture show.

"(BLACKOUT)"

ACT 1. Scene 2.

SETTING: The Beach.

AT RISE: Minutes later. Allegra and Violet are walking along the beach carrying their shoes. Allegra is wearing an elegant beach ensemble while Violet is wrapped in her beach blanket wearing s floppy hat and dark glasses.

ALLEGRA
Do you really think you're up to auditioning for Arsenic and old Lace?

VIOLET
Are you afraid of the competition? Want me to drop out and strengthen your odds?

ALLEGRA
Oh no, no. It's just that you were complaining about your health and I thought maybe it would be too much for you.

VIOLET

I'm doing fine. It was my decision to retire. I changed my mind.
The holistic physician I'm seeing thinks being involved with the
world is nature's best medicine.

ALLEGRA

I wonder what a real doctor would advise.

VIOLET

She is a real doctor. Her approach is sort of "New Age," and I like
it. Look Allegra, if you want to work on someone work on Liz.
I'm not backing out.

ALLEGRA

Well you do have the advantage of playing the part so many times
for so many years.

VIOLET

Like I said I can do it in my sleep. I even look the part. You don't.

ALLEGRA

Well you don't think I'm going to pay a visit to the theater looking
like this. I'll find some frumpy clothes.

VIOLET

You don't own anything frumpy enough and I'm not loaning you
anything of mine.

ALLEGRA

Did I ask you?

(Violet shakes her head.)

I'll just sashay downtown to the Goodwill store in Asbury Park
first thing in the morning and find something that reminds me of
you.

VIOLET

I doubt if you'll find anything there with a fine lace collar. Martha
always wore fine lace collars.

ALLEGRA (EXHAUSTED BY THE CONVERSATION)
I'll make do. I'm a survivor. (beat) Is your agent still calling you
with work?

VIOLET
Not much. My agent's not that interested in actresses our age.
The last few parts I got I stumbled on myself.

ALLEGRA
Is your son bringing in a steady salary?

VIOLET
Jimmy's doing well. His teaching is steady and his concerts are a
bonus. We have my social security. We get by.

ALLEGRA
I have one audition coming up in September. You know that
tedious part Liz and I are up for- a geriatric Nancy Drew. After
that, who knows what? I can't live on social security and the
maintenance on my co-op is going up again.

VIOLET
You've been spoiled by the good life. Maybe you should consider
a roommate.

ALLEGRA
What do you do with a roommate when you want to have a man
stay over?

VIOLET
Forget it. You don't need that headache. Besides what would you
do if he had a heart attack and died in your bed?

ALLEGRA
At least he would die with a smile on his face. (pause) Do you
remember the first time you fell in love?

VIOLET
Everyone does.

ALLEGRA
Do you remember those magical feelings, the glow?

                        VIOLET
Come now, do you really think you're going to have any more love
affairs?

                        ALLEGRA
Where there's life there's love. I'm not dead yet.

                        VIOLET
Oh Allegra, you've always been a free spirit, like Isadora Duncan.
You prefer to cast your fate to the wind. I put my fate in the hands
of the Lord.

(Allegra trips over a body wrapped in a blanket.)

                        ALLEGRA
Oh, oh! I'm terribly sorry.

              VIOLET (SCREAMS IN HORROR.)
It's a corpse!

                        ALLEGRA
No Violet, it's moving. It or he's alive!

                        VIOLET
Thank God. I almost lost my teeth.

(TED scrambles out from under his blanket. The women pull back in apprehension.
Allegra seems to have injured her ankle. Ted sounds a bit like Count Dracula, looks
a bit like Cary Grant.)

                        TED
Good evening.

                        ALLEGRA
Good afternoon.

(Allegra rubs her ankle dramatically. Ted is overly concerned. Violet avoids looking
at him.)

TED (SQUINTING)
Is there still some sun?

ALLEGRA
I hope I didn't damage any part of you when I tripped.

TED
All the important parts feel in order.

ALLEGRA (FLIRTING)
Oh, I can see that.

(She reaches for his arm. Violet pulls her back.)

VIOLET
Don't touch him. We don't know where he's been.

TED
I've been here too long. It's time for me to wake up and get moving.

VIOLET
Are you living on the beach?

TED
I'm living. I'm on the beach.

VIOLET
What I mean is do you live here?

TED
No. Do you?

ALLEGRA
He's obviously just here for a nap.

TED
Obviously. (to Allegra) How's your ankle?

ALLEGRA (MILKS IT)

A little sore. It's all my fault. I wasn't watching my way. Meeting you has distracted me from my pain.

TED

Please let me take a look at your ankle.

(He lunges toward Allegra. She trips backwards. Violet catches her before she falls.)

TED (CONT.)

I have never met a woman with such elegantly shaped legs.

ALLEGRA

Your legs look so muscular. I bet you're an athlete. (He nods.) What do you play?

TED

Tennis and golf keep me in shape for more challenging indoor sports, if you get my drift.

ALLEGRA

You can drift in my direction. I love playing indoors.

VIOLET

Allegra dear, I think we should head back to the Hotel.

TED

(He takes a bottle of champagne out of a cooler under his blanket.)

Would you ladies care for champagne?

(Allegra goes to sit down and Violet pulls her back.)

ALLEGRA

I adore champagne.

TED

I'm sorry it's only Korbel.

VIOLET

Alcoholic beverages aren't allowed on the beach. There are signs all over. Don't people read signs anymore?

TED

I won't tell, if you won't tell. (He reaches under his blanket.) Look, I even have paper cups.

ALLEGRA

How charming. Are you always prepared?

TED

I'm always prepared.

ALLEGRA

Sit Violet. We can trust him; he's a boy scout.

(Violet obeys with apprehension. Allegra sits.)

VIOLET (TO ALLEGRA)

I'm glad I didn't let you go out alone.

ALLEGRA (FLIRTING)

I'm not. I wouldn't mind some privacy now.

VIOLET (SITS BETWEEN THEM)

I'm not leaving.

TED (POURS CHAMPAGNE)

I'm sorry I have no snacks. I usually carry something nonperishable.

ALLEGRA

Like a jar of caviar? (He nods.)

TED

How did you guess, psychic?

ALLEGRA

I can read some people's minds. I foresee some great times in our future.

TED

Next outing I promise Petrossian caviar.

ALLEGRA

Oh I love this man and he knows where to shop.

VIOLET (SHAKES HEAD DISAPPROVINGLY)

We should leave the beach before the drugstore closes so that we can buy an ace bandage for your ankle.

ALLEGRA (SIPPING CHAMPAGNE)

This is the best medicine for my poor foot.

VIOLET

Don't blame me if you can't walk tomorrow, if you ankle becomes deformed or...

TED

Please let me take a look.

(Allegra poses her leg before hi. Violet pulls it back.)

VIOLET

Really sir, I think that's much too intimate a gesture. We don't even know your name.

TED

I'm Ted Eastman. I'm a physician.

ALLEGRA

Oh a doctor. I'm impressed. My name is Allegra Whilde. I was a Rockette.

TED
I'm not surprised. You blew me away. With legs like yours I knew you were a dancer.

ALLEGRA (PUTS LEG ALMOST TO HIS FACE)
Dr. Eastman is certainly qualified to examine my poor little wounded leg with his strong gifted hands.

VIOLET
He can examine your ankle, but not the whole leg. Besides how do we know he's a doctor? He doesn't look like a doctor.

TED
I am retired.

VIOLET
So am I, but I'm properly dressed. Do you have a card?

(He reaches into his beach bag, pulls out a card and hands it to her. She reads it.)

VIOLET (CONT.)
This says Eastman Imports. (hands card to Allegra)

ALLEGRA (EXAMINES CARD)
Yes, but he has an MD next to his name.

TED
Eastman Imports is my family's business and my hobby since I retired.

ALLEGRA
I believe him.

VIOLET
You'd believe Judas if he had a good tan.

ALLEGRA (TO TED)
Do I need a cast?

TED
Are you doing a show?

ALLEGRA

Oh, did your psychic ability tell you we are actresses?

TED

You don't have to be psychic to read your talents. I think your ankle is fine, but I'd like to double check at dinner tonight.

ALLEGRA

I'd love to, but I'm busy tonight. How about tomorrow?

TED

It's a date. Where do I call for you?

ALLEGRA

At the House by the Sea on Ocean Avenue.

VIOLET

Call for her at the front desk and wait for her in the lobby.

TED

Please let me walk you ladies back to your hotel.

ALLEGRA

I could use a little help. Even though I know my ankle is fine, it is a bit sore.

(Ted and Violet flank Allegra as they leave the beach.)

TED (TO ALLEGRA)

If you have any discomfort later on tonight, please don't hesitate to call me.

ALLEGRA

Violet we are so fortunate to have found such a handsome capable gentleman to concern himself with us.

VIOLET

Us?

TED

You know ladies, I love the theatre. I go regularly. I may have seen you on stage.

ALLEGRA

I'm sure you have. Currently, I'm between engagements. I hope to be back on Broadway this fall in a wonderfully glamorous part. The role suggests a Myrna Loy, Greta Garbo type sleuth.

TED

No Tome for Crime?

ALLEGRA

Honey you are psychic. How did you ever?

TED

My brother, Tom's, a backer. Says it's going to be a big hit.

VIOLET (SUSPICIOUS)

Has he backed any other shows?

TED

A few. He put money in Hello Dolly, Equs, Hair, to name a few. He also heads Eastman Imports.

ALLEGRA

I'm so impressed. Aren't you Violet?

VIOLET

Hair is obscene. I turned down comps for that show. It's shows like that that paved the road to immorality.

TED

I'm afraid that's a well paved road these days.

VIOLET

I'm looking forward to the Mercury theater's production of Arsenic and Old Lace.

TED

I can understand why you'd prefer that.

ALLEGRA
I try to keep an open mind.

TED
You know I can see Allegra in Hello Dolly.

ALLEGRA
Really? I'd love to play Dolly. Any chance for a revival?

TED
There are rumors in the air.

ALLEGRA
Do you think I could meet your brother Tom sometime?
Informally, of course.

TED
Of course. I'm sure he'd love to meet you. Like me, he enjoys the
theatre and the company of beautiful intelligent women.

ALLEGRA (CUDDLES CLOSE TO HIM)
Teddy honey, something tells me we are going to become great
friends.

TED
Together we can Light Up the Sky.

(They share laughter as they head back to the Hotel.)

"(BLACKOUT)"

ACT1. Scene 3.

SETTING: Front Porch of Victorian Hotel.

*AT RISE: Next evening. Liz is seated in rocker doing needlework and singing "Long
Ago and Far Away" (Kern/Gershwin 1944) Ted is listening from adjoining Hotel
parlor.*

LIZ

"Long Ago and Far Away

I dreamed a dream one day.

And now that dream is here beside me.

(She drops her needlepoint and can't find her needle)

Damn my eyes! It's so hard to hear anymore

(She gets down on her knees to look for her needle. When she finds it and looks up, Ted is standing above her holding a rose.)

TED

I wish I had Aladdin's lamp.

LIZ

To turn back time? (He helps her up.)

TED

No to turn your head around so that I can see you.

(He helps her up and looks into her eyes)

LIZ

I don't know what to say.

TED

Then let's continue singing. (he sings)

"Chills run up and down my spine

Aladdin's lamp is mine...

TED/LIZ (SING TOGETHER)

"The dream I dreamed was not denied me...

Just one look and then I knew that all I longed for was you."

(He goes to kiss her and she pulls away).

LIZ
Don't tell me you're a song and dance man.

TED
I'd tell you anything to get you to smile.

LIZ
You're a charmer. You must be here for Allegra.

TED
I'm supposed to meet her at 8. I'm early. Nervous.

LIZ
Anxious?

TED
I do feel some anxiety, but it's because of you.

LIZ
Do I make you nervous?

TED
Oh no, pardon me. I meant that in a positive exciting way. I am delighted to meet you Liz. My name is Ted, Ted Eastman.

(She lets him kiss her hand, then giggles.)

LIZ
Oh so you're the doctor Allegra fell for on the beach.

TED
I'm at a disadvantage. You know about me and I only know that you have a lovely voice. I would love to learn more.

LIZ
What would you like to know?

TED

Are you single?

LIZ (GIGGLES)

Oh My Lord! I haven't been asked that in years.

TED

Are you married? I noticed you're wearing a ring.

LIZ

Yes. I mean no. I'm a widow. I never could take the ring off.
Ours was the perfect marriage.

TED

Being a widower I understand.

LIZ

Stan and I were in love from the moment we met. He was a
director. That's how we met. We were working on Showboat.

TED

I bet you played Magnolia.

LIZ (NODS)

I admire a man who knows theatre.

TED

I know Showboat.

LIZ

Did you also have a perfect marriage?

TED

Gladys and I loved each other very much. I promised her that
when I retired we would see the world.

LIZ

And?

TED

A month before we were to leave for Rome she had trouble
breathing. Her doctor found a mass in her chest. She had
advanced lung cancer.

                        LIZ
Oh My God, how terrible.

                        TED
It came as a total shock. She never smoked, nor did I. It was a
medical mystery.

                        LIZ
I am so sorry. I'm sorry she had to suffer and that you are still in
pain. How long ago did it happen?

                        TED
Three years and six months ago. Before she died she insisted that
I take the trip we planned with my nephew.

                        LIZ
At least you weren't alone.

                        TED
I cried a lot.

                        LIZ
Crying can blur your vision.

                        TED
I hardly saw a thing. That trip made me realize how flat the world
is when seen through only one pair of eyes.

*(Allegra enters looking stunning. Violet, like a shadow is at her heels. Ted stands,
kisses Allegra's hand and gives her the rose he's been holding.)*

                        VIOLET
It feels chilly out here.

                        ALLEGRA
Lizzy why don't you join Violet for some hot tea or brandy in the
Bar.

                        LIZ
Yes, I'd like something warm.

(Allegra takes Ted's arm to leave.)

                         TED
Goodnight ladies. I look forward to seeing you again. (He winks
at Liz as they exit.)

"(BLACKOUT)"

ACT II. Scene 1.

SETTING: Hotel Bar.

*AT RISE: Minutes later. Violet is drinking tea and Liz is drinking a Jack Rose at a
corner table. Sam uses matches to light the candle lamps at all the bar tables.*

                         LIZ
I wish I knew where we could get a copy of Arsenic and Old Lace.

                        VIOLET
The library is closed by now.

                         SAM
I have a copy in a play collection upstairs. You ladies can share it.

                         LIZ
Share? (To Violet) How about if you and I share the play and don't
tell Allegra?

                        VIOLET
You know I can never lie dear.

                         LIZ
I'm not asking you to lie. I'm merely suggesting that we don't
volunteer any information.

                        VIOLET
All right dear if it will make you happy, but a lie of omission is
still a lie.

                         LIZ
Allegra's out anyway. She won't be able to read the script with us.

VIOLET

I don't need the script. I've done the part, remember, but I'll be glad to read with you.

LIZ

I'm at a disadvantage. The last time I read that play was more than 30 years ago when I auditioned for the part of the ingenue, Elaine.

VIOLET

Oh yes and Helen Brooks got the part. I remember how disappointed you were.

LIZ

Devastated. It could have been a turning point in my career.

VIOLET

No sense crying over missed opportunities. We've all had our share.

LIZ

What was yours?

VIOLET

I have no regrets. My energy is low and I don't have the stamina for another show. I know it's best if I do retire.

LIZ

With few opportunities I feel like I'm on forced retirement I'm anxious to see that script.

SAM

All right... I'll go get the script, but I don't feel good about not telling Allegra.

LIZ

I guess you couldn't use a little extra cash.

VIOLET

Liz, really! Bribery is a crime.

SAM

I'll go get the book, but I don't want to get in the middle of a squabble with you ladies or look like I'm showing favorites. If Allegra asks me where you got the play I will tell her.

VIOLET

That's a good boy darling. You must always tell the truth.

SAM

I won't volunteer information. I don't want any grief. I don't want anybody mad at me.

(He exits.)

VIOLET

Be grateful dear. You now have an edge on Allegra.

LIZ

Providing the director even asks us to read.

VIOLET

We are presuming a lot. However, my intuition tells me he'll be thrilled to have one of us.

LIZ

Thrilled or overwhelmed. The three of us may be too much for him.

VIOLET

Let's leave it in God's hands. I'm feeling a little tired. I think I'd like to go take a little nap before dinner and our play reading.

LIZ

(Takes photos out of her handbag)

Violet you haven't looked at my photos from last summer yet.

VIOLET
Later dear. I'm really feeling a bit light headed. Let me rest a bit.
(She gets up)

LIZ
(She studies one of the photos. Violet refuses to look.)

You have to look at this photo of Allegra from last year. She has
less wrinkles this year. I'm convinced she had a face lift. She'd
never admit it.

VIOLET
We're not getting any younger. I feel like I have one foot in the
grave and the other on a trap door.

LIZ (TO VIOLET)
See you later Love. Get a good rest.

(Sam enters with book, passing Violet as she exits upstairs. Sam hands Liz the book
and goes back behind the bar.)

LIZ (CONT.)

(Alone at her table she seems mesmerized by her photos and talks to herself. Sam
watches.)

I wonder if they'll notice I haven't taken any photos yet this year…
Last year we were so gay and carefree. Lillian looked so lovely
in her royal blue silk dress. She had such classic style. I wonder
what her sister did with that dress.

SAM
Liz would you like another Jack Rose?

(He gets no response and busies himself drying glasses.)

LIZ (PREOCCUPIED)
We're not getting any younger.

(She holds photos to candle lamp and burns them.)

SAM

(Runs to her)

What are you doing? Do you want to burn the place down?

LIZ

(On the verge of tears)

I'm sorry. They couldn't take the time…

SAM
How could you burn your precious pictures?

LIZ
No one has enough time.

SAM
I hope you saved the negatives.

LIZ
Yes. They're back in New York. New pictures will have to wait until we meet again.

(She collects ashes from photos and sweeps them with her hand into their former envelope.)

SAM
Why? Liz, I don't understand. Do you plan on saving those ashes?

LIZ
Ashes to ashes. Dirt to dirt. Dust to dust. Who are we anyway?

(She hands Sam the envelope.)

Here, throw this out with the rest of the trash.

SAM
I'm sure Violet and Allegra really wanted to see your photos.
They were just waiting for the right time.

LIZ
Who has the right time?

SAM
Your photos are important documents. You ladies are legends
here.

LIZ
Legends fade, like old photographs. If we are lucky we glow for a
moment. The next moment we are star dust.

"(BLACKOUT)"

ACT II. Scene 2.

SETTING: Hotel Bar.

AT RISE: Next day. Violet, Allegra and Liz are seated at a table and appear quarrelsome. Sam is behind the bar.

LIZ
Mine are shapely and firm from years of ballet.

ALLEGRA
Ballet or burlesque?

LIZ
At least I danced. All you did was tap your heels at Radio City.

ALLEGRA
Our classic routines glorified the all American girl.

LIZ
Now you glorify the American Gothic.

VIOLET
Girls, girls stop this banter. I'll acknowledge mine are the shortest
and dumpiest

SAM
Would you ladies like another round?

VIOLET
These gals could go at least another round.

ALLEGRA (STANDS)
Sam honey, I want you to sashay over here and tell us who has the
best legs

SAM
I ah never think about those things.

LIZ (STANDS)
Sam darling, hurry over here before your daddy comes down.

SAM
Maybe my father should decide. He's more experienced in these
matters.

VIOLET (STANDS)
I hope we're not corrupting the poor boy.

*(The women stand in chorus fashion and lift their skirts slightly. Sam is embarrassed,
but tries to cooperate.)*

ALLEGRA
It's about time the boy becomes acquainted with the facts of life.

LIZ
Knowledge is power darling.

                    SAM
I know, how about I decide tomorrow at the beach when you're all
wearing bathing suits.

(The ladies pull their skirts up a little higher.)

                    VIOLET
You know Sam, men really prefer skirts to swimsuits. It has to do
with mystery.

                    SAM
What can I say? (studies legs) You know they all appear smooth,
strong, angular...

                    ALLEGRA
Save the fish metaphors for your novel honey.

                    LIZ

(Takes Sam's hand)

Feel this calf.

                    SAM

(He touches her leg while looking away.)

Good muscle tone. I can tell you studied dance.

                    ALLEGRA (SEXY)
Aren't mine lissome and willowy? The classiest show girls have
thighs and calves like mine.

                    VIOLET
Oh my God Allegra. Back off.

                    LIZ
Don't frighten the poor boy. Nervous anxiety could hinder his
concentration.

SAM

Please, please don't make me do this. How can I decide?

(The girls study him sternly.)

SAM (CONT.)

Could I close my eyes, spin around a few times, see where I land
and tag one?

LIZ

Sounds like pin the tail on the donkey.

ALLEGRA

I'd rather play post office.

VIOLET

I like Sam's idea. It sounds kind of spiritual. Let's spin him
around. See how he lands.

(Front door bell rings.)

SAM

(Looks out window)

Ah, it's the UPS truck. I'll have to run and sign for something.

ALLEGRA

Choose!

SAM

I have to...

LIZ

Choose darling.

(Doorbell rings again.)

SAM

(Yells to lobby)

I'm coming.

THREE WOMEN IN CHORUS

Choose. Choose! Choose!

SAM

I choose ah ah Liz's legs.

(He escapes to lobby. They return to table.)

LIZ (TEASING)

It feels good to know that I'm the sexiest gal here.

VIOLET

Maybe we should have given Sam more time.

ALLEGRA

We gave him too much time. Sam's a thinker, an intellectual like
Lizzy. He was judging from his mind rather than his masculinity.
He wouldn't recognize a good body if he tripped over one.

(Sam enters with a box)

SAM

Ladies this came for you.

(They freeze. He sets the package in the middle of the table.)

VIOLET

Oh, oh God. I have to sit down.

ALLEGRA

Back to reality.

LIZ

Mortality. Don't unpack the box. If I see the container I'll die.

ALLEGRA

Then we can have a double ceremony. Do you want to be cremated or thrown in a box?

LIZ

If you want to know I plan on resting in the family vault.

VIOLET

I'm having a traditional Catholic funeral.

ALLEGRA

My lawyer has instructions to just dump my body in the East River and have a big party with whatever money I have left. So if I'm the next one to go you ladies will be treated to the party of your lives.

VIOLET

You're not allowed to dump bodies in public rivers. It's against the law.

ALLEGRA

Fine, they can arrest me on judgement day. For now, what do we do with this box?

VIOLET

Should we open it?

LIZ

Lillian's instructions specified we have to dispose of her remains off the fishing pier into the ocean.

ALLEGRA

And follow a script she wrote for us. Let's do it sunset Friday.

VIOLET

You know this plan is illegal. What if we get caught tossing those ashes?

                        LIZ
Oh stop! Do you really think some cop is going to take us to jail
for tossing ashes in the sea?.

                      ALLEGRA
If The Press covers it that will and we make a lot of noise one of
us will definitely get the part in "Arsenic and Old Lace."

                        LIZ
What have we got to loose at our age?

                      VIOLET
Saturday would have been Lillian's 75th birthday.

                      ALLEGRA
We always celebrated her birthday down here.

                      VIOLET
Then Saturday it is and a great day to think about Lillian and
celebrate her life.

(They clasp each other's hands and look at the package, as if it is about to explode.)

                        LIZ
Where should we keep the ashes until Saturday?

                        SAM
Would you like me to keep them in the safe? Or behind the bar?

                      ALLEGRA
Oh, behind the bar.

                      VIOLET
I don't know. They could fall, be mistaken for something else
or...

                        LIZ
I think Lillian would like resting behind the bar. We shared so
many fun evenings in this room.

(They smile together as Sam takes the package away.)

SAM

You ladies didn't tell me how you made out with Joe, that director you saw this morning.

ALLEGRA

He wasn't interested in making out. Which is a pity because he is truly adorable...big blue bedroom eyes.

VIOLET

Much too young for your consideration.

ALLEGRA

He's a baby. I always loved babies

LIZ

Then why didn't you have one?

ALLEGRA

Why didn't you?

LIZ

You know how much I always wanted one, but Stan had this problem and...

VIOLET

Let's get back to our interview. Sam's not interested in babies.

ALLEGRA

We have to at least find him a girlfriend first.

SAM

(Embarrassed)

Well, will Arsenic and Old Lace open or not?

                    LIZ
Joe said the actress who played Martha is in very poor shape and
will not be well in time. He's postponing the opening for two
weeks and hopes to hold auditions on Saturday.

                  ALLEGRA
He said any one of us could do it, but being he put an ad in
Backstage he wanted to be fair. So we'll audition with others on
Saturday and may the best one win.

               LIZ (TO ALLEGRA)
I was surprised how familiar you were with the role. I thought you
said you never read for it before.

                  ALLEGRA
I didn't. Last night I had Teddy drive me to Barnes and Noble
where I bought a copy of the script and read it before I went to
bed.

                   VIOLET
Very clever dear. However, I noticed you didn't dress down.

                  ALLEGRA
Teddy suggested that looking glamorous would make me more
memorable than looking like all the other frumps who would be
after the part. I noticed you loaned Liz one of your dresses.

                    LIZ
Violet didn't think I should wear black.

                  ALLEGRA
I suppose that's an improvement.

                    LIZ
Allegra became downright obsequious when Joe told us he was
paying scale.

                  ALLEGRA
It's no secret that my income doesn't measure up to my lifestyle.
Besides I got really turned-on when he said he was going to try to
take the show to New York.

LIZ

I don't act for the money.

ALLEGRA

You never had to.

VIOLET

I'm not adverse to making a little extra money. I don't like being so dependent on Jimmy.

LIZ

You could still do commercials or voice- overs.

VIOLET

When I look back on my life all I see is a parade of costume changes. From now on my wardrobe will be simple.

LIZ

No more romantic leads.

ALLEGRA

I think a woman's romantic scenes are more touching after menopause.

VIOLET

I for one don't miss those tedious love scenes where you are glued to a sweaty man with bad breath for hours.

LIZ

Then he tells you that you ruined his love scenes because you're frigid and wear the wrong perfume.

ALLEGRA

Then two months later he's serving you a steak at Sardis.

LIZ

What we do for love.

ALLEGRA

For love and money.

                    LIZ
Speaking of love Allegra. Did you tell Sam about the man you fell
for or fell over on the beach?

(Sam nods and continues to listen, while he busies himself at the bar.)

                    VIOLET
The alleged Dr. Ted Eastman.

                    ALLEGRA
Oh, Teddy.

                    LIZ
What does Violet mean by "alleged doctor?"

                    VIOLET
Violet means that she's suspicious. He makes me uncomfortable.
For one thing I don't like the way he looks at Allegra.

                    ALLEGRA
He suffers from myopia.

                    VIOLET
If he's a doctor and he suffers from myopia, you'd think he'd have
enough money to buy proper glasses. I asked Jimmy to make
some calls and check him out. I think your Teddy is just another
Stage Door Johnny.

                    ALLEGRA
I don't believe this. Do you realize how embarrassed I'll be if
Teddy finds out that we doubted him.

                    LIZ
Especially if his brother is a backer for No Time for Crime.

                    ALLEGRA
Point well taken Lizzy. We should all know the value of having a
friend whose brother is a producer.

VIOLET
We'll know his value soon. His brother is probably a big Butter and Egg man. Jimmy's checking him out as well.

LIZ
Can't be too careful these days.

ALLEGRA
Instead of getting senile, the two of you are getting paranoid in your old age. I'd trust Teddy with my life.

VIOLET
You'd trust Jack the Riper if he carried an American Express card.

ALLEGRA
The two of you are just jealous because he's a debonair and sexy gentleman who likes me.

LIZ
I don't know if he told you, but we did a little duet out on the porch. He has a very nice voice.

VIOLET
We all know there's no room in Liz's heart for anyone but her beloved Stanley.

ALLEGRA
What about Harry?

LIZ
What, what about Harry?

ALLEGRA (SINGING)
You were just wild about Harry.

LIZ
And he was just wild about you. You stole him away from me and broke my heart.

ALLEGRA
You've never forgiven me for that and it wasn't my fault.

VIOLET
Harry's ancient history, before Stanley, over thirty years ago.

ALLEGRA
Lizzy went into apoplexy over Harry. He was dating the two of us and he chose me. It happens all the time.

LIZ
You teased poor Harry; held him at your beck and call; cheated on him. The more you tortured Harry, the more he loved you.

ALLEGRA
Harry was a jerk.

VIOLET
I thought he was a lawyer.

LIZ
Harry was brilliant; ran for the senate.

ALLEGRA
He didn't run fast enough. He lost, twice I believe.

VIOLET
Where's poor Harry now?

ALLEGRA
Oh Harry's been dead for years.

VIOLET
Maybe it's time to let the issue rest in peace.

ALLEGRA
Tell her. My act was a blessing in disguise. She didn't realize that my dating Harry freed her to meet her precious Stanley.

LIZ (TO ALLEGRA)
People never see you for who you are. They are enchanted by the actress, not the woman.

ALLEGRA
The actress is the woman.

LIZ

(She waves her white napkin in truce as Allegra rolls her eyes.)

Let's bury Harry's memory.

VIOLET

Personal histories are a comedy of errors.

ALLEGRA

The scenes ferment with age, but the bitter seeds remain.

LIZ

Do you trust your memory Allegra?

ALLEGRA

Impeccably. I always said I'd know that I'm old when I can no longer recall the order of my lovers.

LIZ

All right smarty, number and name them.

VIOLET

Liz, that's very personal information.

LIZ

For some people, but our Allegra prides herself on being a celebrity, a public person.

ALLEGRA

I could write them down.

LIZ

All right. Sam, do you have a pen and paper? A large pad-the size of a phone book.

SAM

(He nods and goes behind bar and gets them.)

All I have is a steno book and a ballpoint pen.

ALLEGRA
Just rip off a few sheets. I'll put them in my bag and work on my
list at my leisure.

SAM
(He gives Allegra paper and pen and exits in a flash.)

I have to check something upstairs.

VIOLET
Allegra, I really don't think this is appropriate behavior. Some
things should remain unsaid, unwritten...

LIZ
Or unread. Maybe Violet's right.

ALLEGRA
Nonsense. I like tests. Besides, writing their names will
recapture lost memories.

LIZ (CAUTIOUSLY)
Do you have any idea of how many dead guys will be on your list?

ALLEGRA
Darling, it's for me to know and you to find out once the list is
revealed.

(She puts her list in her purse and smiles at their anticipation.)

"(BLACKOUT)"

ACT II. Scene 3.

SETTING: Split focus. Scene moves between Porch and Hotel Bar.

*AT RISE: Early next evening. Allegra and Ted are seated on rocking chairs, holding
hands. A bottle of champagne and a dish of strawberries are on a table near them.*

*Violet, Liz and Sam are at a table near the bar having drinks. They seem distracted,
as if straining to hear and see what is happening on the porch.*

SAM

I really enjoyed the show last night.

VIOLET

We were so happy that you could join us my dear.

LIZ

I would have been happier if they performed inside, not under a mildew tent.

SAM

Yeah. It seemed like a lot of the lines sort of faded into the night air.

VIOLET

That was bad acting honey. Actors aren't taught how to project anymore. Everything is internal, an outgrowth of the moan and groan theatre of the 60's. They no longer consider the audience. Everything is here (pointing to her head). Not here (holding her heart).

LIZ

That show infected my whole body with mosquito bites. The stage lights attract those nasty creatures and the junk food gives them the strength to breed and steal the show.

SAM

They should spray.

VIOLET

No they shouldn't. Insecticides are toxic. The chemicals damage your lungs, cause cancer, irritate your eyes…

SAM

What about the ozone layer?

VIOLET

Do we still have an ozone layer?

LIZ

All right. All right. Sorry I mentioned it. Next time I'll scratch quietly and think of Little Shop of Horrors.

(Porch: Allegra and Ted entwine their arms as they toast with their glasses of champagne)

TED

Here's to my seeing you glow in many shows after Arsenic and Old Lace.

ALLEGRA

Here's to your being near enough to heal all my wounds.

TED

I'm amazed at how well you're managing in high heels this evening.

ALLEGRA

I'm in good hands.

(She nestles closer to him.)

TED

You are a hardy lady.

ALLEGRA

Hardy as a rose in your garden?

TED

Not just any rose. You are like a tea rose or a grandiflora. I'll name one after you this year - a blend of elegant yellow and pink.

ALLEGRA

Oh I hope I'll get to see it. Roses are my favorite flower. I'm so happy.

(She kisses his forehead.)

TED

I'll send you a dozen Allegra roses a week. If I close my eyes I can smell my roses.

(She sets their glasses down, closes his eyes with her fingers, then closes hers. They embrace.)

(Bar: Violet and Liz crane their necks to get a glimpse of the action on the porch. Sam busies himself.)

                    LIZ
They made it to kissing. They can't really go any further on the porch

                  VIOLET
Oh, no no. I don't believe it. Sam honey let me have the newspaper over there . I need to fan myself.

(Sam gives her the newspaper. She fans herself.)

                    SAM
Should I turn on the air conditioner?

                    LIZ
No dear. I feel a chill.

(She puts her shawl around her shoulders.)

Allegra must be rehearsing for Lolita.

                  VIOLET
Certainly not The Nun's Story. How indiscreet. There's a time and a place for everything. What must Sam think?

                    SAM
Sam thinks people should do what makes them happy.

              VIOLET (TO SAM)
What would your father say if he saw you with a girl on the front porch?

> SAM

He's never said anything.

> VIOLET

So our Sam has a girlfriend. I knew it.

> LIZ

I've noticed he spends a lot of time at Caroline's boutique.
Caroline is a sweet little girl.

> VIOLET

She's no little girl. She's at least 21.

> SAM

Caroline is 23. We're good friends.

> VIOLET

It's best to start as friends and gradually build a relationship.
Romance should be an learned blessing, not false illusion and
impulse.

> LIZ

(She checks Allegra and Ted through window.)

They stopped kissing.

> VIOLET

Maybe they'll join us soon.

> LIZ

Not too soon. He's pouring them more champagne.

*(Porch: Ted is feeding Allegra a strawberry. They continue to feed each other
strawberries and champagne throughout the scene.)*

> ALLEGRA

Oh ambrosia. I didn't expect to dine with a God tonight.

TED

Is my Venus pleased?

ALLEGRA

Let's fly to the moon.

TED

I'm not a pilot, but I'm a great sailor. I'd love to take you out on my boat sometime.

ALLEGRA

Imagine, owning your own boat. Is it a big one?

TED

It's a replica of an 1860 schooner. It's 60 feet long. I call it "Cotton Blossom."

ALLEGRA

Like Showboat, my favorite musical, how cute.

TED

We'll have to waltz around my deck sometime.

ALLEGRA

People will say we're in love.

TED

OKLAHOMA.

ALLEGRA

A man who knows his theatre. I'm impressed.

TED.

It didn't matter, Till there was you.

(They embrace and begin a waltz.)

ALLEGRA

My Music man.

(He sings as they dance.)

TED
"There were bells on the hill, but I never heard them ringing, No, I never heard them at all. Till there was you........."

(Bar: Violet is having trouble opening her handbag.)

LIZ
What's wrong? Is the catch stuck? Can I help you?

SAM
Maybe I can help.

VIOLET (DISORIENTED)
I can't. I can't. Damn it!

LIZ
Damn what? You're not all right.

SAM
Your diabetes?

VIOLET
No angina. I have pills somewhere in this old bag.

LIZ
Why didn't you tell us about your condition? I'll get Ted; he's a doctor.

VIOLET
Supposedly. Don't disturb them.

(She gets bag open and the pills spill on the floor. Sam helps her pick them up. He reads the label on the bottle.)

SAM
Your prescription says take two pills three times a day. Have you
taken any today?

*(She shakes her head. He reaches for a glass of water on the table. He holds it as she
struggles to drink it.)*

LIZ
Why didn't you take your medicine?

VIOLET
What for? Sometimes I forget. Who cares?

LIZ
I care. We all care. I'm getting Ted.

(Violet is shaky, pale and weak. Liz runs to porch.)

SAM
Hurry. I'll hold her.

(PORCH; Liz interrupts Allegra and Ted's passionate embrace.)

LIZ
Ted. Come quickly! Violet is having an attack.

TED
(Jumps up and follows Liz)

Of course. What is it?

ALLEGRA (TO LIZ)
I hope this isn't some ploy to sabotage my evening.

LIZ (SHOCKED)
I would never...

(They trail Ted to the Bar.)

(BAR: Ted checks Violet's pulse and studies the prescription on pill bottle. He opens pills and give them to her with water)

ALLEGRA (TO VIOLET)
Why didn't you tell us about this problem?

VIOLET
Please don't yell at me.

LIZ
Allegra be kind.

ALLEGRA (EMBRACES VIOLET)
I'm sorry darling, warmth is not my specialty. I'll never play Mother Teresa.

SAM
Should I call the hospital's rescue squad?

TED
No. That's not necessary. She's coming around.

VIOLET
Thank you. I am feeling better.

TED
She should go to her room and rest. Sam could you fix her a snack, maybe some fruit, cheese and crackers and a cup of tea?

SAM
Sure, no problem.

LIZ
I'll take her.

ALLEGRA
No. I will take her.

VIOLET
Please don't fight. I can take myself upstairs. I don't need anyone.

ALLEGRA
We all need someone . I probably need you more now than you
need me. I want to stay with you until I know you're all right.

LIZ
All right. I'll take my drink on the porch and unwind.

TED (TO ALLEGRA)
I'll help you make Violet comfortable upstairs.

(PORCH: Liz gazes at stars leaning against porch rail.)

LIZ

(She sips her drink in a melancholy mood. She softly hums and sings "I'll be seeing you" (Sammy Fain, 1938). Ted returns to the bar and listens to her by the porch window.)

"I'll be seeing you In all the old familiar places that this heart of
mine embraces all day thru…

(She stops and talk to herself, teary eyed.)

Who will I be seeing next year. I feel Lillian's spirit all around me
and now…

(Ted enters cautiously.)

TED
May I join you for a moment?

LIZ
Of course. Pardon my tears.

TED

(Puts his arm around her shoulder)

I understand. You had a terrible scare this evening.

LIZ

How is Violet?

TED

Violet is going to be fine. How are you?

LIZ

Just a touch of heartburn. It will pass.

TED

If there's anything I can do.

LIZ

Tend to Violet. Are you sure she'll be all right?

TED

The nitroglycerin helped. She'll feel better in the morning. She needs to rest and take her medicine as prescribed.

LIZ

I don't understand why she didn't tell us about her condition.

TED

She probably didn't want to burden you. What could you do? She may need an operation this fall.

LIZ

Oh no.

TED

Don't worry. She has a good chance. She's a strong woman. You're all strong women.

LIZ

Lillian was a strong woman. She's gone. Allegra is probably the strongest of us left.

TED
Allegra's a fine lady; enchanting.

LIZ (SARCASTIC)
So she's been told many, many times.

TED
Liz you are a very beautiful woman.

LIZ
Please don't patronize me.

TED
I mean it. You are lovely. But why the black dress? Are you in
mourning?

LIZ
No. I always wear black. It's one less decision I need to make.

TED
Decisions are roadblocks in our pursuit of happiness.

(Allegra appears, unnoticed at doorway, barefoot, holding her shoes.)

LIZ
Life is too short.

TED
Because life is short, try to jazz it up a bit. I 'd like to see you
dressed in a bright sparkling pink.

LIZ (ON THE VERGE OF LAUGHTER)
I can't see myself in shocking pink. How about flamingo red?

TED
Lovely. Go for it.

LIZ (WIDE-EYED)
Do you really think so?

TED
I know so. Just the mention of it draws a sparkle from your eyes.

(Allegra caresses her sore ankle as she studies them with a cat's stare.)

> LIZ (MOVES CLOSER TO HIM)
> Allegra would die if she knew you thought I could be attractive.

> TED
> You are beautiful.

> LIZ
> I'd settle for comely.

> TED
> "She walks in beauty, like the night. Of cloudless climes and starry skies. And all that's best of dark and bright...

> LIZ (TEASING)
> Are you really Lord Byron in disguise?

(Ted kisses Liz's hand. Allegra drops her shoes and startles them. She appears from the shadows and greets them coquettishly.)

> ALLEGRA
> Anyone for a night cap?

"(BLACKOUT)"

ACT III. Scene 1.

SETTING: A seaside restaurant that is large enough to have a dance floor.

AT RISE: Early evening. Allegra and Ted are seated at a table with an ocean view. They have the restaurant almost entirely to themselves..

> ALLEGRA
> Teddy, are you a betting man?

> TED
> I'll bet you get the part you want in Arsenic and Old Lace, even though I think you're too young for it.

ALLEGRA

I bet you say that to all the girls.

TED

Why do you want to play an eccentric old lady?

ALLEGRA

Good actresses can play any age. If I get that part I'll just put off my face lift a little longer.

TED

I don't understand why a woman as beautiful as you would even consider plastic surgery.

ALLEGRA

It's a tough market out there honey. I have to maximize my options. Twenty years ago I had to fight the wolves off with a club. Now I have to dress up as Little Red Riding Hood and spike the wolf's all bran.

TED (LAUGHS AND SHAKES HIS HEAD.)

I can't believe you're unhappy.

ALLEGRA

Believe it. I'm unhappy because I never met a gentleman like you to take care of me.

TED

Come now Allegra, I'm nothing special.

ALLEGRA

I wish I met you twenty years ago.

TED

I was married then.

ALLEGRA

Thirty years ago?

TED

Married.

> ALLEGRA

You weren't born married.

> TED

I was born to be married.

> ALLEGRA

Do you remember the first time you fell in love?

> TED

Yes, like it was yesterday.

Gladys, though gone still own a piece of my heart.

> ALLEGRA

You are so lucky to have married the love of your life.

> TED

I was lucky.

> ALLEGRA

I want to love again.

> TED

All of us who have lost long for love again. It's part of the human condition. I hope we both find what we need.

> ALLEGRA

Do you think you could need me?

> TED

I appreciate the simple life. I can't imagine you crawling around my garden.

> ALLEGRA

I wouldn't crawl. I could wear garden gloves and a sun hat.

> TED

And you'd look elegant my dear. You're a woman of much taste

> ALLEGRA

Much taste indeed. I bet you reel the gals in with that line.

TED

No. I hardly fish or date. Tonight dear, I only have eyes for you.

ALLEGRA

I feel a song coming on.

TED

I want to dance with you, hold you tightly in my arms.

ALLEGRA

Teddy, it's too early. The band won't be here for hours.

TED

We don't need a band. Let's relive the songs of yesterday.

(They rise to dance, creating their own music.)

ALLEGRA

Remember "The Gay Divorcee?" (he nods.) I feel like Ginger
Rogers and you're my Fred Astaire. I see myself wearing a long
sexy black satin gown, split up the side so I can move with ease.
You're wearing tails.

(Ted sings "The Way You Look Tonight," (Dorothy Fields & Jerome Kern, 1936)).

TED

"Some day when I'm awf'ly low.

When the world is cold, I will feel a glow

just thinking of you And the way you look tonight…"

*(His song moves her to dance slowly with him as he sings more of the song. She joins
him in the refrain while dancing.)*

ALLEGRA/TED

"Lovely, never, never change,

Keep that breathless charm,

Won't you please arrange it,

Cause I love you,

Just the way you look tonight..."

(They hum some more of the song as they dance.)

TED
"Just the way you look tonight..."

(They dance out to the terrace. The scene ends with their embrace.)

"(BLACKOUT)"

ACT III. Scene 2.

SETTING: The Beach. Two large umbrellas and blankets are set-up facing the ocean.

AT RISE: Liz is under one umbrella putting on sun tan lotion as her radio plays "Eine Kleine Nachtmusik." There is no one under the other umbrella though personal items suggest someone will return. When she's finished oiling herself, she picks up her copy of Arsenic and Old Lace and studies it. Ted approaches her from the back armed with a bag of food. He startles her when he takes her book out of her hands.

TED
Don't overdo it darling. You'll be fine.

LIZ
You can't possibly understand how important getting this part is
to me.

TED
You're right. I don't understand how you can torture yourself over
some rinky-dinky stock production.

LIZ

I torture myself over every audition. I can't explain why, but I have to get this part. I know I can do it.

TED

Of course you can do it. I can do it. Who cares? This isn't New York. But I do have genuine New York hot dogs for us. And two foaming draft beers.

LIZ

Marvelous. I love the Boardwalk stands. The girls refuse to eat there. This is such a treat for me. Did you get mustard?

TED

Of course. I'll get whatever your heart desires. Now put away that script and let's enjoy our picnic.

LIZ

I haven't had a meal like this since... a very long time ago.

TED

Were you obsessed with your career when you were married?

LIZ

Stan and I were both born into show business. Our parents were vaudevillians and they knew each other so we sort of grew up together on the road. I don't know if you can imagine what that was like.

TED

I can't imagine it. I don't understand show business. My brother Tom lives breathes Broadway.

LIZ

Stanley and I understood and supported each other through everything. I remember after he died, when the numbness passed, a sense of panic set in—panic and intense loneliness.

TED (NODS)

I understand those feelings.

LIZ

Through all the rough emotional times I had the solace of my work. My work enabled me to take care of myself and happily blend with society.

TED

You remind me so much of my wife Gladys.

LIZ

You're nothing like Stanley.

TED

Gladys was an avid reader. Did I tell you she was an English teacher?

LIZ

Oh really.

TED

Really. She also directed some of her school plays and coached the debating team.

LIZ

So she was interested in theater, interesting. Stanley was always in motion. His energy fueled our lives and drove us through some hard times. When he wasn't doing a show, he'd be organizing closets or painting the woodwork.

TED

May I ask how he died?

LIZ

(She moves out from under the direct sun, repositions her blanket under her blanket and puts on her dark glasses.)

It happened ten years ago. There was a terrible snow storm. Stanley insisted on going out and getting the Sunday paper. I didn't want him to go, but he thought I was silly. The store was only two miles away. In younger days we would have walked.

TED

Car accident?

LIZ

No. It was weird. He got a flat tire. While he was changing it he got a heart attack. I'll never know how long he suffered or how long it took the police to find him When the cops came to my door I was speechless. I knew he was dead; I felt it.

TED

I'm so sorry.

LIZ

I remember all the times I complained about his chronic singing or whistling of show tunes. He couldn't relax. Imagine someone up at the crack of dawn fussing around the house in rhythm to his rendition of "Ole man river" or "Some enchanted evening." After his death I tried so hard to hear his version of those melodies. His music was lost, with him, forever.

TED

Some of Gladys' dresses are still hanging in her closet. I can't bring myself to give them away. (She nods knowingly) Sometimes when I touch her clothes I can still smell the faint aroma of Joy, her favorite perfume.

LIZ

I can't bear to give up the West Village apartment we bought together, though I sold the house in Connecticut shortly after Stanley died. The Village apartment is so cluttered with memories.

TED

I understand.

LIZ

You're a very kind man Ted.

TED

Thank you. You're not only kind, but sensitive and comfortable to be with.

                    LIZ
What about Allegra?

                    TED
Allegra would make a great army sergeant, the way she keeps men
in line.

                    LIZ
Or a ballet master, keeping men on their toes.

                    TED
What a great image. I can see twenty potbellied, bowlegged
elderly men trying to leap through hoops while on their toes under
Allegra's direction. (They laugh together.) You're fun to be with.
I hope you'll have time to see me when we get back to New York.
Perhaps we could have dinner.

                    LIZ
Perhaps. Or I could make us dinner. I love to cook, but rarely do
anything fancy for myself.

                    TED
I'd love something fancy. One night I'd like to take you to my
favorite fancy restaurant. It's in your neighborhood; La Tulipe.

                    LIZ
Oh, I've always wanted to go there. It's so chic!

                    TED
And you are such a chic lady. They have a dessert there that is to
die for. It's called La Tulipe Javanaise-a creamy coffee ice cream
with chocolate sauce in a flower-shaped pastry shell.

                    LIZ
Sounds divine. My birthday's in September.

                    TED
Good, then we have a date.

                    LIZ
O.K. And one night I'll make you scaloppina alla francese.

TED

Wonderful! Now we have two dates.

LIZ

I feel a little chilly. I should head back to the hotel soon. I need to study the script more. Audition's tomorrow.

TED

Stop worrying. You have greater victories ahead.

LIZ

No Time for Crime?

TED

Remember my brother wants to meet you.

LIZ

Your brother? Oh, Tom, the producer. I almost forgot.

TED

You're shivering. Let me keep you warm.

(He cuddles next to her. She submits coquettishly.)

LIZ

You are so warm and your arms are so strong.

TED

I can feel your heart beat.

LIZ

And to think just yesterday I believed these days were over.

TED

This is only the beginning.

(They kiss.)

"(BLACKOUT)"

ACT III. Scene 3.

SETTING: Fishing pier.

AT RISE: As sunset approaches Allegra, Liz and Violet are on a windy fishing pier that stretches from the boardwalk over the ocean. Allegra is holding container with Lillian's ashes. Violet is holding a bouquet of lilies. Liz is holding a large envelope with a speech she will read shortly.

                    VIOLET
Need I remind you we could go to jail for this.

                    ALLEGRA
You need not. There's not a cop in sight and if one should appear
he wouldn't believe this.

                    LIZ
We're good actresses we could convince him we're doing
something else.

                    ALLEGRA
Like casting fate to the wind.

                    VIOLET
I wish Lillian's sister would have sent this dedication earlier so
that you could have memorized it.

                    LIZ
This makes it more like an audition.

                    VIOLET
Do you think she can hear us?

                    ALLEGRA
Let's get on with it. If we wait until the sun sets Lizzy won't be
able to read.

                    LIZ

(Opens envelope)

Oh my God!

ALLEGRA
What? Don't scare me. I don't want to loose these ashes.

VIOLET
What does she say?

LIZ
She doesn't say anything. It's an extract from a poem.

VIOLET
I hope it's not vulgar.

LIZ
It's from the "Rubiyat of Omar Khayam."

ALLEGRA
Well at least it's not "Murphy at the bat."

LIZ
You mean "Casey at the bat."

VIOLET
Don't mention bats. It's getting dark. Who knows what flies around here after dark.

LIZ
Can we get started, please?

ALLEGRA
Would you rather I read it?

VIOLET
Lillian wanted Liz to read and me to throw the lilies into the water, followed by you tossing the ashes into the flower's wake.

LIZ
Places? (ladies fall into place) Then I'll begin. (pause)

"I sent my soul through the Invisible,

Some letter of that After-life to spell:

And by and by my soul return'd to me,

And answered. I Myself am Heaven and Hell."

                    ALLEGRA (PAUSE)
Is that all there is?

                        VIOLET
I'm next.

(She tosses lilies gently into the surf.)

                        ALLEGRA
My turn.

(She opens canister and tosses ashes. A gust of wind blows the ashes back onto them. They react.)

                          LIZ
Oh my God! I'm covered with her ashes.

                        ALLEGRA
That's what you get for wearing black.

                        VIOLET
I sort of like having Lilian's ashes on me, It's sort of spiritual like divine blessing.

                        ALLEGRA
Or intervention.

                  VIOLET (STARTLED)
Look behind us!

                    LIZ (ANXIOUS)
What? What?

                        VIOLET
Those lights.

LIZ

Street lights?

ALLEGRA

Fog lights.

LIZ

It's eerie, gloomy.

ALLEGRA

Lillian would love it.

VIOLET

It's like the set from The Hound of the Baskervilles.

LIZ

Or Dracula.

ALLEGRA

Or Star Wars.

LIZ

Or a deserted beach on the brink of a storm.

VIOLET

We better head back before it rains.

(A gust of wind almost knocks them over. They scream and fall into each other's arms.)

ALLEGRA

Be careful we're near the edge.

LIZ

Why do we keep hurting each other? We should love each other
after all these years?

ALLEGRA

We do love each other. We just hate getting old.

VIOLET

Nonsense, everyone gets old.

ALLEGRA

(Pushes up her breasts)

And battles with gravity. Now our bodies keep letting us down till there's no getting up.

LIZ

We're loosing time, energy and teeth.

VIOLET

Last year Lillian and I went to church together. Now I go alone. Maybe next year my pew will be empty.

LIZ

Please let's not quarrel anymore. Let's try to cherish the moments we have left. Let's promise to meet again next year.

(They stand like the three graces reaching and respond in unison.)

ALL

I promise. (look to the sky) God willing.

ALLEGRA

Let's try to cherish each other.

VIOLET

Number our days.

(They hug each other. Then they step back, looking to the sky for answers.)

LIZ

That poem was too short. I really didn't put much feeling into it. Please let me read it again.

ALLEGRA

Sure, why not? Lillian's encore.

LIZ

(Unfolds paper to read)

"I sent my soul through the Invincible...

(A gust of wind blows the poem from her hands.)

ALLEGRA

(They try to retrieve poem.)

The word was invisible Lizzy, not invincible...

(Catches herself) I'm sorry Liz, darling.

(The poem flies away from them in the wind.)

LIZ

Oh! It's beyond our reach.

VIOLET

It looks like a seagull.

ALLEGRA

We have our answer.

"(BLACKOUT)"

ACT III. Scene 4.

SETTING: Porch of Hotel.

AT RISE: Violet is seated in a rocking chair humming "I'll walk Alone" (Cahn/Styne, 1944). Sam enters with a coke for himself and a lemonade for Violet. He sits next to her.

VIOLET

(She leans toward him in confidence.)

I got the part.

SAM

How wonderful.

VIOLET

Hush. Hush. It's our secret.

SAM

It can't be our secret for long.

VIOLET

Dear, I have to refuse. I'm just not that strong, physically.

SAM

Then why did you try-out?

VIOLET

Pride.

SAM

And you love acting.

VIOLET

Theatre is magical. And magic is temporal. All spells need end.

SAM

Ted spoke of some surgery you plan on having.

VIOLET

By-pass surgery. No reason to get the girls upset.

SAM

I'm glad you have Jimmy to look after you.

VIOLET

I wish he didn't have to be so responsible for me. Sometimes I
feel I'm holding him back; keeping him from getting married and
starting a family of his own.

SAM

Why can't he have both?

VIOLET

I pray he'll be happy. I also pray that you'll be happy; publish
your book, fall in love..

SAM

Thank you. Now what are you going to do about your part?

VIOLET

I am going to savor the victory for one day. Today I will enjoy my
gift. Tomorrow I will call that director and recommend Allegra
for the part.

SAM

Why Allegra?

VIOLET

First, she is wonderful, though Liz is quite fine. Secondly, Allegra
needs the work and the money. Liz has an income.

SAM

Are you sure the director will take your advice?

VIOLET (NODS)

I think he may see it as a toss up between all of us anyway. Don't
say a word to either of them about this. Promise. (He nods.)

SAM

My lips are sealed.

VIOLET

Would you like to share any of your secrets with me?

> SAM

You mean Caroline?

> VIOLET

Yes Caroline. She's lovely. The girls and I think she may be a suitable girlfriend for you.

> SAM

If the girls think so it must be true. Anyway I do find her attractive and I think she likes me.

> VIOLET

Rumor has it that she likes fishing.

> SAM

No kidding. I know she's an avid reader. Maybe I should show her my novel,

> VIOLET

Or maybe she'd like to go fishing with you.

> SAM

Great idea! What could be more romantic than a day out on the water? Why didn't I ever think about that?

> VIOLET

You have to be taught.

> SAM

Before I get caught. Oops, another fishing metaphor.

> VIOLET

Getting caught is part of the game. Try to be more romantic. Send her flowers. Read her poetry.

> SAM

I knew you were a romantic. Was there one great love in your life?

> VIOLET

I loved Jimmy's father. He was killed in the war.

SAM

World War II?

VIOLET

Battle of the Bulge.

SAM

I read about that, Horrible blood bath.

VIOLET

He died two months before Jimmy was born. Jimmy was of course named after his father.

SAM

So sad-sad for you and sad for Jimmy. By the way what was that tune you were humming before?

VIOLET

Before? Oh "I'll Walk Alone," another war time song. I sang it a lot when Jim was away. I thought he'd hear me. I'll never forget him.

SAM

What are the words?

VIOLET

I'll try to remember, excuse my rough singing voice.

"I'll walk alone because to tell you the truth I feel lonely.

I don't mind being lonely when my heart tells me you are lonely too.."

(Her voice cracks a bit.)

Excuse me, my memories are distorting the melody. The last verse is something like this...

"I'll always be near you where ever you are each night in every prayer, If you call I'll hear you no matter how far just close your eyes and I'll be there."

ACT III. Scene 5.

SETTING: Hotel Porch.

At Rise: The next day. Ted and Liz are seated together on the porch swing.

                          TED
        I want to sing you a love song.

                          LIZ
        Sing away.

                          TED
        I can't think of our perfect song. My head is too clouded with
        images of us.

                          LIZ
        Our song will come. It takes time.

                          TED
        I'll practice a few songs and sing the to you when we meet in New
        York next week.

                          LIZ
        Next Saturday night at La Tulipe. I can't wait. I hope you won't
        forget.

                          TED
        Forget you? Never.

(As they start to kiss a commotion is heard in the Bar)

                          LIZ
        What's could be going on?

                          TED
        Let's go together and see.

(He takes her hand and leads her to the Bar. Violet and Sam are at a table while Allegra is milking her grand entrance, lighting up the room)

ALLEGRA

Elderberry wine for everybody!

LIZ

(To Allegra)

You got the part? (Allegra nods) Congratulations!

ALLEGRA

I know you're happy for me honey.

LIZ

You'll be sensational!

TED

Spectacular!

ALLEGRA

(Excited)

I know! I know!

VIOLET

You'll be competent my dear. I couldn't have taken the role, even if it were offered to me.

ALLEGRA

(To Violet, with forced sympathy)

I know, I know dear.

LIZ

(To Violet)

You've played Martha hundreds of times before. I never have. Maybe I will some day.

TED

There are hundreds of roles you can play dear.

ALLEGRA

There's still "No Time for Crime."

TED

Oh Allegra, my brother can't wait to meet you. He's coming down for your opening night.

ALLEGRA

Yes, Tom. Could you please leave me his address so I can send him a personal announcement.

TED

I'll drop off all his numbers and addresses when I stop by later on my way home.

VIOLET

Then you won't be joining us for the theatre tonight?

TED

Unfortunately not. Business calls.

(He kisses Liz and throws kisses to others as he exits)

SAM

Allegra, the closest thing I have to elderberry wine is blackberry brandy. Unless you think it may be closer to port.

ALLEGRA

Sam honey, why don't you try mixing port with blackberry brandy and we'll live dangerously.

SAM

Fine. I'll add some club soda and a slice of lemon and we'll have invented a new concoction.

ALLEGRA
Go for it! I love to experiment. How about you Liz?

LIZ
I never liked living on the edge. I'll stay in the safe zone with my
Jack Rose.

VIOLET
I'll stay safer with diet ginger ale.

SAM

(Takes out a pitcher and experiments)

Let's see I'll take two ounces of blackberry brandy, three ounces
of port, some powdered sugar and…

VIOLET
Don't forget the club soda and maybe some ice.

SAM
Let's see I'll add three ounces of club soda and a twist of lemon on
the glass.

ALLEGRA
Oh I'm so excited. It's so pretty!

LIZ
It looks so bloody purple.

VIOLET
Looks deadly. Add some ice Sam. (he obeys) Ah, now it almost
looks violet.

SAM

(Pours drinks for Allegra and himself as Liz and Violet raise their glasses to toast)

To love, life and theatre!!

(They touch glasses in toast)

I know we'll call this drink the Allegra. I'll tell Dad to add it to the Bar menu.

ALLEGRA
I'll drink to that!

SAM
I like it. It's fruity and refreshing, maybe a tad too sweet.

ALLEGRA
Just like me?

LIZ
A tad too sweet?

ALLEGRA
(To Sam)

I'll have to kiss you for this honey.

(Sam blushes as she kisses him, but cooperates)

ALLEGRA-CONT.
Sam is so cute and talented. I just know he'll be a great writer.

VIOLET
Tell him, not us Allegra.

LIZ

(She toasts him)

To Sam, the next Hemingway!

SAM

I don't know if I would want to be like Hemingway. He was never happy.

ALLEGRA

Happiness is not the point. Stop spending so much time in the safe zone, watching. Get out there and Act! Take some chances. Don't restrict your life to the comfort of your imagination. Define your goals. Visualize yourself achieving them. Makes things happen!

LIZ

(To Sam in a more comforting tone)

Allegra's right. Discipline is also important. Take one day at a time.

VIOLET

A little prayer and meditation will also center your spirit and strengthen your heart.

SAM

Thank you ladies. I'll write your advice in my journal and reflect on my future. I'll be a new man when you see me next year.

LIZ

We'll be here. Make sure you write our reservations in you Daddy's book.

(He nods)

ALLEGRA

(To Liz)

You haven't snapped your camera once this year.

LIZ
I'll take some before I leave.

VIOLET
I was looking forward to seeing those photos. I don't understand why you're hiding them.

LIZ
I'm not hiding anything. They got damaged. I'm sorry.

SAM
I accidently spilled Liz's Jack Rose on them when she was showing them to me.

ALLEGRA
How peculiar. You mean the liquor destroyed them?

VIOLET
Liquor destroys more than pictures. Pictures can be replaced, livers cannot.

LIZ
The negatives are back in New York. I send all of your prints when I get home.

VIOLET
That's very kind of you dear. You tell us how much they cost and we'll reimburse you.

ALLEGRA
(She opens her handbag and takes out her list.)

Ta Da! My list! Are you ready for the intimate details of my life?

(She hands out copies, even to Sam.)

LIZ

You finished? I'm impressed.

VIOLET

I don't approve of this. I'm not sure Sam should have a copy without his father's permission.

SAM

I need a copy. Research. My next book will be a romance.

ALLEGRA

Sam needs inspiration. He's a budding writer. This list steams with imagery.

SAM

You ladies are a constant source of inspiration.

ALLEGRA

Pull up a chair Sam darling. I haven't enjoyed anything so much in years. It's complete from High School sweethearts to what's his name?

LIZ

You mean Ted?

ALLEGRA (TO LIZ)

Yes Teddy. You won that prize my darling.

VIOLET

You even included places. I'm shocked.

(Though shocked she continues to look.)

LIZ

(She puts hands over her eyes.)

Oh this is more than I expected. My eyes are burning. I don't think I should look. I'm so (peeks through fingers) embarrassed.

ALLEGRA
There's nothing to be embarrassed about. Look how many I've had since Harry.

LIZ (LOOKS)
And before.

SAM
Harry's number six.

(They are all having fun with this game.)

VIOLET
There's another Harry number twelve.

LIZ
Are these all affairs or just dates?

ALLEGRA
Affairs, boyfriends, beaus. I leave the torrid details to your imagination

LIZ
No, no. You couldn't have with Dr. Long.

VIOLET
He's our dentist.

LIZ
He looks like Woody Allen.

ALLEGRA
Looks have nothing to do with it.

LIZ
Was he? (slaps herself) I don't want to know.

ALLEGRA
Dr. Long, Shelby, was kinky. He had to floss every time
we kissed.

VIOLET
At least he never had bad breath.

ALLEGRA (TO LIZ)
Why don't you give him a call?

LIZ
Actually I do need a check-up. He's a good dentist.

VIOLET
I thought he retired.

ALLEGRA
He'd come out of retirement for Liz, the new femme
fatale of the geriatric set.

SAM
Does he really look like Woody Allen?

ALLEGRA
Liz can close her eyes and think of Hollywood.

VIOLET (PLAYFULLY)
Or Gary Cooper or Clark Gable or...

LIZ
Violet stop it, stop it! They're all dead. They can only
perform in our dreams.

ALLEGRA
Look Liz, if you're afraid to call Shelby, I'll call him and
try to set something up for you.

LIZ

Let's talk about it tomorrow. Tomorrow is another day.

ALLEGRA

Look Liz, maybe it's time for you to work on developing your list.
Work on it all year and bring it next summer.

LIZ

I'll work hard at it. Competition helps keep us alive . I'm so
thrilled we'll all be here next year.

VIOLET

God willing.

ALLEGRA

I'm happy to start rehearsing at the Mercury theater next week.
They're putting the actors up at the Lilligard Hotel.

SAM

I'll miss you. I will come see the show.

ALLEGRA

The Lilligard doesn't have a bar, so you'll continue to see a lot of
me. And I'll send my fans here to try an Allegra cocktail. I love
it!

SAM

I'll make sure Dad imprints the Allegra on the bar's permanent
menu. We'll run it on special the week of the show.

ALLEGRA

A special-I love it! Feature me with oysters.

LIZ

Tomorrow we start our good-byes. I hate good-byes. Last
summer we said good-bye to Lillian believing we'd see her again.
(becomes weepy)

VIOLET

In all good-byes we believe we have tomorrow to say good-bye
again.

LIZ

I've learned to take nothing for granted.

ALLEGRA

Oh Violet, Sam, Lizzy Liz, you know parting is such sweet sorrow.

VIOLET

Let us number our days.

LIZ

With luck, the best is yet to follow.

SAM

Tomorrow, tomorrow and tomorrow.

"(BLACKOUT)"

ACT III. Scene 6.

SETTING: Porch of Hotel.

AT RISE: Evening. Liz and Violet make their entrances dressed in beautiful brightly colored dresses and shawls. They sit on rocking chairs as Sam serves them drinks. He gets himself a coke and joins them.

VIOLET

Why does it always take Allegra so long to get dressed?

LIZ

She has the most to conceal.

VIOLET

Be nice dear. Remember you have a truce. Allegra has behaved very well today.

LIZ

The cat who ate the canary. People don't change, they just get older.

>   VIOLET
> We all have our days in the sun. Let her enjoy hers and let's bask
> in her radiance.

*(Allegra enters. She looks elegant. Sam hums something like the "Miss America"
theme as she enters.)*

>   SAM
> Here she is… Our All-eg-ra…

>   ALLEGRA
> My last grande entrance of the season.

>   SAM
> What about Arsenic and Old Lace ?

>   ALLEGRA
> Oh honey in that play I portray a frump. Frump's don't have
> spotlights. Frumps have sagging bosoms and fallen arches.

>   VIOLET
> Count your blessings my dear.

>   ALLEGRA
> Oh, I am grateful for the role. It's just not glamorous. It's not
> Hedda Gabler.

>   SAM
> Let's see tonight you ladies are seeing The King and I, right?

(They nod)

>   LIZ
> I wonder who'll play the King.

>   VIOLET
> No one can replace the great Yul Brynner.

ALLEGRA
We're all replaceable honey.

VIOLET
And interchangeable.

LIZ
Sam honey can you join us tonight?

SAM
I'd love to but I've made other plans.

VIOLET (TEASING)
A date?

SAM (BLUSHES)
Yes, Caroline.

VIOLET
Caroline is such a sweet little girl. (to others) She owns that
darling boutique in town.

ALLEGRA
Oh, I've shopped there many times. It's a very successful business.

LIZ
I actually pointed Caroline out to Sam last summer when we saw
her at the beach.

VIOLET
It really doesn't matter who saw her first. What matters is that
Sam likes her and he is going on a date.

LIZ
Who knows we may be coming back here for a wedding soon.

ALLEGRA
Let's not push the boy into marriage. He has a challenging career
in front of him. It's getting late and we must get to the theater.

VIOLET
Our calling.

LIZ

Magic time.

ALLEGRA

Our curse and our blessing. How about a picture Liz?

LIZ

(She takes her camera out of her handbag.)

Oh I almost forgot.

(She hands camera to Sam.)

Could you please?

(He nods, takes camera as the ladies line up and smile for the shot. Violet complains.)

VIOLET

I wasn't ready. Could we do another please?

(He shoots another, then Liz takes the camera and motions for Sam to get in the picture. Then they make their exit from the hotel slowly.)

SAM

Please send me copies. You better hurry. It's getting late. Have a nice evening ladies. I'll see you tomorrow.

ALLEGRA (KISSES HIM)

Don't you rush back for us honey. You have a splendid date. Don't do anything I wouldn't do.

VIOLET (TO SAM IN CONFIDENCE)

Don't do anything she'd do.

LIZ
Don't listen to anybody. Do what's best for you and enjoy!

(Hand in hand the ladies walk the shoreline path from the hotel. Sam calls to them. They look back and see Sam with his arm around Caroline. They look very happy. The ladies wave, smile and continue their journey.)

ALLEGRA
That Caroline is a real knock out.

VIOLET
Her dress was a little short.

LIZ
They looked happy. We look happy.

(They approach the shore.)

ALLEGRA
Look the tide's in

LIZ
I love to take deep breaths of pure sea air.

(They take a deep breath together.)

ALLEGRA
Each breath empowers me.

(They breath again.)

LIZ
Let's enjoy the rest of our journey.

                    VIOLET
God will guide us.

                    ALLEGRA
Let's continue to daydream life's possibilities.

                    LIZ
Sketch our entrances, sorrows, joys, exits and encores.

                    ALLEGRA
Time well lived…

                    VIOLET
Loved and remembered…

                    ALL
God be with you, till we meet again.

(They continue their journey to the theater singing the last verse of "Sentimental Journey" (Green/Brown/Homer 1945) with affection and glory).

                 ALL (CONT.)
"Never thought my heart could be so yearning.

Why did I decide to roam.

Got to take a sentimental journey. Sentimental journey home.

 Sentimental journey."

                "(BLACKOUT)"

Earthly Remains
A Comedy in Two Acts

THE CAST OF CHARACTERS

MARTHA WHITMAN: an artist homemaker.

HORACE WHITMAN: Martha's husband, a retired minister.

MARY BACHE: Martha's sister, a gym teacher.

DOLLY WHITMAN: Martha and Horace's daughter, a playwright.

STANLEY REICH: Dolly's fiancée, a math professor.

SOPHIE REICH: Stanley's mother, a nurse who recently arrived from Poland.

REV. JEFFERSON DAVIS SMITH: Horace's cousin, a minister.

THE SUPPORTING CAST

Monuments to the dear departed: statues, mannequins, urns, TV testimonials, stuffed animals and death masks, all displaying name tags. Portraits grace the walls.

GRACE: Martha's mother; wears a lot of jewelry and make-up.

AUNT SARAH: Grace's younger sister, frail martyr.

AUNT JOAN: Grace's older sister, wealthy, haughty and arrogant.

KRISTEN: Aunt Joan's 21-year-old daughter; Ivy league cheerleader.

UNCLE BEN: Grace's brother; lawyer/realtor, a box of Kleenex at his side.

LARRY: Martha and Mary's brother, a minister, commodities broker and playboy.

GREAT GRAND AUNT MADELINE: Grace's maternal aunt who was married to an Italian Duke. She wears a tiara.

TAFFY: Martha's Pekinese.

SPOT: A Doberman that belonged to Aunt Joan.

CLEO: Grace's Siamese cat.

PRETTYBIRD: a caged parrot that belonged to Aunt Sarah.

TIME: 1970's.

SETTING: a large old house in upstate New York.

ACT I. Saturday

The Living Room, afternoon.

The Garden, before dinner.

The Living Room, after dinner.

The Garden, 11 P.M.

ACT II. Late Saturday Night

Dolly's bedroom/Garden, midnight.

The Living Room, Sunday morning.

Dolly's bedroom, late morning.

The Living Room, afternoon.

The Living Room, late afternoon.

Act 1.Scene 1. Living room, afternoon. At rise Martha is tending the monuments: dusting, grooming and embracing some. She is wearing a frilly dress and a red, white and blue apron. Horace, dazed and frozen in thought, is sitting in a wheelchair, facing the arched windows that frame the garden.

He is wearing an ascot with well worn, but expensive clothes. When he speaks it is as though a statue has come to life.

HORACE

Martha. Martha! Martha, stop fussing.

MARTHA

What do you want now Horace? Can't you see I'm busy caring for the family?

I have a lot of work.

HORACE

I have nothing.

MARTHA

Stop mumbling. Don't look out the window when you speak. Look at me!

HORACE

Your constant activity makes me dizzy. You're a thundercloud always ready to storm.

MARTHA

Horace, you're too old to speak in metaphors.

HORACE

(Turns to face her)
Metaphors are all I have left. I don't see anything now or in the future, except statuary. The sameness stifles me. I just see my past reflected in those windows. Our daughter is getting married this weekend and I'm trying to remember what our wedding was like, who we were, are, will be. You and I vowed to grow old together; not to change.

MARTHA

All you do is sit around here and make up things to fret about. I haven't changed.

This is the same dress I wore at our twentieth or twenty-fifth anniversary. Remember?

MARTHA

HORACE

Yes, it's a lovely dress. You've always had exquisite taste.

MARTHA

I inherited my sense of taste from my dear departed mother. (She embraces Grace)
Look at her, she is still stylish after twenty years.

HORACE

She hasn't changed a bit. She still stares at me with those beady eyes and sour mouth.

MARTHA

I promised mother I would maintain order in this living room. My past, present and future are alive here. What will happen when I'm gone? (She looks at Grace for an answer.) You'd think my lazy sister would help me, especially this weekend. This is her family too.

She spends her life lifting weights and batting balls around.

HORACE

Mary's concerned with sports. You're concerned with ceremonies and rituals.

MARTHA

(On the verge of tears)
I just can't do all this alone. I need a break. I need help.

HORACE

Don't look at me. I'm incapacitated.

MARTHA

You're probably constipated. I bought you that powdered laxative the doctor recommended to mix in your juice, but you don't like the taste.

HORACE

That glob makes me gag. You'd probably like it if I gagged to death. When I drop dead you'll have a lot of money to squander. Take that trip you always nag me about.

Go to Greece, where they have more statuary than our living room.

MARTHA

I refuse to stand here and argue with you. (She addresses her mother) See what I have to deal with? Who is going to help me with our daughter's wedding?

HORACE

(Waves his arms at the supporting cast)
You have a room full of relatives. They have all the answers.

MARTHA

(To supporting cast)
They're the only ones with any brains around here. They can see my burdens are too great!

HORACE

(To the windows)
Like a mule, Martha denies her burdens Grace.

MARTHA

(Puts her arms around GRACE)
Don't bring mother into this conversation.

HORACE

Grace never speaks to me.

MARTHA

(To Grace)
Oh, Mother, do you believe my little girl is getting married? Remember the day we brought her home from the hospital? She was the best baby; so quiet and still. Aunt Sarah mistook her for a baby doll. That's why we named her Dolly.

HORACE

(Looks out at garden)
Dolly spent her childhood in that garden. Now it's overgrown.

I hope she'll weed this weekend. (Pause)

HORACE

What happened to the garden swing? It used to hang between Grandfather's Elms. Where are my grandfather's elms?

MARTHA

(To Horace)
Calm down! Stop talking to yourself!

HORACE

Who else do I have to talk to?

MARTHA

Mary will be here any minute. You must compose yourself.

HORACE

(Mimes conducting the statues)
De-com-pose. De-com-pose. Deeee-compose.

MARTHA

(Refers to supporting cast)
He thinks he's so funny. I don't hear them laughing. (To Horace)
Horace, please try to conduct yourself like a gentleman this weekend.

HORACE

(Mimes conducting himself as a gentleman)
In control. Heads will roll. Then we'll all bowl.

MARTHA

Stop rhyming!!!

HORACE

Just my way of having fun. Remember fun, Martha?

MARTHA

I have no time for triviality. Mary will be here any moment. She hasn't seen you since your stroke.

HORACE

Who has she seen?

MARTHA

Some distant relatives who I've lost touch with.

HORACE

Did you invite any of my family to the wedding?

MARTHA

Your family has been here for generations.

HORACE

This is my family home. My ancestors created all the noble traditions that you cherish. It was their idea, not yours, to always perform wedding and funeral rites in this living room... (Calms down)
Did you remember to get the candles for the ritual?

MARTHA

Who else? (Refers to supporting cast) Do you see any of them running to the store? (Confides to Horace) Do you remember how carefree we were at Dolly's age? Remember those wild parties at Divinity School?

HORACE

(He nods)
Oh yes, those were the days. I remember how I held you in my arms when we danced to "Unchained Melody." (She nods then turns away.) Now I just have a blanket to hold.(He refers to supporting cast.) Now you take better care of them than me.

MARTHA

Times change. Now my family makes demands of my free time.

HORACE

You have no free time. If there are demands, there is a price.

My family never made any demands.

(The doorbell rings. Neither moves to answer it.)

MARTHA

Your family never made anything, except money. Then they died.

(Horace shakes his head in frustration and turns back to the window. Someone tries the door, knocks. Neither move.)

MARTHA-CONT.
Mary? Mary, is that you?

(MARY enters through the garden doors. She looks athletic, carries a tote bag.)

MARY
(Addresses Martha and supporting cast)
Hello everyone! Don't anyone get up or move for me. Stay cool.

MARTHA
It's about time. I thought you'd never get here. (She gasps at Mary's sneakers and casual attire.) Football practice?

(Horace is motionless, as if in a trance.)

MARY
Started jogging again this morning. (Jogs in place) I feel great!

How's Horace?

MARTHA
Don't ask.

MARY
Did it affect his brain?

MARTHA
Who can tell?

MARY
(Turns Horace's wheelchair so that he faces her. He doesn't respond.)
Horace, do you know who I am? Do you know me?

(She waves her hand in front of his face.)
Do you know who I am?

HORACE
(Blank stare)
Don't you?

MARTHA
He only responds when he wants to. What did I do to deserve this?

MARY
You have it rough, Sis. Who's delivering dinner tonight?

MARTHA
It's another difficult decision. Dolly likes Chinese food, but we can't eat it in front of Aunt Sarah.

MARY
Put a sheet over her. (Martha agrees.) While you're at it, put a wet towel over Larry's bust. I don't want to look at his face.

MARTHA
Larry was our brother. You have to forgive him.

MARY
All right, but agree to turn his face around when I'm in the room.

MARTHA
(Turns Larry's face away from Mary)
His monument should have been a public address system. He was such a brilliant trial attorney.

HORACE
Talking shrines amuse me.

MARY
Is Larry's head still in the freezer?

MARTHA
(Nods)
Yes. We couldn't handle the whole body. There have been great advances in cryonics. He may return to us soon.

MARY
If they find a cure for his disease he just has a head, no body.

HORACE

Don't worry. Martha can make him a perfect body. She could make him look like Michelangelo's "David." She's very creative.

MARTHA

Thank you Horace. I appreciate your support.

HORACE

You're welcome, my dear.

MARY

(Runs her fingers through Uncle Ben's hair.)
Uncle Ben always said I was creative. He said I had great taste.

MARTHA

That to do with art, not with life.

MARY

I finally got around to drawing up my will. I'm leaving Dolly my entire collection of surrealist paintings.

MARTHA

(Grimaces. Takes brush out of her pocket to groom Taffy.)
I hope I die first. That painting you have with all those eyes gives me nightmares.

MARY

My most recent painting has a penis.

MARTHA

Oh good. You always wanted one.

(Doorbell rings)

HORACE

Could that be dinner?

(Doorbell rings again. No one moves to answer it.)

MARTHA

All you think about is your stomach. It's only three o'clock.
(Looks reproachfully at Mary.) I wish I could find someone to
open the door, vacuum, dust... (She gives in and gets the door)

(Dolly and Stanley enter. Mary slips Horace a cigar. They all embrace)

DOLLY

Mother, I can't believe you changed the locks again.

HORACE

(Does his Groucho Marx imitation.)
Everybody is dying to get in here.

(Dolly slips her Dad a candy bar as Stanley, somewhat puzzled, examines the supporting cast.)

MARTHA

(To Dolly)
So this is Dolly's mathematician.

DOLLY

Stanley knows all about things like Game Theory and Nonlinear
Vibrations.

MARTHA

That's nice dear, but does he know how to mix cement?

STANLEY

You certainly have a lot of... art? (Confused) Dolly said the whole
family would be here.

MARY

I don't have a name tag, but I do have a lot of warm blood and
expectations.

MARTHA

(Takes Stanley's arm)
Let me introduce you to the supporting cast.

(SPLIT FOCUS. Dolly is at her father's side. Stanley and Mary follow Martha's tour. Cast interacts with supporting cast whenever possible.)

DOLLY
Father, you look troubled.

            MARTHA
            (Embraces Grace). Weddings were Horace's
            mother's passion.

HORACE
Someone took your swing out of the garden.

            MARY
            And she only married once!

DOLLY
We'll put up another swing.

            STANLEY
            (To Martha) You and your mother look so
            much alike.

HORACE
(Looks at Martha) Someone destroyed the elms.
DOLLY
Grandfather's elms are gone!

            MARTHA
            Mother died of heart failure.
            MARY
            Uncle Ben died of pneumonia.
            (Takes tissue out of Ben's box And dusts
            him off)

HORACE
I miss Grandfather.
DOLLY
Hard to believe he's been dead twenty years.

            STANLEY
            Sorry to hear that.

HORACE
Grandfather and I used to sit here for hours and
play chess.
Your mother thought I was having too much fun
and put him in the barn.

            MARTHA
            Aunt Sarah was devoted to birds.

MARY
(Teases parrot)
Uncle Ben liked to cook birds…
They fought all the time.

DOLLY
Let's visit him later.

STANLEY
Is that why they're facing away from each
other?

HORACE
Martha arranged all of my family in the barn.
I don't care about my uncles, aunts, cousins
or even my parents, but I was so close to my
Grandfather. He should witness your wedding
vows. (Dolly wheels him toward the Others for
tea.)

MARY
(Nods) Could never see eye to eye. Aunt
Joan always acted as coach. (She picks up
bust of Larry)
Don't we look alike?
STANLEY
(Nods. Trips over Pekinese dog)
I thought it was…

DOLLY
What will mother allow you to eat?

MARTHA
Alive? Taffy was so playful.

HORACE
Crow.

MARY
Taffy is still cute. (Pets him) A Pekinese
with a sense of humor. My brother Larry
lacked humor. He ruined my life.

DOLLY
I never ate crow. I'm so hungry I could die!
MARTHA
(To Mary) He didn't ruin your life; he saved your life. (Mary
shakes her head and puts Larry's bust out of sight.)

285

(To Dolly)
Now I don't want to hear any more talk about dying. You can't die before your wedding dear. Besides, it's time to serve tea.

DOLLY
Shouldn't we wait for Stanley's mother?

MARTHA
Stanley's mother is late. We can't keep tea waiting.

STANLEY
(Pets Taffy) My mother loves dogs.

MARTHA
Does she love tea?

MARY
(To Stanley) Sometimes having tea in this place is like playing musical chairs. Martha is always moving everyone around.

Let me show you the garden. (She leads him out)

HORACE
(Slips Dolly a candy bar from under his blanket)
Our secret.

DOLLY
(Puts candy bar in her pocket and acts innocent)
Aunt Mary is looking well.

MARTHA
Let's hope she stays well. We don't want her to move in here.

HORACE
You could always put her in the barn.

MARTHA
Your family liked her less than mine.

HORACE
If you don't like her, why did you invite her to our daughter's wedding?

MARTHA
She's family. You can't turn your back on family.

HORACE
Especially if they carry knives.

MARTHA
Don't bring my father into the conversation. His memory upsets
me more than life itself.

DOLLY
Mother, don't allow yourself to get upset. Think about dinner.

What are you planning for our rehearsal dinner?

MARTHA
Aunt Joan would approve of Kentucky fried chicken.

HORACE
Another fowl meal. I'll be cackling soon.

MARTHA
Be polite! Wail until the guests leave.

HORACE
I haven't had a home cooked meal in years.

DOLLY
I could fix something tonight. Is there anything in the freezer
besides Uncle Larry's head?

MARTHA
Oh there's a lot of stuff. We belong to a freezer club. I think there's
some steaks, ribs, pig's knuckles and some ice cream.

HORACE
Martha only cooks when she has to. She always freezes leftovers.

DOLLY
Why did you take Uncle Larry out of that cryogenic place?

MARTHA
My poor brother didn't leave enough money.

HORACE
His credit cards expired. Bad credit follows you into eternity.

DOLLY
I'm sorry about Uncle Larry, but we need to order dinner.

Stanley and I haven't eaten all day.

MARTHA
I'll take care of it darling as soon as I find the portable phone. I can't imagine what I did with the phone. I'll also check on the catering for tomorrow.

DOLLY
Oh mother, you are so organized. I don't know where you find time.

MARTHA
My family found time and passed it on to me.

DOLLY
I hope I inherit that trait. I never found the right wedding dress.

I hope you were able to dig something up.

MARTHA
Grandma's coming-out dress would look lovely on you.

DOLLY
Isn't that the same dress she was laid out in?

MARTHA
(Nods)
I had it cleaned and pressed the other day. French lace over white satin... You look so much like my mother. You could also wear Great Grand Aunt Madeline's tiara. I wore it at my wedding.

DOLLY
Oh that tiara will make me feel like a princess.

MARTHA
Don't forget that Great Grand Aunt Madeline was married to an Italian Duke.

You need to record our family's history for your plays.

Horace shakes his head and pulls his blanket tighter.

DOLLY

Oh I will Mother. I plan to research more this weekend.

HORACE

(To Martha with affection)
Dolly looks like you. I'll never forget how beautiful you were on our wedding day. We were so much in love. Remember?

MARTHA

How could I forget? It was filmed and my wedding portrait hangs outside our bedroom.

HORACE

Where do feelings hang?

MARTHA

(Kisses his forehead)
I must have feelings. I'm here. (Pause) Now look at Dolly next to Mother.

(She places Dolly's face next to Grace for comparison)

HORACE

They do look alike. Something happened to Grace's nose. It used to be longer.

MARTHA

We look like the three graces. Mother is faith. Dolly is hope and I'm charity.

HORACE

(To Martha)
Isn't charity supposed to begin at home? You're always chiseling.

MARTHA

I work. You watch.

HORACE

He also serves who only watch and wait…

MARTHA

It's been ages since someone has served me. I'll die first.

(She moves affectionately around monuments.)
There are those who appreciate my efforts.

HORACE

Martha has the advantage… all the voters come from her district.
My constituents reside in the barn.

DOLLY

(Takes a notepad from her purse.) I'm missing a lot of good lines.

I should be taking notes.

*Mary and Stanley enter from the garden. Mary holds a bouquet of wild flowers. Mary
adorns some of the monuments with the flowers. Martha eyes her critically.*

MARTHA

(To Dolly)
Working on another play, dear?

DOLLY

Immersed.

MARTHA

Our home provides such inspiration.

STANLEY

Dolly's last play got rave reviews in Boston. Her new one "Alien
Doctors," is a riot. I'm so proud of her.

Stanley takes Dolly in his arms.

MARTHA

I hope to see one of her plays some day. It's so hard for Horace and I to get away. As you can see there is so much to do here. We can't afford help.

MARY

I saw her last play, "Broken Hearts." It was about cannibalism.

MARTHA

Distasteful topic. Dolly should write happy romantic plays.

She should write about Aunt Sarah, Uncle Ben, Aunt Joan and maybe a little tidbit about your love story Mary.

MARY

No one cares about lost loves. (She gives Martha and then Horace a sharp stare and exits to the garden.)

MARTHA

Mary spends too much time outside. If she's not playing ball she's gardening. The sun will kill her.

STANLEY

Mary's worried about the weeds in your garden strangling the plants.

HORACE

What about the weeds in here?

MARTHA

Did I hear another metaphor Horace?

HORACE

Sorry dear. I'll watch my words.

DOLLY

Everyone will get a preview of my writing tomorrow. Tonight I will finish the fifth draft of our wedding vows.

MARTHA

Shouldn't the script be ready for tonight's rehearsal?

DOLLY
I'm still working on it. I want every word to be perfect.

MARTHA
Perfect is a weak word. Maybe you should consult Uncle Ben's thesaurus, under his podium. I can still hear him reading from it. He would have made a great playwright. You know most playwrights are men my dear. I'm glad you're getting married.

STANLEY
Dolly is a great playwright. She will never stop writing. She is the love of my life and we are getting married because we are deeply committed to each other. (He kisses Dolly passionately)

DOLLY
Thank you darling. Mother, see, this is what our life is based on.

I want my wedding to be like the opening night of a new play.

MARTHA
(Pulls Dolly away from Stanley and embraces her)
That was a lovely simile my dear. In rehearsal we can run through the actions of the ceremony and you can supply your words tomorrow.

It is so wonderful having a writer in the family. We never had a writer in our family.

HORACE
My Uncle James was a writer!

MARTHA
He was a newspaper reporter.

HORACE
He was nominated for the Pulitzer Prize.

MARTHA
Yes, but he didn't get it.

STANLEY
I think I need some air. I'll help Mary weed.

Stanley kisses Dolly and exits to the garden. Martha rearranges or removes flowers that Mary had put on the monuments.

DOLLY

Where is Uncle James? He used to stand behind the desk.

MARTHA

That was before I had the new phone installed. (Absent mindedly) That reminds me, I need to find the phone. I need to order dinner.

HORACE

Uncle James is in the barn. (He wheels himself back to his spot by the windows to shut down)

MARTHA

(To Dolly)
Where is Stanley's mother? She's awfully late. She should call.

DOLLY

(Shrugs her shoulders)
I don't know. I sent her directions and a map with her wedding invitation.

MARTHA

Why hasn't she called? (Distracted) At least if she'd call we'd hear the phone and be able to find it.

DOLLY

I hope she's not lost or in an accident.

(Hits herself on the head in an effort to gain control.)
Dolly, stop imagining the worst. Why do people always imagine the worst?

MARTHA

I promised you nothing but pleasant dreams. What went wrong?

DOLLY

(Looks out the windows at garden)
Mother, what happened to Great-grandfather's elms?

> MARTHA

When your father was in the hospital I had them chopped down.

They were too big, threatened our home. Look how bright
everything is now!

> DOLLY

How could you have Great grandfather's elms chopped down?

> MARTHA

I found a tree surgeon in the phone book. Any service I'll ever
need is listed in that great book.

> DOLLY

I can't believe you could do such a thing.

> MARTHA

I don't even think he noticed. Calm down. Don't upset your father.
Remember he had a stroke. (Dolly nods and tries to compose
herself)
Well I'm going outside to see what they are up to in my garden.

*Martha exits to garden and Dolly moves to her father by the window. He wheels
himself around to talk with her. She gives him a hug.*

> DOLLY

Oh Daddy. I do miss this place, but mostly I miss you.

> HORACE

I could have the guesthouse renovated if you decide to move back
home.

> DOLLY

That was my playhouse as a child. That's where my writing
career started. Remember how I wrote little skits for my dolls to
perform?

(He smiles with memory) Are all my dolls still there?

HORACE

I don't know love. I haven't been out there in years. Your mother uses the place for storage.

DOLLY

Maybe if Stanley's job wasn't so far away we could live here.

HORACE

Stanley could teach down here. I still have connections.

DOLLY

That would be wonderful. Do you really think you could get him a job at the college in town?

HORACE

Done! I could use another man in this house. Nice boy, this professor.

After you move in he could help me with a few little things. For now, do you think he could help me get grandfather out of the barn?

DOLLY

Stanley's the most compromising man I've ever known. He'll do anything I want.

HORACE

My Dolly with a logician. Lord knows this house is plagued with problems in higher mathematics.

DOLLY

Oh Daddy, someday you'll love Stanley as much as me.

HORACE

As well, but never as much.

DOLLY

You say the most clever things. I think I'm a writer because of you.

I still remember all the stories you told me about your youth.

HORACE

I have a lot more stories my dear. After you are married I'll tell
you the whole story of my courtship with your mother.

DOLLY

That might be too personal. I don't know if mother would like it.

HORACE

Oh don't worry about that. Characters never recognize themselves.

They are so busy searching for meaning that they never find it.

The journey is the meaning. The destination is the end.

DOLLY

Oh father, daddy. I can see why you became a minister. You are a
True philosopher. Did you ever think of writing a play?

HORACE

I think I'd make a better stand up comic.

DOLLY

Do you mind if I join my groom in the garden?

HORACE

Oh no go to him my dear. I'll take a little snooze before dinner.

Dolly kisses him on the forehead and slips him a candy bar.

DOLLY

One of our secrets.

*She puts her finger to her lips in a hush and exits. Horace wheels himself over to Ben's
podium where there is a box of tissues. He blows his nose and tosses the tissue on the
floor. He takes another and wheels himself back to his window perch. He watches the
activity in the garden. He takes out a candy bar.*

HORACE

I don't even have my own tissues. Candy is a blessing. It took me a long time to learn the facts of life around here. You get nothing you don't die for.

Act.1. Scene 2. Garden, before dinner. Dolly weeds as Stanley paces. Horace watches them through living room window and comments to the audience in George Burns style.

STANLEY

I wish I didn't leave my math books home.

DOLLY

Do you miss them Stanley?

STANLEY

I was working on the most beautiful proof.

DOLLY

You talk about numbers the way other men talk about sex.

STANLEY

The beauty of a mathematical problem lies in its process.

I wish you could understand.

DOLLY

Aunt Joan used to say it wasn't as important to understand as to accept.

STANLEY

Like this arcane marriage ritual. Why is it so important for us to be married in that creepy living room?

DOLLY

As long as anyone can remember, weddings and funerals in the Whitman family were always performed in the living room.

STANLEY

Could we stretch tradition a little and have the ceremony out here where there's fresh air and breathing space?

                    DOLLY
Oh no! I'm afraid to think what might happen if the chain of
traditions is broken.

                    STANLEY
Chains not only secure, they strangle.

                    DOLLY
Invisible chains can't harm anyone. Aunt Sarah said that our
traditions form a mythical bond with the past.

                    STANLEY
What could happen if we break tradition? Are you afraid of being
struck by lightening or turned into a frog?

                    HORACE
I like multiple choice questions.

                    DOLLY
Aunt Sarah said never to test fate. Or was that tempt fate?

                    STANLEY
Let's tempt fate, see what happens.

                    DOLLY
I can't . I just can't. There are secrets buried in that room.

If I follow the rules I'll know the truth someday.

                    STANLEY
You are talking in circles, making no sense. It's like I left a
different woman in Boston. I don't recognize you here.

                    DOLLY
Aren't people always different around their families? Wait until
your mom gets here. You'll turn into the little boy I never met.

                    STANLEY
Unlikely. I've always been very serious and grounded.

The only one in your family I can relate to is Mary. She has
common sense.

DOLLY

I wonder who she got it from. My mother gets so jealous of Aunt Mary. I suppose it could be related to common sense.

HORACE

My father wanted me to marry Mary. My heart chose Martha.

STANLEY

That's silly.

DOLLY

No, serious. My Uncle Larry introduced my father to Aunt Mary and they went out for awhile. They were engaged when my mother met him.

STANLEY

Why did he choose Martha?

HORACE

How many people have the opportunity to hear their pasts dissected?

DOLLY

He met my mother at his and my aunt's engagement party. It was love at first sight. My Dad was mesmerized.

HORACE

I should have been analyzed.

DOLLY

The family couldn't believe what a civilized broken engagement Father and Aunt Mary had. The only one who cried was my Grandmother. She was afraid Aunt Mary would never marry.

STANLEY

And she never did marry, did she?

HORACE

Mary makes waves. Martha floats.

DOLLY

I'm worried about my father's condition.

STANLEY
Your father uses his illness as a mask. He doesn't want to be well.

HORACE
If he's so smart, perhaps he can tell me what I DO want.

STANLEY
He wants a live audience.

DOLLY
You'll like my father when you get to know him.

STANLEY
I didn't say I don't like him. He seems like a nice enough guy for a father-in-law who you'll only see two or three times a year.

HORACE
People see what they choose and hear what they need to.

DOLLY
It will be so much easier when we live here.

STANLEY
What are you talking about?

DOLLY
Father said he could use his connections to get you a job at the local community college. Then we could all live together,

STANLEY
What? And leave Harvard?

DOLLY
It would be so much easier for you at the local college. Not so many boring intellectuals.

STANLEY
Just what boring intellectuals are you talking about?

DOLLY
All you friends.

STANLEY

I thought you liked my friends. I thought you were my friend.

You went to Radcliff for Christ's sake. If that doesn't make you an intellectual who or what are you?

DOLLY

I'm a playwright, an observer. I don't live in the world of ideas.

I dwell in the tangled web of my imagination.

STANLEY

This place could fuel a donkey's imagination. That living room probably hosts enough mold and molted fur and hair to feed a flea circus.

All of a sudden Dolly becomes visibly upset and tearful. Stanley is confused.

DOLLY

You are nothing more than a barbarian with a slide rule.

STANLEY

Who uses a slide rule anymore? Why are you hysterical?

DOLLY

I'm not hysterical; I'm very worried. My world is falling apart on the eve of my wedding.

STANLEY

Our wedding. What could go wrong? You wrote the ceremony?

DOLLY

It's not the words that worry me; it's our actions.

STANLEY

What actions?

DOLLY

Our secret .You know.

STANLEY

Which secret?

DOLLY

(Stage whisper)
My virginity.

STANLEY

What virginity?

DOLLY

That's the problem. Intellectually I'll always be a virgin.

HORACE

It will unnerve Martha if the candles flicker.

DOLLY

This is no time for jokes. I feel so guilty. I never lied before,
except maybe lies of omission, but they don't count. If it wasn't for
that, our wedding would make so many people happy.

STANLEY

What percentage of your family can feel or emote happiness?

DOLLY

Don't make fun of my family. They're loving and close- knit.

STANLEY

Like muscle around a spinal chord.

DOLLY

Exactly. Blood ties.

HORACE

Life-like impressions in cement.

STANLEY

Dolly, why can't we just tell everybody the truth and have a
friendly little party?

DOLLY

Oooh! The truth would kill everybody.

STANLEY
They are already dead.

DOLLY
Stanley. You don't understand. You're becoming hostile.

STANLEY
I am hostile. I feel like a new resident in the state of confusion.

DOLLY
If we get through the wedding without any incidents we'll be home free.

STANLEY
And free to go home. (Teasing) Are you sure you're not a virgin?

She puts her fingers to his lips to silence him. He kisses her fingers. Doorbell rings. Martha enters the living room. Horace pretends he's asleep.

MARTHA
Dolly, Dolly, could you get the door, please?

DOLLY
In a minute mother.

Dolly takes Stanley's hand and leads him into the living room. Martha exits to the kitchen. The doorbell rings again and then knocking is heard. Horace wakes up.

HORACE
(Takes candy from under his blanket)
Anyone for a Mounds bar?

STANLEY
No, but I'd love a drink. Any vodka?

Horace points to a liquor cabinet. Mary enters with a bat and ball.

HORACE
Help yourself my boy. Get acquainted with the place.

Learn where the keys are.

Mary answers the door. It is SOPHIE, Stanley's mother. She is weighted down with various sized cake boxes and bags. Stanley and Sophie kiss.

STANLEY
Mother, I'm so glad to see you. I was starting to worry. You're always so punctual.

SOPHIE
I got lost. Couldn't find signs on roads.

DOLLY
Did you have trouble reading the map I drew?

SOPHIE
(Kisses Dolly)
You make lovely drawings darling, a little abstract.

DOLLY
Drawing relaxes me. I draw almost as much as I write.

SOPHIE
My Stanley is lucky to find such talented girl.

Sophie hands bundles to Dolly and Stanley. Horace reacts with interest to foodstuffs.

SOPHIE-CONT.
I don't know what everyone like so I got little of everything;
cheese buns, crullers, rolls, dried fruit and some candy.

Dolly leads Sophie to Horace. Sophie is confused and overwhelmed.

DOLLY
Come meet my father. He's recovering from a stroke.

MARY

Nice to meet you Sophie. It may take a while for Horace to respond. He likes to be coaxed.

HORACE

Coached is more like it. Mary and I tried out for the same team. I was too weak to make it.

MARY

Maybe in you're next life you'll make it. Think immortality.

HORACE

Now I think immobility. I'm hungry.

MARY

Martha couldn't find the phone so she's cooking tonight.

HORACE

Oh God no. (He takes the phone out from under his blanket.) Look what I found!

MARY

Are you creating a new parlor game Horace? (He laughs and tosses It to Mary who treats it like a hot potato) I'll put it back before Martha returns. (She quickly returns phone to its cradle) I wonder what mystery meat Martha defrosted.

STANLEY

Would that mystery meat come from the same freezer where Uncle Larry's head is stored?

HORACE

Afraid so. I hope she doesn't make mock turtle soup again.

MARY

Martha is the mistress of mockery. In this house you never know who or what will show up for dinner. Maybe she'll dig up a few extra guests.

HORACE

(To Stanley)
You look like you need a drink, my son. (Reaches under his

blanket)
Here's the key to the liquor cabinet.

Horace hands Stanley the key and points to cabinet. Stanley rushes to open it, finds a big bottle of vodka and no glasses. He takes a slug from the bottle, toasts the supporting cast, closes the cabinet then carries the bottle around with him.

STANLEY
Anybody else need a drink?

SOPHIE
Later honey. I will wait for glasses.

HORACE
Don't bother re-locking it my boy. This will be a long night.

DOLLY
I'll go to the kitchen and see if I can help Mom.

HORACE
Make sure everything is well done or well preserved. No surprises.

SOPHIE
(To Dolly)
Let me help darling.

DOLLY
Oh no. You relax . You had a long trip. (She exits to kitchen)

HORACE
Relax Sophie. Stay in here and get acquainted with the family.

(Stage whisper to Sophie) The most esteemed family members are in the barn. Maybe Stanley will take you there later.

Sophie sits and stares at the supporting cast in confusion and disbelief. Martha enters with a tray holding paper plates, plastic glasses and napkins etc. She sets it down, wipes her hands on her apron and sizes up Sophie.

MARTHA

So you and your son want to join our family.

SOPHIE

I'm here for wedding.

HORACE

Dolly said you were a nurse. (Sophie nods) Good, I may need one.
Sophie is confused and overwhelmed.

Stanley takes a plastic cup and fixes his mother a drink. Sophie extends her hand to Martha who backs off and puts her hands in her apron pockets.

MARTHA

Sorry I need to wash my hands. I still have some blood on them
from the roast. We'll get to know each other later.

MARY

Stanley, want to go outside and hit a few balls with me before
dinner?

STANLEY

Sorry Mary, I'm not up to ball playing right now. I need to drink
more and reflect.

MARTHA

Don't reflect too hard Stanley dear. You wouldn't want to crack
any valuable mirrors.

STANLEY

I think I'll go upstairs and rest up for dinner.

MARY

Get a good nap. This is your last day as a single man.

*Stanley exits to his room with vodka bottle. Mary is playing with her ball in the living
room which disturbs Martha.*

> MARTHA

When we were children I wanted dolls, Mary wanted balls.

> MARY

Now we both have what we want. When will we eat Sis?

> MARTHA

I better go back to the kitchen. All I do is work. (Refers to Mary).
And all she does is play.

> SOPHIE

I can help. Before I was nurse, I was cook.

> MARTHA

Guests here don't cook or nurse. Have another drink Sophie.

Horace sneers as Martha exits to the kitchen.

> MARY

Horace, want to go out and play with me?

> HORACE

Love to, though I'm not much of a player anymore.

How about Sophie?

> SOPHIE

I feel cold. I stay in here and rest. I see garden later.

*Mary wheels Horace out to the garden. Sophie, left alone, explores the room, reads
the name tags, fixes herself another drink, takes a framed photo of her husband and a
small shopping bag out of her suitcase and sets them on the floor behind a chair..*

GARDEN. Mary plays catch with Horace until he's too tired, as they speak.

> HORACE

Remember how beautiful this garden once was?

MARY

Gardens, like hearts, need to be maintained.

HORACE

I've grown a heavy heart. I wish I could turn back time to when love ruled our lives.

MARY

Does anything turn you on anymore?

HORACE

Laxatives and cold baths.

MARY

You always had the most disgusting sense of humor; definitely not suited to the ministry.

HORACE

My life didn't work out as I planned. I guess yours didn't either considering all you're interested in is flexing your muscles.

MARY

I'm jealous of big happy families. I do get some pleasure flexing my muscles around here. It makes Martha nervous.

HORACE

Jealousy will rot your bones then all you'll have left is muscle. I don't know any men who find big muscles on a woman attractive. Have you ever thought of wearing a dress?

MARY

I'm not interested in what men think. You were the last man I tried to impress and you dumped me for Miss Prim, Proper and Deranged.

HORACE

You don't know how many times I replayed that old scenario. I wondered how my life would have been different had I married you. You were grounded and sensible and you dressed better then. I certainly would have gotten a good church. You would have been wonderful for the youth in the parish. When I met Martha I lost all sense of reason. It was love at first sight. It was magic.

It was…

MARY

Your penis talking. You never thought about sex with me.

We played tennis, soccer, volleyball and danced a little. We were
in constant motion.

HORACE

It wasn't romantic, it was calisthenics. I do remember we had sex.

MARY

Thanks for the memory. Just how are you and Martha getting on?

HORACE

Maybe you should ask her.

MARY

We're not exactly close. I'm supposed to be the one angry at her
and she always acts like she was the one hurt.

HORACE

We were happy for a few years. Then after your father and Larry
died]she became hostile. Instead of coming to me for comfort she
took to plaster and went on a crusade to claim the living room as
her own.

MARY

She works well in plaster. It's a shame she never practiced her art
on the outside. She's talented and still quite beautiful in her frilly
way. She's made mother into quite the lady. She never looked that
good when she was alive.

HORACE

Shhh! Suppose she hears you.

MARY

I don't talk to statues and I believe when someone is dead he
or she is gone forever. I think you and Martha should spend
sometime in the real world and give up listening to shrines.

HORACE

Shrines and monuments can't hurt anyone.

MARY

Maybe they already have.

HORACE

Can we continue this conversation later tonight, under the stars?
Midnight.

MARY

The bewitching hour. Sure, why not. Do I detect a romantic tone
in that gruff voice of yours?

HORACE

The same muse who inspired me, crippled me.

MARY

Oh Horace, you are such an enigma. If you loose your mind,
please don't loose your sense of humor.

She kisses him on the forehead and wheels him back inside.

HORACE

I'll have it preserved in formaldehyde and will it to you.

*Act 1. Scene 3. Living room, after dinner. At rise Horace is alone smoking a cigar.
When others arrive he puts it out in a plant near by.*

HORACE

When you're my age, talking to yourself is one of life's pleasures.
Who else do you end up talking with anyway?

No one listens. (Refers to monuments) They might listen, but they
can't smoke or drink really good wine. They're a captive audience.
They can't even fart. At my age I can say and do anything I want.
Everyone excuses you... "It's his age."

"You know he had a stroke. Poor old thing..." I don't spend too
much time talking to myself. I spend too much time listening.

Mary and Stanley enter sipping sherry in elegant glasses.

> STANLEY
> If I solve the problem I'm working on, I can pick any Chair in mathematics in this country.

> MARY
> Only this country?

Dolly and Sophie enter with coffee.

(SPLIT FOCUS.) Horace listens attentively to both sides.

STANLEY
Mathematics is a universal language.

> DOLLY
> I hope my mother got a photographer.

MARY
Math and physical ed. were my best subjects in
school.

> SOPHIE
> I brought big camera.

STANLEY
You are a very attractive woman.

> DOLLY
> My uncle Ben was famous for his
> photographs. You should get to know him.

MARY
Older women turn you on?

> SOPHIE
> I try. Sounds like you were close to him,
> darling. Do you miss him?

STANLEY
Their faces have more character.
MARY
Check out aunt Joan. She was born old.

> DOLLY
> Why would I miss him? He's always in the
> same place.

STANLEY
Too stiff!

SOPHIE
I work on getting to know entire family.

MARY
A life devoted to mathematics would kill me.
Too many laws to memorize.
STANLEY
It's when you get beyond the rules that the
beauty of logic becomes obsessive.

DOLLY
(To Stanley)
Aunt Mary helping you to solve the problems of the world?

STANLEY
No. She's helping me to create new ones.

DOLLY
Conflict moves the action forward.

STANLEY
For every action there is an equal and opposite reaction.

MARY
For every old fool, there's a young fool.

STANLEY
And for every action of a fool there is an equally foolish opposite
reaction.

DOLLY
I'm confused. (Takes notepad from purse) I think I should be
writing this down.

STANLEY
(To Dolly)
Honey, let's go outside and get some air.

Dolly and Stanley exit to the garden. Martha enters with after-dinner mints.

                    MARY
It's hard to visualize a wedding here. This place needs a little
pizzazz, ornamentation...

                    HORACE
Life.

                    SOPHIE
Streamers. Paper bells. Almond candies wrapped in net...

                    MARTHA
No! Oh no! This is not a firehouse or a catering hall. This is an
historic home.

She turns to her mother (Grace), speaks to her and imagines a response.

Why are these occasions so complicated? Why didn't you prepare
me for this? Sure, you knew all the answers and you took them to
your grave.

                    MARY
You were always so hard on Mother. She did the best she could.

                    MARTHA
You were Mom's favorite. I was Aunt Sarah favorite. (Points to
Sarah) See how she looks at me.

*Mary takes a camera out of her backpack. She plays with viewing the room from
different angles. She's all over the room, making Martha nervous. Martha motions
for Stanley and Dolly to come back in and leads Sophie over to Larry.*

                    SOPHIE
It must be hard losing brother.

                    MARTHA
He's not lost. He's in the freezer. Some day medical science will
find a cure for what killed him and he'll be back.

He hasn't taken his eyes off you since you arrived.

SOPHIE
I could never love anyone like my Bela. When he die part of me was lost.

HORACE
Which part? Maybe Martha could make you a new one.

Mary continues to fuss around with her camera. Horace encourages her because it's making Martha more nervous.

MARTHA
(To Mary)
Can't you stay still? This isn't a ball field.

MARY
I'm glad you told me. I was just going to steal home base.

DOLLY
I really would like a wedding rehearsal family portrait.

MARY
It's so hard to get everyone in focus at the same time.

MARTHA
(To Sophie)
I hope Mary watches her manners tomorrow. She's spent her life embarrassing me and my family. Aunt Joan always said Mary couldn't be taught manners.

The combined family poses for their portrait.

HORACE
Manners are false feelings.

MARTHA
Manners serve society.

STANLEY
Manners create comfortable distances between people.

MARY

Manners are things other people watch.

SOPHIE

Manners are different in other country. We kiss more in Poland.

DOLLY

(Takes her notebook out and writes)
Manners are everywhere. I need to write all this down.

MARTHA

(To Mary)
Everyone expects you to dress and act properly tomorrow.

MARTHA-CONT.

No whistle tomorrow and No sneakers!

MARY

(Salutes her)
Aye aye Sis. Whatever makes you happy.

MARTHA

I better get back to the kitchen. It won't clean itself.

DOLLY

I want to go up to bed early. I'll have a long day tomorrow.

SOPHIE

I feel tired too. (To Dolly) Can you show me my room dear?

Dolly, Stanley and Sophie head upstairs.

MARY

I have to go unpack my car.

MARTHA

Make sure you take all your belongings upstairs.

Don't clutter up the living room.

MARY

I'll be tidy Sis.

Mary goes out to her car.

HORACE

I think I'll do a little reading.

MARTHA

After I finish the kitchen I'll take a bubble bath before my much needed beauty sleep.

HORACE

You were never lovelier.

MARTHA

What are you talking about?

HORACE

Remember our wedding day?

MARTHA

As if it were yesterday. How did we grow so old and so far apart? Life hasn't been good to us.

HORACE

Maybe we haven't been good to life.

MARTHA

There you go talking in riddles again.

HORACE

I wish we could find those lost feelings.

MARTHA

I'm sure they're buried somewhere.

HORACE

Somewhere outside the living room. Will you try and help me find them?

MARTHA

Don't be silly Horace. Only a miracle could recapture our youth. Our future is here.

HORACE

I want my future to be more than reruns of "The Twilight Zone."

MARTHA

Aunt Sarah always said you were too fresh.

HORACE

Now I'm stale.

Martha kisses the top of Horace's head then heads to the kitchen. Horace looks at her longingly and stands up and looks outside.

Act 1. Scene 4. 11 p.m. Sophie and Dolly are in the garden. Horace is in the living room, at his perch, near the windows; eavesdropping.

SOPHIE

I wish your mother would let me help more with Wedding preparations.

DOLLY

I wish I had a clear grasp of what I want. I can't visualize the ceremony. That's why I've rewritten the script so many times.

SOPHIE

Have you consulted Bride magazine?

DOLLY

(Shakes her head)
No. Every time I wanted to buy Modern Bride Stanley would laugh at me and say how silly I was.

SOPHIE

Men are hypocrites! Do you know how many back issues of "Playboy" I throw out last week? Stanley had them arranged, in neat little piles, under his bed.

DOLLY

Do you believe he calls me his "complex variable?"

SOPHIE

I believe that. Men are alien sex. How many men can talk about feelings or appreciate beauty of traditions?

HORACE

I'd like a vote on those issues.

SOPHIE

I worry about your lack of bridesmaids, outside relatives and friends.

DOLLY

Doesn't cousin Kristen count? Mother will dress her as my maid of honor.

SOPHIE

What about friends from Boston?

DOLLY

Stanley said we could have a little wedding party when we get back. There's really no room here for more guests, especially if we bring some of Dad's clan from the barn.

SOPHIE

I know everyone will understand. I look forward to meeting your Dad's family

HORACE

She better not try taking anyone home with her. You can't trust those foreigners. I better warn Grandfather tomorrow.

SOPHIE

(Opens her pocketbook and takes out gift)
I like you to have my grandmother Katrina's diamond locket.

DOLLY

How sweet of you! This can be my something old with Great Grand Madeline's tiara! (Sophie helps her put it on.)

SOPHIE
Do you have your something new?

DOLLY
My wedding ring? My shoes?

SOPHIE
Probably shoes because you don't wear them all of time.

Something borrowed?

DOLLY
Aunt Mary's pearl earrings.

SOPHIE
Something blue?

DOLLY
Gee no.

SOPHIE
Just in case I pack a few blue things in suitcase.

I didn't know your taste, so I bring a blue trimmed garter, robin egg's blue hanky and royal blue elastic hair band.

DOLLY
Can I wear more than one blue thing? The garter would be nice.

I'm supposed to throw that. I can use the elastic band because I want to wear my hair up.

SOPHIE
I don't know darling. Would anyone know?

DOLLY
Aunt Joan, but she isn't saying much lately.

SOPHIE
Joan's pose yells to you. Did she die like that?

DOLLY
No. The pose was Daddy's testimonial. She would have liked it.

HORACE
It's easiest to pose those who can't please themselves.

SOPHIE
So who, in your family started tradition of family preservation?

DOLLY
Legend has it that my paternal grandfather's grandfather, (Points
to his headstone) the son of a Revolutionary War hero, thought
there should be a monument to his father, a hero among men. Then
he realized that all men and women are heroes of some sort, if not
on the battleground, then within their homes.

Since then, whenever anybody in the family died a bust, statue or
some likeness was created as a memorial. Aunt Sarah called them
memory banks. Uncle Ben called it plastic nobility.

HORACE
I call it plastered mobility.

SOPHIE
Now your mother continues tradition only with her family.

DOLLY
Mother says people's conceptions of heroes change with the times.

Every once in a while she brings out one of Daddy's relatives.

SOPHIE
On birthdays? Holidays?

DOLLY
Sometimes, if she remembers.

HORACE
Martha remembers to forget.

*Sophie retrieves the framed photo she had hidden earlier and presses it to her chest
with the face pressed against her heart.*

                    SOPHIE
I have surprise to show you. (She reveals photo)
This is all I have left of Stanley's father.

                    DOLLY
(Takes photo and studies it)
Stanley looks so much like him.

                    SOPHIE
He was my Bela. We named our son Stanislaw, after my father.
When Stanislaw got to Harvard he became Stanley. Now he's
American. He does not like being called Stanislaw.

                    DOLLY
I like the name Stanislaw. Maybe I can get him to change it back.

                    SOPHIE
That would make his father happy. Can I put Bela on the mantle?

                    DOLLY
Let's ask mother first. She's always very careful about placing
people.

                    SOPHIE
Maybe I'll take him to bed with me and you can discuss him going
to wedding with your mom later. (Dolly nods.)

*Stanley enters. He looks at the photo of his father suspiciously. Sophie presses it
against her chest.*

                    DOLLY
(To Stanley)
Hi darling. Sorry I didn't make up your bed yet.

                    STANLEY
Don't worry. I may not use it.

                    DOLLY
Why don't you stay and talk with your Mom for awhile. I'll go
make your bed.

Stanley seems edgy. Dolly exits upstairs.

STANLEY

I see you brought Dad's picture. You should have left it home. He never would have related to this menagerie.

He would have left in a jiffy.

SOPHIE

He would have sacrificed principles to see you happy.

STANLEY

Do I look happy?

SOPHIE

Wedding anxiety?

STANLEY

I feel uneasy here. Dolly seems transformed in this house. I see a side of her I don't like. It scares me. The Dolly I love is smart, sensitive and sexy. In this place she acts like a princess in a lost barbaric civilization.

SOPHIE

They have microwave, dishwasher and cable. This has to be America.

STANLEY

I feel when I say anything no one hears me around here.

SOPHIE

Maybe you need to speak louder.

STANLEY

You know how much I love you Mother, but even your behavior has changed since you got here. I fear they are getting to you.

SOPHIE

They are nice people who worship past.

STANLEY

Their lives are buried in the past. I want to be buried in the future.

SOPHIE
You are embarrassed because I'm immigrant; no living relatives; no traditions; no old silver or portraits.

STANLEY
Don't be ridiculous. I never think about such things.

SOPHIE
What do you think about when you pass family portraits that line Whitman halls?

STANLEY
I think they need dusting.

HORACE
The dust conceals their blemishes.

SOPHIE
I want you to be happy. Why don't you get some sleep?

You will see world more clear in the morning.

STANLEY
Why don't you go on to sleep. I may spend the night in the garden.

HORACE
That place is reserved at midnight.

Dolly heads downstairs and enters in a long elegant negligée. Horace feigns sleep Sophie seems impressed and Stanley seems shocked.

SOPHIE
Oh my Dolly, how beautiful you look, like goddess.

DOLLY
It's Victoria's Secret.

STANLEY
Where is the sweet simple playwright I feel in love with?

Why are you dressed like a showgirl? What is this all about?

SOPHIE

Stanislaw, tell her how beautiful she looks. (Pause)
I'm going up to bed my dears. Good night.

Sophie exits as Stanley backs away from Dolly. He rubs his forehead with his hands in frustration. Dolly seductively dances around him.

STANLEY

I am so confused. I don't know you anymore Dolly.

(Turns to her) Who are you?

DOLLY

Why don't you come up to my place and find out.

She leads him upstairs. After they exit Horace wheels himself to the garden.

Act. 2. Scene 1. Midnight. Action moves between garden and Dolly's bedroom. At rise Dolly is sprawled out on her bed as Stanley tidies up her messy room.

DOLLY

Why are you always cleaning?

STANLEY

Someone has to. This place is filthy. Don't you ever hang anything up? .

DOLLY

There are more closets in Boston. This house has more open
space, high ceilings, beautiful antiques...

STANLEY

Catacombs, old bones, stale air and more dust than the Mohave
desert.

DOLLY

You need to be more positive. A negative attitude wills things to
go wrong.

> STANLEY

If anything can go wrong, it will.

> DOLLY

You lost your positive attitude. Remember when you made that big speech at one of our parties about how much we will grow together because playwriting is so much like mathematics?

> STANLEY

What did I say?

> DOLLY

You said we both solve problems, make order out of chaos.

You deal in numbers; I deal with characters.

Stanley sinks into a chair next to her.

> STANLEY

We can't solve any problems here.

> DOLLY

I know. We can create new ones.

She unpacks her suitcase into her bureau. Stanley notices that she tosses things, doesn't refold. It makes him crazy, but he doesn't do anything but shake his head.

> STANLEY

We've already created a new problem. I'm just here for the Wedding.

> DOLLY

OUR Wedding is a major act in my play

> STANLEY

A whole act?

> DOLLY

It's more than one scene. It's the pivotal event of our lives.

STANLEY

Maybe it's our final curtain.

DOLLY

Don't say such things Stanley. That's bad luck. Remember the Whitman ritual.

STANLEY

Sounds like Voodoo. Next thing you know they'll be sacrificing virgins. At least we know you won't have to worry about that.

DOLLY

I do worry about that. We never should have had sex until we got married.

Stanley opens the dusty curtains and notices a full moon.

STANLEY

Full moon. Figures. You sound like a lunatic.

DOLLY

If we didn't have sex I wouldn't have been able to get you here.

STANLEY

Are you saying this is a trap? Are you saying you let me knock you up so you could knock me down?

DOLLY

(Whispers, as if walls had ears. Teases him)
Shh! Don't be a silly Billy. You know I love you. Sometimes the only way you can get to a man is through his...

STANLEY

What is done cannot be undone.

DOLLY

Darling please don't add guilt to consequence.

STANLEY

In Boston you were my Juliet. Here I can almost see you as Lady Macbeth.

DOLLY

You know, maybe I should have been an actress.

STANLEY

Save you from having to carry that notebook all the time.

DOLLY

Instead of writing about other people's lives, I could live them.

She sets herself back on the bed, leaving her bureau draws open. He closes it.

STANLEY

Acting has to come from experience.

DOLLY

I grew up very sheltered around here. I haven't experienced much.

He climbs onto the bed next to her. She backs off.

STANLEY

Come on. Now you are being silly. You've experienced Radcliff, having your plays produced, boating on Walden Pond, cold nights snuggling with me by the fire and..

DOLLY

(Takes out her notebook)
I think I know where this is going.

STANLEY

Put down that notebook and kiss me.

DOLLY

Not tonight. Remember the Whitman ritual.

STANLEY

I've had enough of this hocus-pocus. If you don't make love with me I'm going home.

DOLLY

Is that a threat or a promise?

STANLEY

For now it's a threat. I'm going downstairs to make us some
drinks. When I get back we'll continue this discussion.

DOLLY

Which discussion?

He slams the door, exits. She sinks into her bed.

Garden. Mary paces as Horace follows her with his wheelchair.

HORACE

Are you ever still?

MARY

I need some exercise. It's so stuffy in that house.

HORACE

Do you miss your bar bells?

MARY

I don't use bar bells Horace. I use hand weights.

You need to build upper body strength. You'll wither away in that
wheelchair.

HORACE

What makes you think I don't exercise?

MARY

You're a big fake, aren't you?

He laughs coyly. She tries to pull his blanket off. He clutches it tightly around him.

329

HORACE
Come sit on my lap, my Dear.

MARY
Don't be ridiculous. I'm happier in motion, thank you.

HORACE
Always the headstrong independent woman.

MARY
Why are a woman's choices always questioned?

HORACE
Why didn't I choose you instead of Martha?

MARY
There's a lot of wisdom in hindsight.

HORACE
Your hindsight doesn't look that bad for a gal of your age. I guess there are some advantages to calisthenics.

MARY
More than you can imagine. The answer to your question is obvious. You made the right choice. Martha was a born hostess with a flair for interior decoration. I was a born crusader with a tendency towards breaking windows.

HORACE
(Shakes his head)
There you go again. Just where has all your running around as a gym teacher gotten you?

MARY
Connection with the outside world.

HORACE
Hogwash. Who needs it?

MARY
Dolly for one.

HORACE

Dolly has everything she needs right here.

MARY

Where? In this garden-cemetery?

HORACE

Don't knock this cemetery. How many families can boast a
Revolutionary War hero in their garden?

MARY

How many families need to?

HORACE

Did you come to this wedding just to spark trouble?

MARY

I came to see my niece married, check out her husband and bring
you some forbidden food.

HORACE

You're a kind soul Mary. You'll probably wind up in the barn.

MARY

When I'm dead who cares? In the meantime I'm having a full
length hologram made of myself to give to Martha for her
birthday. That way I can haunt her while I can still breathe, laugh
and taunt her.

HORACE

(Laughs)
Maybe you aren't such a kind soul.

MARY

Dolly will love the hologram. It's so theatrical.

HORACE

Oh Mary, I never forgave myself for hurting you.

MARY

(Kisses his head)
You're forgiven.

> HORACE

How about one last thrill?

She laughs as he tries to pull her on his lap. She teasingly resists then takes his blanket off his lap which causes candy, cigars and junk to scatter on the ground. They try to control their laughter.

Dolly's bedroom. Dolly is in bed. Stanley enters with two martinis.

> STANLEY

Looks like you have given my offer some thought.

> DOLLY

Yes. I'm not having anymore sex with you until after we're married.

> STANLEY

If you love me then leave with me tonight and marry me in Boston.

> DOLLY

If we don't get married tomorrow in the living room my whole family will disown me.

> STANLEY

That may not be such a bad thing.

> DOLLY

Stanley, I really want to live here.

> STANLEY

Then you should. I won't.

> DOLLY

If we're married, then we have to live together.

> STANLEY

I've had enough of this!

DOLLY
Do you want me to call the Wedding off?

He throws his drink against the wall.

STANLEY
Call the wedding whatever you like. I'm leaving.

DOLLY
What about all the plans, preparations, your mother?

STANLEY
It's your call honey. Are you coming with me or do you plan on being preserved downstairs?

DOLLY
I have to stay. I belong here.

STANLEY
Enjoy! I'm out of here. Call me in Boston and let me know whether you want me to send you your things or have them preserved.

He leaves and she throws her drink at the door and sobs. Martha comes to the door to see what the commotion is. When she sees her daughter crying, she sits on the bed and embraces her.

Garden. Mary is using Horace's blanket as a shawl. The ground is still cluttered from before.

MARY
What kind of shrine is Martha constructing for herself?

HORACE
We never discuss the future.

MARY

Do you discuss your relationship?

HORACE

We've grown apart. I do wish there were a way to go back and
find those lost feelings. Life is too short for us to live in banter and
misery.

MARY

Have you thought about marriage counseling?

HORACE

Do you know any shrinks who make house calls?

(She shakes her head then bends down to pick up some debris.)
Maybe this is what getting old is like.

MARY

It doesn't have to be. Maybe you could go away together take a
cruise.

HORACE

Martha always wanted to see Egypt. Imagine a cruise up the Nile.

MARY

The sphinx could inspire Martha's sense of design.

HORACE

She'd really love it if she gave it a chance.

MARY

Maybe the two of you could rediscover your relationship and give
your love and marriage new life.

HORACE

You have truly given me food for thought my dear.

Now give me a piece of candy.

*Mary bends down to get candy then drops some as Horace catches her off guard and
pulls her on to his lap.*

MARY

(Giggling)
I didn't notice any Viagra under your blanket.

HORACE

I'm not ready for that yet.

Martha enters the garden in a huff, hysterical not quite noticing the scene.

MARTHA

The Wedding is off! Dolly is destroyed! We have to... (Gasp)

Martha almost falls over the wheel chair. She sees Mary on Horace's lap and braces herself on a high tombstone.

MARY

Not to sound cliché, but this is not the way it looks Sis.

As Mary gets up from Horace's lap she trips on debris and falls back onto him.

MARTHA

I can't believe this. I can't believe I had two tragedies in one day!

First my daughter is jilted on the eve of her nuptials and now my husband and sister have betrayed me.

HORACE

We were just playing a harmless little game.

MARY

I'm really sorry. We were just playing.

MARTHA

Life is more than playing. I am a feeling person. I am hurt.

MARY
I think you're jealous. I didn't think Martha had a jealous bone in her body.

HORACE
Maybe she found some new bones.

Mary and Horace laugh. Martha is not amused.

MARTHA
This is not a laughing matter. My heart is breaking!

Martha holds her heart and gasps for breath. She trips on debris then faints on them knocking them and the wheelchair over.

Act 2. Scene 2. Living room, mid-morning. Dolly is writing in her notebook next to Aunt Sarah. Sophie is sobbing near Dolly. Horace is seated at his perch near the window reading. Martha is fussing, rearranging the monuments and dusting.

SOPHIE
(To Dolly)
I can't believe my Stanislaw could leave his true love on wedding day. I am so sorry darling.

DOLLY
Writing my feelings help me to control them.

Sometimes the best writing comes from pain.

SOPHIE
Sounds like Tolstoy.

MARTHA
You can't mention Tolstoy in this house Sophie.

He was a big trouble maker and look what he had poor Anna Karenina do.

HORACE

You only know Tolstoy from the movies. You never read anything he wrote.

MARTHA

I'm not speaking to you Horace, so anything you say doesn't count. You just keep looking at that barn, your destiny.

And don't think for a moment that I'm going to allow my sister there.

She's lucky if she makes the basement.

HORACE

(To Sophie)
Will you please tell my wife she jumped to ridiculous conclusions last night? Things are not always what they appear to be.

MARTHA

(To Sophie)
Will you tell my estranged husband that the only thing he jumped was my sister's bones. There's truth in consequence.

HORACE

(Wheels himself toward Martha, she backs off)
Martha, that was almost profound. You know how philosophy turns me on. Remember the days we read Aristotle together? Stendhal on love?

Martha dusts Horace's head with a feather duster. He sneezes as Mary enters with her suitcase. Dolly continues to write and ignores her. Sophie hides behind Uncle Ben.

MARTHA

Go take a cold shower. (Looks at Mary) Maybe your paramour would like to join you.

MARY

Martha, what can I say to help you understand?

MARTHA
What would mother or Aunt Sarah say?

MARY
Why don't you ask them?

MARTHA
Just look at them. Their eyes are shooting daggers at you.

MARY
You touched up their eyes this morning, didn't you?

You turned the whole room against me!

MARTHA
I said there is truth in consequence. Write that down Dolly.

DOLLY
I already did. There's so much going on I can't take it all in.

SOPHIE
Maybe we should blame it all on full moon.

MARTHA
What do you mean by "all" Sophie. Do you think you son's actions were influenced by the moon?

SOPHIE
I just want everyone to get along. I want everyone to make up and be happy.

HORACE
Martha's in charge of make-up. If she wanted to she could put a smile on everyone's face.

MARY
I guess I should leave.

DOLLY
It looks like there won't be a wedding. If I keep writing I won't cry or think too hard.

MARY
(Extends her arms to Dolly)
Come sweetie give me a hug.

Dolly puts down her writing and moves towards Mary. Martha stands between them and shows Mary the door.

MARTHA
If Dolly hugs anyone it will be me!

Martha and Dolly stiffly hug.

MARY
You both need more of that. After you hug Dolly hug your husband.

MARTHA
Why don't you take Horace with you. It would mean one less piece of furniture to dust.

MARY
I told you I was sorry. I didn't do anything wrong. Horace and I were just playing, teasing, having fun.

MARTHA
The only person Horace is legally bound to have fun with is me.

MARY
You're actually jealous of what happened last night, aren't you? Admit it.

MARTHA
I don't get jealous. I get even.

MARY
Instead of putting so much effort into game playing and creating trophies of dead people why don't you make an effort to bring more fun and lightness in here. Open the drapes and open your heart to your husband.

Dolly runs back to her notebook.

DOLLY

I miss Stanley. How could he leave me?

SOPHIE

I know Stanislaw loves you. He told me. Is hard for men to say
such things to mothers. It must be true.

MARY

You know that old saying if you love someone let him go. If it's
meant to be he'll come back.

SOPHIE

Let fate and stars guide us.

HORACE

Fate isn't in the moon or stars it's in our hearts. Love fails when
our hearts fail.

MARTHA

Horace should practice what he preaches.

MARY

Maybe you should let him. I'm going, I'm going.

I don't even want to be invited back until there's peace and light in
this house.

MARTHA

Don't hold your breathe and have a pleasant trip.

*Martha opens the door for Mary to exit. She kisses Dolly and Sophie and throws
a kiss to Horace. As she exits she bumps into Stanley who is holding a bouquet of
flowers, drops them and becomes all frazzled. Mary drops her suitcase and freezes.*

MARY

Looks like fate has just walked in the door.

DOLLY
It's just Stanley and I'm not speaking to him.

SOPHIE
Stanislaw, how could you treat Dolly so bad?

STANLEY
In America I am Stanley. I didn't treat her bad, as you say.

We had a misunderstanding.

HORACE
Misunderstandings seems to run in this family.

MARTHA
Horace, you are to keep your mouth shut until we get the bride and groom back on the wedding cake.

MARY
I'm staying to help.

MARTHA
You can start in the kitchen.

MARY
Fine, as long as I don't have to go in the freezer.

Stanley puts his arm around Dolly as she snuggles with him in happiness.

DOLLY
I was so scared. I couldn't face never seeing you again.

All the free writing in the world couldn't heal my wounds.

STANLEY
I'm sorry. (He looks around room) I guess I was scared too.

I missed you the moment I walked out the door.

Mary exits to kitchen. Horace follows Martha around with his wheelchair.

                              HORACE
What's my penance?

                              MARTHA
Don't speak to me for the rest of the day.

                              HORACE
That's not a penance; that's a blessing.

                              DOLLY
You have to speak with each other. It's my wedding day.

Everyone is excited at the news. Stanley accidentally bumps Uncle Clyde's ashes off the fire place and the urn breaks.

                              STANLEY
I'm so sorry.

                              MARTHA
Stop being sorry.

                              SOPHIE
More bad luck?

                              MARTHA
Not a problem. I was thinking of getting rid of him anyway.

He never added to a conversation.

                              SOPHIE
I will clean it up.

                              MARTHA
No, let Mary to it. (Calls to kitchen) Mary, we have some clean up
work here.

Mary comes in and collects ashes and urn and takes them into kitchen without a word.

DOLLY

Mother, you and Dad need to speak and get our wedding in order.

MARTHA

All right, we can speak, but we don't have to say anything.

Martha gets her make up case and works on the monuments. Sophie picks up the rest of Clyde's remains and heads to the kitchen. Dolly, Horace and Stanley huddle near the window facing the barn.

HORACE

(To Stanley)
Are you sure you want to be part of this extended family?

STANLEY

The only thing I'm sure of is my love for Dolly.

HORACE

Nicely put son.

DOLLY

He's not your son yet.

HORACE

Trouble in paradise?

DOLLY

Stanley and I need to talk more about earthly matters.

STANLEY

Country matters.

HORACE

So you're really serious about this job of your in Boston?

STANLEY

I'm really serious about mathematics and they pay me at Harvard.

HORACE

Come on boy we both know those Ivy schools are over rated. I went to Yale.

DOLLY
It's more than Harvard. Stanley is working on a very complicated math problem, something to do with reverse logic.

MARTHA
(From other side of room)
Is that the problem that could make him famous?

HORACE
He could be famous here.

MARTHA
Stanley may have a point. Maybe he can win the Nobel prize or something . Maybe them living in Boston for awhile isn't a bad idea.

HORACE
But Martha, I thought you wanted them here.

MARTHA
Maybe I was wrong.

Everyone is awestruck.

HORACE
When did the thunderbolt hit her or me? Martha admitting she could be wrong. The end of the world is near.

DOLLY
Daddy, the bottom line is that Stanley doesn't want to live here and I want what Stanley wants.

STANLEY
(Takes Dolly in his arms)
Oh my love, my woman.

HORACE
I don't know what to say.

MARTHA
Then shut up and let them live their lives their way.

HORACE

Speaking to me?

MARTHA

I'm thinking about it. (Pause) Dolly, it's about time you go upstairs and start getting ready for your wedding ceremony.

DOLLY

I could sit at my old dressing table. I used to play make up there when I was a little girl.

STANLEY

That sounds so cute. What should I do?

MARTHA

Why don't you go to the den and work on that brilliant problem of yours?

STANLEY

Which one?

MARTHA

The math problem you're always talking about, something about reverse logic, the proof that will make you famous.

STANLEY

You want me to do mathematics on my wedding day?

MARTHA

This should be the happiest day of your life. Maybe you'll get lucky.

Stanley and Dolly exit. Martha sits down with Horace.

HORACE

Will you ever forgive me for last night?

MARTHA

You only need forgiveness if you did something wrong. Did you do something wrong?

HORACE

It was just a silly moment. It really didn't mean anything.

MARTHA

I often wonder why you chose me over Mary.

HORACE

I'm surprised. You really think about that? (She nods) I

Thought it was obvious.

MARTHA

What I saw last night was obvious. I confess I did feel jealous, something I hadn't felt in years. I was afraid of losing you, afraid of our world crumbling apart.

HORACE

Instead of constructing monuments let's work at reconstructing our world.

Let's turn our days of wine and roses into days of fresh air and sunflowers.

MARTHA

Sounds romantic. I wonder if I can ever feel romantic again.

HORACE

I love watching Dolly's excitement over her romance. It reminds me so much of how we were. At her age we were carefree lovers.

Remember? (She nods) When you were around me it was like I needed to be grounded from your electrical field. Sparks were always flying.

MARTHA

Remember what we did the night we met? (He nods) No one who knows us today would believe how passionately we rolled around naked in the hay loft of that barn and made love with only faint moonlight seeping in.

HORACE

You smelled of Windsong, your hair was long and unruly and your lips were so sweet and soft.

MARTHA
What happened? How did we grow apart?

HORACE
We got into a routine. Our lives became complicated. We
renovated this place and we lost our dreams.

MARTHA
Do you think we could ever find those dreams again?

HORACE
I don't know. Do you want to look?

MARTHA
I feel scared.

HORACE
What are you frightened of?

MARTHA
Feelings.

HORACE
Maybe Mary's right. Maybe we need get away from here, clear the
air between us, to talk openly and try to learn how to love again.

MARTHA
I don't want her in our plan.

HORACE
Stop acting jealous of Mary. It doesn't become you. Mary is your
sister and she loves you. She wishes us the best.

*Martha nods agreement and takes Horace's hands to her heart. Sophie enters. She's
carrying a tray of small sandwiches and a pitcher of iced tea.*

SOPHIE
We all need little nourishment before wedding.

The three sit down for a snack together.

Act 2. Scene 3. Dolly is alone in her bedroom, sitting at her dressing table, fixing her hair. Her wedding gown is hanging outside the closet door behind her.

DOLLY

Stanley likes my hair up. He says it makes me look sophisticated

And a little arrogant, like a ballerina.

She demonstrates as she speaks.

What he likes best about my hair is letting it down; taking out the pins and watching my long hair fall down my shoulders.

He finds that sexy.

Oh Stanley, Stanislaw, as your mom would say… Today you will be my husband. Aunt Joan said the word husband meant "frugal manager."

Aunt Sarah preferred the term "consort." I like "consort" better;

Sounds more like a compromise than a commandment.

She opens table drawer, takes out a variety of make up.

Make-up; another skill I've failed to master. Do these colors really attract and seduce men? Crystal violet, desert sky, silvered wine, gray silk, sweet cucumber. Their names are part of the code; part of the mystery.

She takes out her notebook to document her venture.

I must record some of my thoughts today. I bought a new lipstick; plum brandy. I bought it when Stanley bought Vitalis. They had Bride magazines at the store. I almost bought one, but chickened out; thought Stanley would laugh at me. Most of this make up is from when I was in High School.

Does it go bad? Anyway, it's probably all wrong now. If cousin Kristen were here she would have insisted that I research the latest colors and styles. Maybe it doesn't matter what colors I choose as long as I put enough on. Why is it that when a woman my mother's age looks attractive people say she's "well preserved?" Though I suppose in my mother's line of work that would be a compliment.

Cousin Kristen believed beauty was hard work. Now her maintenance is Mother's work. One of my family crusades involved women helping women to be beautiful. "A mother's work cannot be done until women's work is completed." Aunt Joan.

She gets up to examine her wedding gown.

It's a pity I only get to wear this once. I can remember as a little girl sneaking into my mother's hope chest, unfolding her long satin gown, putting it on and parading around the room. The long train twisted around my bare feet, making it hard to move. Once I fell asleep on my mother's bed in her yellowing gown. She awoke me in a terrible fit and said that I should never touch her gown again. Of course I dressed up in it again, even ventured downstairs and put on Great Grand Aunt Madeline's tiara and paraded around in her duchess persona. I never got caught again. It was so much fun playing pretend. Now I get to play dress-up and bride for real.

She sits down and writes in her notebook.

My parents wedding was one of the most regal events this quaint town ever witnessed. Grandma said my mother looked like Princess Grace and my father looked like an undertaker. Now people compare my mother to Eleanor Roosevelt and Daddy still looks like an undertaker.

I truly believe my parents love each other. They simply view the world through different lenses. Each constructs a separate landscape. When Daddy says something is green, Mother says it lacks color. When Mother plans a party, Daddy digs graves.

When my mother has Daddy's ancestral elms cut down he doesn't
get a better view of the garden.

She puts on lipstick and licks her lips with her tongue.

Why do I always expect lipstick to taste like candy?

Well, I guess this is it. I can't think of another thing to fuss about.
Though I suppose there's always time for some more notes;
reflections.

She makes a few more notes while talking.

It's too soon to go downstairs. Downstairs... the living room.

I'll have to keep my fingers crossed that nothing will go wrong.
But then how will I hold my flowers? I know I'll simply fall apart
if someone faints, falls or candles flicker. Luckily it's a short
ceremony and everybody loves me. God, the burden of it all. Why
must we worship so many shrines?

*Act 2, Scene 4. Living room is showered in lilies and mums. Martha, alone adorns the
supporting cast for the wedding.*

MARTHA
(To Grace)
I know Mother, it's a bit overdone. Mary ordered the flowers a
dozen of everything; like choosing teams.

She takes a pink lace dress out of a box, lays it out and prepares to
dress Kristen.

Smell those lilies, look at the size of those spider mums.

It's like a funeral in a Mafia family. Kristen is so pretty. Every day
she looks more and more like Aunt Joan.

She holds dress up to her body.

This gown is going to look lovely on Kristen. I wore it to my Spring Cotillion when I was eighteen. Kristen will always be twenty-one.

She talks to Uncle Ben while dressing Kristen.

Doesn't Stanley remind you of Uncle Eric, Father's family ... downstairs? You used to call him a ferret; the way he rolled his eyes; looking everywhere at once. You said his black eyes went beyond undressing women; he read their thoughts.

She is distracted by some noise outside the window. She sees Stanley wheeling Horace's grandfather on a dolly from the barn. Horace leads them in his wheelchair.

That Stanley has a lot of nerve! That boy can't live here. His sympathies are with the other side.

Stanley, Horace and his grandfather enter through the garden door.

MARTHA
(To Horace)
So you got your way; as always. Where are we going to put him?

HORACE
How about giving him Aunt Joan's place? Her order is decaying.

MARTHA
No one is leaving this room!

HORACE
We could put Grandfather on the far side of the fireplace.

MARTHA
Opposite Uncle Ben? They never got along.

HORACE
They don't have to face each other.

Stanley rolls and spins Grandfather's body to accommodate direction.

MARTHA
Don't destroy the symmetry of the room.

HORACE
Then move Kristen. She's in the wedding party. Put her next to the
fireplace and give Grandfather her place.

MARTHA
Let's try it; see how it looks…No, No your Grandfather simply
doesn't belong in here.

HORACE
HE belongs here more than YOU do!

MARTHA
Now the truth comes out! You don't want me here.

HORACE
I didn't say that.

MARTHA
You inferred it.

HORACE
I thought we were going to try and get along; compromise.

MARTHA
You know I've never been good at compromise. Things are
changing too fast.

I'm getting dizzy. I don't what to think.

HORACE
You are free to do or think whatever you like.

MARTHA
(Sobs as she looks around the room for support)
If I left here, where could I go?

Stanley, uneasy with the situation, places Grandfather and exits up the stairs.

HORACE
If you need room to think, go stay with your sister.

MARTHA
Never! Between the cats and the barbells I'd go insane.

HORACE
Calm down, calm down. You know I don't want you to leave. We made it together this far. The rest is gravy.

MARTHA
Gravy? The next thing you'll want is dessert.

HORACE
I want our lives to be more than a series of double entendres.

We haven't talked honestly in a long time.

MARTHA
Did we ever have much to say to each other?

HORACE
(Wheels himself closer to her)
I think we have a lot to say, but without an audience. (Supporting cast)
I'd like to share with you my feelings about how much more I value life after surviving a stroke.

MARTHA
You almost died. I was so scared.

HORACE
I know you were scared. I saw it in your eyes. I pray we survive.

MARTHA
What should we do? How do we survive?

HORACE
Breath together, take a break from the burdens of this place.

Live simply.

MARTHA

I could never live simply. I suppose I could try. Just don't ask me to go camping. I don't like being that close to the earth.

HORACE

What do you want?

MARTHA

I guess I want what everybody wants, a loving relationship; true intimacy.

I just don't know how.

HORACE

How about starting with sex?

MARTHA

We never needed sex.

HORACE

We needed more. He pulls her close. He suddenly seems stronger.

MARTHA

It's hard to have sex around here.

HORACE

I thought about that. After the wedding I'll share some strategies with you.

MARTHA

Perhaps part of my strategy should be tending less to my ancestors and more to you.

HORACE

That's a good start; a big compromise.

MARTHA

Remember when we put each other's needs first?

HORACE

Oh yes. I need and want only you.

MARTHA

It's so hard for me to say those words, but you know I love you.

HORACE

I know. Now give me a kiss. Say it during the kiss. Talk to my heart.

MARTHA

(She says the words during a long kiss which sounds garbled)
I love you.

They giggle and Horace stands up.

Act 2. Scene 5. The Living room, late afternoon. Mary sneaks Spot into the room and places him next to Aunt Joan as Sophie puts Bela's pic on the mantle. Martha enters with her make-up case to put some finishing touches on the supporting cast Then Mary and Martha light the ritual candles in ancient silver holders on the fireplace. Stanley stands next to the fireplace with his mother. Dolly, struggling to keep the large tiara on her head, is on the opposite side of the room preparing to go down the aisle with Horace who is in his wheelchair.

MARTHA

Magic time!

DOLLY

(To Horace)
I am so scared.

HORACE

The best way to face your fears is to confront them.

Martha puts on a scratchy recording of Mendelson's "Wedding March. "Horace wheels himself slowly down the aisle with Dolly beside him. Spot keels over next to Aunt Joan with a loud flop. Martha stops the music and everyone freezes. She notices Bela's pic on the mantle, but says nothing.

MARTHA

(To Mary)
Put Spot back in the kitchen. Why did you bring him in here?

A wedding is no place for a Doberman.

(Pause) Let's start again. Magic time!

Horace and Dolly continue to the podium, near the fireplace. Martha clings to her Mother with Mary on Grace's other side. When Horace reaches the podium he supports himself up to a standing position and starts reading the paper in his Bible.

HORACE

(He joins Dolly and Stanley's hands)
Dolly Whitman and Stanley Reich have decided to go through life together as man and wife. We have come here together that this woman and this man might bear witness before you and to the world of the oneness that has grown up between them; that they might affirm this oneness and this oneness and this dedication here, as they have affirmed it to each other. As they now exist as one in their own eyes, so may they exist in your eyes. This mysterious union of two persons in marriage has already occurred in them in the giving and receiving of their love. In witness to this mystery they do pledge their love and the sharing of their lives.

SOPHIE

So beautiful! Did you write that Dolly? Dolly nods and a candle starts to flicker. Martha gives Sophie a disapproving stare.

HORACE

Now let me read their vows. (Pause) Dolly and Stanley wish to plow through life together.

SOPHIE

(Confused)
Plow? Did he say plow? Like fields or something?

MARY

(Blows her whistle)
Silence during the ceremony!

Martha shakes her head. She becomes more nervous as the candles are not still.

> STANLEY

We wish to clear and cultivate new paths with our love.

> DOLLY

You were supposed to say fields, not paths. Didn't you memorize the script I wrote?

> STANLEY

Sorry dear. Should I say it again? (Dolly and Horace nod)
We wish to clear and cultivate new FIELDS with our love.

> SOPHIE

I new it was something about fields.

Mary goes to blow her whistle again and Martha takes it from her and throws it out the window into the garden. The candles flicker more.

> DOLLY

(Watches candles as she speaks)
We hope our love will bear fruit and grow.

Sophie stops herself from commenting.

> HORACE

Stanley, do you take Dolly for you loving wife; to give and share for as long as you both grow and flourish?

> STANLEY

I do and vow my love.

> HORACE

Dolly, do you take Stanley for your loving consort; to give and share as you both shall grow and flourish?

> DOLLY

I do and vow my love.

> STANLEY

(Confused)
Consort? A candle goes out and Dolly becomes nervous.

                    SOPHIE
The vows are most sacred moment.

Mary re-lights candle. It goes out again.

                    HORACE
With the power invested in me by the state of New York I now
Pronounce you man and wife. Now you may kiss the bride.

*Stanley kisses Dolly, who then runs from his embrace, to the garden. Another candle
goes out. Silence; the rest of the party is in shock. Martha runs to garden to Dolly.*

                    MARY
(To Horace)
This is just like what happened at your wedding. Remember?

Horace puts a finger to his lips to silence her.

Garden.

                    DOLLY
(In tears)
I'm so ashamed, embarrassed. Now that the candles went out
everyone will know the truth. What must everybody think?

                    MARTHA
It was a beautiful wedding dear... A little short, but all the
important parts were covered.

                    DOLLY
I wanted everything to be perfect.

                    MARTHA
If Aunt Joan were more alert she would have assured perfection.
We have no organizers in this generation.

                    DOLLY
Mother, I'm already "married," in the Biblical sense.

MARTHA

Yes. I was there. Everything was fine. Now compose yourself and tend to your guests.

HORACE

(Back in his wheelchair near the window)
Martha never listens. Dolly never knows when to stop talking. Some things are better left unsaid.

DOLLY

(Stage whisper to Martha)
I'm not a virgin.

MARTHA

Big deal! Neither am I. Our words our safe in the garden only the walls have bugs.

DOLLY

I'm not pure.

MARTHA

Purity of thought is all that matters. Look dear, stop fretting.

Everything is fine.

DOLLY

Oh Mother, you're making me feel so relieved; absolved.

MARTHA

Do you want me to paint a smile on your face?

DOLLY

(Smiles)
I am happy mother. Marriage makes the world so orderly.

MARTHA

And the important things legal. Let's rejoin the party.

No more unpleasant thoughts today.

DOLLY

You've always made things easier for me.

MARTHA

I tried my best. Now it's Stanley's turn.

DOLLY

I love you Mother.

MARTHA

I know I don't say it a lot, but I love you my darling.

Martha and Dolly walk arm and arm into the Living room.

STANLEY

(Stage whisper to Dolly)
Did you tell her the truth?

DOLLY

Everything is fine and will be even better in Boston.

Dolly and Stanley kiss. Martha hands Mary a tray of glasses filled with champagne, to serve the guests. Dolly and Stanley extinguish the candles together then toast the supporting cast. Then they take their champagne upstairs.

HORACE

(Takes out a cigar)
Weddings are grace periods. We can eat and drink to excess, all in the name of tradition.

MARTHA

Oh Horace, I don't know what to do with you.

HORACE

Let me be and I'll be with you.

As Martha passes him, he pinches her on the behind.

MARTHA

Horace, please!

HORACE

Would you, like me to do it again?

MARTHA

Not here.

HORACE

(Playful)
You always had a nice ass.

MARTHA

Shh! Shh! Quiet! Remember where you are.

HORACE

And who you are.

MARTHA

My ass. Is that why you married me?

HORACE

I liked the way it related to the rest of your body. I'd like to take that body on a cruise.

MARTHA

Up the Nile?

HORACE

Or up the creek. Whatever will make you happy babe.

MARTHA

(Caresses him)
Oh Horace, you really want to make me happy.

MARY

You kids need some fun. Life doesn't provide round-trip tickets.

Mary picks up her neglected camera. She snaps a few photos. Sophie gets her camera and snaps more photos.

MARTHA

(To Horace)

Nothing like taking photos after the fact. We should have hired a professional photographer.

Horace shrugs his shoulders. Mary and Sophie take more pictures.

HORACE

Better late than never.

MARY

(To Martha)

I'm sending you something that will really startle you.

MARTHA

A jeweled football?

MARY

(Winks at Horace)

A hologram.

MARTHA

What is a hologram?

MARY

You have to wait until your birthday. You'll be amazed.

I must go in a minute.

Stanley and Dolly descend the stairs. Mary and Sophie snap a photos of them. Then Mary Hugs Dolly and Stanley as she gets ready to leave. Dolly puts tiara back on Great Grand Aunt Madeline.

MARTHA

Leaving so soon?

MARY

It's a long ride and I have a busy day tomorrow. Bye bye bye!

(Exits)

MARTHA
(To Horace)
You'd think she'd stay long enough to help clean up.

HORACE
Martha, Martha, you worry and fuss too much. You live your Life
and let Mary get on with hers.

DOLLY
(Takes Stanley's arm)
And my husband and I with ours.

STANLEY
I already packed our bags. We're ready to fly.

MARTHA
I thought you were leaving tomorrow.

HORACE
Live for tomorrow; today never comes.

*Stanley gets their bags from top of the stairs. Sophie pours leftover champagne into
her glass. She seems to be bonding with the statuary.*

DOLLY
Stanley is so quick. He never wastes time.

MARTHA
Everyone is leaving me with a big mess.

DOLLY
Maybe instead of cleaning up you should simply throw everything
out.

STANLEY
Or have it preserved.

SOPHIE
Have safe trip and stay good to each other.

They all hug. Stanley and Dolly pause at the door and give the room another look.

> HORACE
>
> Don't do anything I wouldn't do.

> MARTHA
>
> Or can't.

> HORACE
>
> Is that a challenge? Do you DARE ME?

> MARTHA
>
> Double dare. You're on!

> HORACE
>
> In the barn.

> MARTHA
>
> That's where it all started.

Dolly opens the front door and the knob comes off.

> DOLLY
>
> Sorry, we'll pay to have it repaired.

> HORACE
>
> Forget it. We don't use it very often. I prefer the garden door.

> DOLLY
>
> I suppose we could stay a little longer and help clean up.

> STANLEY
>
> No, No dear. I want to get on the road before dark. (They exit through garden)

> SOPHIE
>
> I guess I should go too.

> HORACE
>
> No rush.

MARTHA

Sophie's family now. She can stay as long as she wishes.

SOPHIE

Maybe I'll stay till tomorrow so I can help you clean up.

MARTHA

Wonderful idea! I'll get you a broom.

HORACE

Stay a couple of weeks. If you want maybe you can watch the place while we're away.

SOPHIE

Really! You're letting me belong. I'm so thrilled!

HORACE

Become part of our extended family.

Martha runs into the kitchen and gets Sophie a broom and hands it to her like a trophy.

MARTHA

I'm going to the barn.

HORACE

I'll join you in a few seconds.

SOPHIE

I could wheel you. I was nurse in Poland.

MARTHA

I could wheel him. I'm stronger than I look.

HORACE

I'll get there on my own. Be patient my dear.

It takes time to grow old together.

Martha heads to the barn through the garden door. Horace anxiously watches her.

SOPHIE

(Sits on the couch and takes Taffy in her lap)
I would love to stay here for awhile… pretend this is my home.

HORACE

Stay a couple of years. I could get you a mortgage.

SOPHIE

I could cry. I'm so touched.

HORACE

JUST A LITTLE TOUCHED…, but aren't we all?

He wheels himself to the garden door, takes his grandfather's cane from the umbrella stand, stands up and walks slowly to the barn.

Sophie kisses her husband's photo and returns it to the center of the mantle. She happily dances and sweeps around the supporting cast with her broom.

THE END.

Shifting Sands
An Intimate Comedy in Three Acts

CHARACTERS

CATHERINE CHASE: an actress.

NICK CHASE: her husband, an architect.

ANNE SCOTT: a professor.

PETER SCOTT: her husband, a physician.

TIME: ca.2006. New Jersey Shore and New York City.

Act I
>   *i. Atrium of an Ocean Front renovated Hotel/Condo Building in New Jersey.*
>   *ii. Chase apartment, evening.*
>   *iii. Atrium*
>   *iv   Chase apartment.*
>   *v. Scott apartment.*

Act II
>   *i. New York pied- a- terre, next day.*
>   *ii. Same, evening.*
>   *iii. Same, following morning.*
>   *iv. Laundry room of NJ Condo, moments later.*
>   v. Chase apartment, evening.
>   vi. Scott apartment, a few days later, early evening.
>   vii. Chase apartment, next morning.

Act III
>   i. Laundry room of Condo.
>   ii. Chase apartment.
>   iii. NYC apartment.
>   iv. Scott apartment.
>   v. Chase apartment.
>   vi Lobby, moments later.

Act 1. Scene 1. The scene opens in the jungle- like two-story atrium lounge of an exclusive ocean-front condominium complex on the New Jersey shore. Catherine, reclining on a wicker chaise, studies lines from a script. She is hidden from the center of the room by huge fichus and palm trees. At one end of the atrium there is a sign on a door to the pool and elevators on the other end. Nick enters with a cup of tea that he places on the table next to Catherine's chaise.

CATHERINE
(Doesn't look up from script)
Oh Darling. How thoughtful! I don't deserve you.

NICK
I thought you deserved a break. I need to be with you whenever I can.

I'll never see you once your show opens. We're newlyweds, remember?

CATHERINE
(Reaches for tea without looking at him)
Yes. I remember. (She puckers a kiss in his direction.)
I need sugar, darling.

Nick reaches in his pocket, takes out a sugar packet, puts it in her tea and stirs it. He kisses her forehead.

CATHERINE
Two sugars, darling.

He takes another sugar out of his pocket and repeats the above action. She looks up. Their eyes meet.

NICK
I love you.

CATHERINE
I know. You are so sweet. (She throws him a kiss)

NICK

Are you throwing me a bone?

CATHERINE

(She looks at him)
No, my love. I'm sorry, Nicky. I didn't mean to sound insensitive.
It's just that I go into rehearsal tomorrow and I'm not totally
comfortable with my lines.

Nick pulls a chair to sit at her feet, then massages her feet and nibbles on her toes.

NICK

I 'm so proud of you returning to Broadway, but I've hardly spent
any time with you since our wedding. How many people get
married and move into a new apartment on the same day?

CATHERINE

How many people need to?

NICK

Everything happened so fast. We met online, dated for a couple of
months and then got married.

CATHERINE

It's all timing love. Everything just fell into place.

NICK

It was extraordinary.

CATHERINE

We are not ordinary people, my love. No ordinary architect could
have the vision to renovate a hundred year old dilapidated hotel
into such a magnificent building. This place makes me feel like a
modern day Queen living in Cleopatra's temple.

NICK

Do you really like it? Do you think we can be happy here?

She puts down her cup, stands up and kisses him on the head.

CATHERINE

I have never been happier. Imagine living in a shrine that your husband designed and will receive great honors for.

NICK

Does that mean you're coming to the awards dinner?

CATHERINE

Of course. I wouldn't miss it for the world.

He stands and they embrace. His back is towards the center of the room. She looks over his shoulder and recognizes a couple entering opposite them. The couple are about their age, dressed casually and almost bouncing as they hold hands and turn towards the view of the ocean. Catherine appears nervous as she pulls away from Nick and back to her work. He understands, gives her a kiss and exits. Catherine reclines and shields her face from the possible view of the couple that she now appears to be spying on.

The couple, Anne and Peter, face the ocean and hold hands. They don't notice Catherine; they only have eyes for each other.

ANNE

(Bubbles with enthusiasm)
I'm so happy. We live in paradise; the most beautiful place in the world.

PETER

Certainly one of the most expensive.

ANNE

We've been here almost a year and every day feels like a new beginning. I love it! I love you!

PETER

You are my little squirrel princess.

ANNE

You say the cutest things. For such a brilliant doctor you can be such a silly silly goose.

PETER

And to think we met because of your silly little nose.

ANNE

My deviated septum brought us together. And now I have the most
beautiful nose and can breathe better because of you.

PETER

(Kisses her nose)
Yes, my skill at septoplasty and rhinoplasty set the stage for our
romance. Now you are the most beautiful squirrel in the world.

ANNE

Oh Goosey. My brilliant goose.

*Catherine, undercover behind her script, hears some of their dialogue and mimics the
"goosey" line, shakes her head and speaks under her breath.*

CATHERINE

Maybe he could sew up her mouth.

*Catherine hardly notices that Nick has returned with a book. He sits beside her
trying not to interrupt her concentration.*

PETER

(Takes Anne's hand)
Let's go for a swim.

ANNE

Not the ocean. It's too cold.

PETER

No. The pool you silly squirrel.

ANNE

My first swim since my surgery. I haven't been underwater in
ages because I was always clogging up.

PETER

Soon you'll be my own little angel fish.

Catherine hears this and reacts by sinking deeper into her chaise with her script over her face.

> ANNE
>
> All right. I'll try the pool as long as you are there to rescue me if I get nervous.

> PETER
>
> I worked as a lifeguard during the summers while I was in college. You know our complex has the biggest indoor pool on the east coast

> ANNE
>
> And I heard it is very deep.

> PETER
>
> Till depths do us part.

> ANNE
>
> Oh Goosey, you say the cutest things.

Anne jumps up and down, hugs and kisses Peter, as he picks her up and carries her to the exit. Catherine becomes more interested, finally notices Nick and his book. After Peter and Anne exit Catherine puts down her script.

> NICK
>
> I missed you. I hope you don't mind.

Catherine looks at his book.

> CATHERINE
>
> Ayn Rand, good. Maybe we should take a break, go out for lunch.

> NICK
>
> Oh, I disturbed you. I'm so sorry.

> CATHERINE
>
> I need a break.

> NICK

What about your work?

> CATHERINE

Look, maybe you can help me run lines later.

> NICK

Oh, I'd love that. How about a swim before lunch?

> CATHERINE

Not today darling. The last thing I need right now is a swim. I just had a shock.

> NICK

A shock? From what?

> CATHERINE

My heart.

Nick is concerned. He moves her feet to sit at the bottom of the chaise. It topples like a sea-saw. They fall to the ground. He comforts her, hugs her. She giggles.

> NICK

Are you all right? Do you need a doctor?

> CATHERINE

No. It was a doctor who shocked me.

He helps her up.

> NICK

Is this part of your script?

> CATHERINE

The one I'm living, not the one I'm rehearsing.

> NICK

Can we speak a common language?

CATHERINE

Okay. I just saw my ex here in the atrium with a mousy woman.

NICK •

I don't understand. What would he be doing here? Didn't you say he lived in Rumson?

CATHERINE

When we divorced over two years ago he was living in Rumson. Now who knows? Maybe that snake charmer he attracted has a condo here.

NICK

It's easy enough to check. The manager has photo Id's of all the owners.

CATHERINE

I was starting to love this place.

NICK

What's the big deal? If she, he or they bought a condo here, so what? This is a huge complex. We'll never see them.

CATHERINE

New York City isn't big enough. I see him all the time.

NICK

Are you speaking literally or metaphorically?

CATHERINE

Both. We share an affinity for Saks. And he's worked on a lot of corporate tycoons. They all look like him. He's a professional narcissist.

NICK

Has he ever worked on you?

CATHERINE

What do you think? I'm an actress---a tuck here, and there, and my saggy eyes. Besides he owed me. I worked "his" way through medical school.

NICK
I hope you're not thinking of going back to him.

CATHERINE   ·
Why? Do you think I need a facelift? Can you see the jowls dragging down my jawbone?

NICK
(Stands and offers his hand)
It's lunchtime. I'm hungry.

CATHERINE
(Takes his hand and stands)
You didn't answer my question.

NICK
I don't answer stupid questions. You know you are a classic beauty. All the tabloids say so. I love being seen with you.

CATHERINE
You know how much I love being out and seen. How about lunch? (He nods) The Captain's Table?

NICK
We have a high tech kitchen we haven't broken in yet.

CATHERINE
High tech? Honey, I'm high maintenance, not high tech. Half of those steel gadgets belong in a torture chamber and the rest confuse me.

NICK
I didn't marry you for your cooking skills.

CATHERINE
I know, you married me because I am such a marvelous actress.

NICK
And you have a perfect butt.

CATHERINE
It's not starting to sag yet. Is it?

They both study her butt and laugh.

> NICK
> Have I told you how beautiful you look today?

> CATHERINE
> Not since breakfast.

He embraces her.

> NICK
> Let's go to bed where you know how to cook.

> CATHERINE
> Let's talk dirty after lunch.

They kiss, walk to the view of the ocean.

> CATHERINE
> We're living in paradise. Our marriage will be one long vacation.

> NICK
> A marriage is not a sojourn. It's a daily commitment; work.

> CATHERINE
> Yes, sure.

> NICK
> I think the perfect marriage is a balance between romance and responsibility.

> CATHERINE
> Sure. Speaking of responsibility, I'll need to spend more nights in New York after rehearsals. I can come back here some nights, but we'll only have one day off a week and rehearsals go from 10 to 6.

> NICK
> I can't spend time in New York right now.

CATHERINE

I should stay alone. It'll be quiet. I'll be back for the architect's awards dinner.

NICK

We've only been married a few weeks.

CATHERINE

We have the rest of our lives.

NICK

I'm not thrilled at your going, but if that's what you need to do, fine. I can't hold you back.

CATHERINE

We're both moving forward in our careers. This is the best time of our lives.

Catherine looks to the door and sees Peter and Anne enter dressed in matching terrycloth robes covering their swimsuits. They are heading to the pool area, which is past another door on the far end of the atrium. Catherine gasps.

NICK

What's happening?

CATHERINE

My heart again. Look!

NICK

I don't understand.

CATHERINE

It's Peter. What should we do?

Peter and Anne approach them.

NICK

Introduce us.

Peter and Anne walk arm-in-arm, smiling. Peter notices Catherine and springs away from Anne.

> PETER

Oh my God!

> CATHERINE

No, that's Goddess, darling.

> PETER

What are you doing here?

> CATHERINE

Enjoying the view. And you?

> ANNE

It is a wonderful view.

> NICK

I designed the it that way.

> PETER

Are we speaking to old Neptune himself?

> CATHERINE

(Takes a deep breath)
No, you are speaking to my husband, Nicholas Chase.

He's the architect who re-designed this building.

> ANNE

(To Nick)
You did a lovely job.

> CATHERINE

Nicky, this is my ex, Dr. Peter Scott and...

They shake hands. Anne clings to Peter.

ANNE

I'm Anne Scott, Peter's wife.

CATHERINE

Congratulations. Best of luck. (Under her breath to Nick) She'll
need it.

ANNE

(Steps back, fearful)
We've been here for almost a year. We're very happy. I suppose
you're Kate?

CATHERINE

I prefer Catherine. (Studies Anne) Nice nose job.

Anne smiles. Peter steps back, tries to control his anger towards Catherine.

PETER

Thank you. What are you doing here?

CATHERINE

We live here. And you?

ANNE

We bought the south penthouse.

NICK

We own the north one.

PETER

We have wonderful light for gardening.

NICK

My garden is larger.

Pause. The contenders compose themselves.

ANNE

Maybe you guys would like to come over for a drink sometime.

                    CATHERINE
The guys do have some things in common. (She grins.)

                      NICK
Sounds nice. Thanks for the offer.

Catherine looks daggers at Nick. He retreats.

                      NICK
Catherine needs to work on her lines for a Broadway play.

                     PETER
I'm surprised she's not in <u>our</u> New York apartment.

                    CATHERINE
I use <u>my</u> New York apartment when I work.

                      NICK
Actually Catherine needs to retreat there to concentrate on her
work.

                     PETER
Kate is easily distracted.

                    CATHERINE
What happened to your house in Rumson?

                     PETER
I sold it to buy here. I thought I was buying into the best
neighborhood.

                    CATHERINE
We are on opposite sides of this huge neighborhood, so it should
be safe.

                     PETER
We'll try not to meet on the rooftops.

ANNE
(Takes Peter's arm tightly)
Let's go for our swim dear. (To others) Would you care to join us?

CATHERINE
Sorry dear. We're off to lunch.

They move in opposite directions (Pool door and exit).

ANNE
(To Catherine)
Maybe we'll meet in the laundry room sometime.

CATHERINE
Laundry? I doubt it. (She turns her back to Peter.)

PETER
Why don't our expensive condos have their own laundry rooms?

NICK
(Defensive)
I know. I know. I hear that complaint all the time. The old hotel
had a huge laundry room. The developers wanted to save it. You
know, historical touches.

PETER
I thought about getting a washer and dryer hook up in the kitchen,
but it's too small.

CATHERINE
(Turns to face Peter)
Some people are never satisfied.

PETER
Some people can't be satisfied.

CATHERINE
Speak to yourself.

PETER
Who else listens?

Anne smiles at Nick and shakes his hand.

ANNE

I like the big old laundry room with its high ceiling, long tables
and overhead lights.

PETER

Maybe they should put in a ping pong table.

CATHERINE

(To Peter)
Why not a bowling alley? Then you can throw big balls around.

NICK

(To Anne; tries to ignore others)
I like to do my own wash. It relaxes me.

ANNE

Me too!

PETER

(To Catherine)
Call me if you want your butt lifted.

CATHERINE

Call me if you want your ass kicked.

NICK

(Pulls Catherine towards him.)
We need to get lunch. I hope the two of you have a lovely day.

CATHERINE

Yes, enjoy the view. Ciao!

ANNE AND PETER

Have a great day!

*Act 1. Scene 2. An hour later. The living room of the Chase apartment which has glass
doors and a terrace facing the sea. Martinis and a shaker rest on the cocktail table.
Catherine walks about the room testing her memory of lines as Nick, seated, prompts
her with his duplicate script. (The play is Noel Coward's "Private Lives" (1930))*

CATHERINE

"I think very few people are completely normal really, deep down in their private lives. It all depends on a combination of circumstances. If all the various thin gummys fuse at the same moment, and the right spark is struck, there's no knowing what one mightn't do."

NICK

What the hell is a thingummy?

CATHERINE

Don't question the words darling; just read the lines. You can't think too much. You need to let the scenes breathe.

NICK

Do people still like Noel Coward? (She shutters with frustration.) Sorry, Cathy. (She grimaces as the word "Cathy")
Please continue.

CATHERINE

"That was the trouble with Elyot and me, we were like two violent acids bubbling about in a nasty little matrimonial bottle."

NICK

(Insecure)
"I don't believe you're nearly as complex as you think you are."

CATHERINE

"I don't think I'm particularly complex, but I know I'm unreliable."

NICK

(More insecure)
"You're frightening me horribly. In what way unreliable?"

CATHERINE

"I'm so apt to see things the wrong way round."

NICK

"What sort of things?"

CATHERINE

"Morals. What one should do and what one shouldn't."

                    NICK
"Darling, you're so sweet."

                    CATHERINE
Darling, this isn't working.

                    NICK
No. You are supposed to say...

                    CATHERINE
I know, something about your taking a bath.

She puts her script down and crosses to look at the view. He follows her, tries to comfort her.

                    NICK
What's wrong, Cathy?

                    CATHERINE
Cathy is wrong. Please don't call me Cathy. I hate pet names.
Would you like it if I called you Rover?

                    NICK
Poor choice, I'm not inclined to ramble or stray. I don't object
when you call me Nicky. I consider it special, endearing.

                    CATHERINE
Like Kate. I cringe every time I hear that special name Peter gave
me.

                    NICK
If it will make you happy, I'll call you Catherine.

                    CATHERINE
Thank you. Can I still call you Nicky?

                    NICK
Sure. I like it. Do you want to finish this act or take a little break?
We've hardly touched our martinis.

CATHERINE

I'm used to martinis made with vodka. I'm not crazy about gin.

NICK

I'm not crazy about gin or vodka. I found the recipe in a
bartender's manual. I never drank during the day before meeting
you. I went out and stocked the bar with the very best for you.

CATHERINE

Peter and I drank too much. It kept the marriage going.

Looking back it was one big stupor.

NICK

I don't want to live in a fog. I really want to see you, get to know
you in a sober way.

CATHERINE

I promise to give up afternoon libation if my show's a success.

If it's not a success I'll start drinking screwdrivers for breakfast.

NICK

I'm afraid alcohol could affect your memory.

CATHERINE

I'm afraid it won't.

NICK

Erase the past. Live in the present.

CATHERINE

(Holds up her empty glass)
I suppose this is how I hold the present.

NICK

(Hugs her)
Hold me. (Pause) Why don't we slip into the bedroom where I can
pour my drink on your naked body and lap it up.

CATHERINE

(Lightens up)
Sounds unsanitary.

NICK

The alcohol will kill the germs. (Pause) What would you like to do?

CATHERINE

Go out for an early dinner and then come back here and work lines some more.

He embraces her from the back then leads her towards the bedroom. She stiffens up, pours herself another drink and sits on the couch.

NICK

We'll go out later. For now, let's have a quicky.

CATHERINE

Where?

NICK

In the usual delightful places.

As he undresses her, she redresses herself.

CATHERINE

I'm hungry. Can't you hear my stomach growling?

NICK

I thought that was your heart. (Kisses her)
I can call for a pizza.

CATHERINE

Pizza's not dinner.

NICK

I'll do whatever you want.

CATHERINE

Why don't you run into the kitchen and make us a new batch of martinis while I change into something more appetizing.

He heads to the kitchen and she to the bedroom.

NICK
(While fixing drinks)
I want nothing more than to please you, my love.

CATHERINE
I hope you're using vodka this time and a lot of olives. I'm hungry.

NICK
Yes dear. I'm using Sky vodka and lots of olives.

She opens the bedroom door and makes her entrance in an elegant white negligee.

He loudly shakes the martini mix.

CATHERINE
Sounds heavenly, like ice in the clouds.

NICK
You look like an angel. (He pours the mixture into glasses while staring at her.) How do you feel?

CATHERINE
(Sexy)
Divine. Simply divine.

They embrace. She continues to sip her drink while in his clutches. He sets his drink down and holds her closer.

Act. 1. Scene 3. Moments later. Atrium. Anne and Peter, dressed in swim suits and wrapped in large leopard print towels sit outside the pool area door. They are alone.

PETER
I want to take you on a real honeymoon.

                    ANNE
Being here with you is all I need. Our honeymoon is now.

                    PETER
You are so sweet. (He kisses her forehead)
Let's wrap our towels together and snuggle.

They wrap themselves with their towels like a tent. Anne notices their reflection in a mirror facing the sea.

                    ANNE
We look like a two-headed monster.

                    PETER
The easier to eat you, my dear.

He manages to get off the bottom of her suit and tosses it. He snuggles and manages to drop his trunks.

                    ANNE
You are my big bad wolf.

                    PETER
Your wet naked body feels so sexy.

                    ANNE
So does yours. Your touch makes my skin feels tingly. My heart is
sending shock waves through my whole body.

                    PETER
We're charged electrical currents. You make me so horny!

                    ANNE
(Almost breathless)
Shock waves. Power surges. I'm exploding.

                    PETER
Tell me, tell me, tell me how you want it.

ANNE

Upstairs.

PETER

There's no one here. I want to do it here.

ANNE

Suppose someone wants to swim and needs to go by us?

PETER

We'll hear the elevator.

ANNE

I can't hear anything, but our breathing.

This is too public. I want to go back home.

PETER

How about going back to the pool? Doing it in the water? We could play the Mermaid and the Shark?

ANNE

I don't care for your shark side. How about going upstairs and playing house?

PETER

I want to play here.

ANNE

Must you always get what you want?

PETER

(He nods)
Yes, I'm spoiled. I want you now.

He tries to lead them to the pool area. She resists. They clumsily walk, wrapped in droopy towels towards the elevator. She manages to pickup their swimsuits on the way.

ANNE

We'll be at home in minutes.

> PETER

I could eat you alive.

> ANNE

I don't want to be your dinner. I'm your wife.

> PETER

If you play dinner, I'll be dessert.

> ANNE

You're playing the Big bad wolf again.

> PETER

The better to eat you my dear.

> ANNE

You should have been an actor.

> PETER

I am an actor.

> ANNE

I'll play the director and lead you upstairs to perform.

> PETER

Sounds like a hit show! I anticipate grand applause and rave reviews.

They exit as one.

Act. 1. Scene 4. Living room of the Chase apartment. They are behind the open door in the bedroom. The sound of a bouncing cocktail shaker with ice is heard. Then sounds of pouring drinks into glasses is heard followed by sighs and groans of sexual ecstasy and breaths of relief. Catherine enters the living room then switches on a bright light. Nick follows her drinking from the cocktail shaker.

> NICK

This is all melting ice and water.

> CATHERINE

I guess it was too hot in there.

NICK

Couldn't we have just cuddled for awhile?

CATHERINE

I'm sorry darling. It's just the combination of gin and vodka got to me. If I don't eat something soon I'll be dreadful.

NICK

It's just that as I was coming you were going.

CATHERINE

Didn't I ever tell you I have low blood sugar?

NICK

If you have low blood sugar you shouldn't drink. When you were married to a doctor didn't he tell you that?

CATHERINE

He couldn't tell me anything. He drank like a fish and smoked like a chimney. At least I don't smoke.

NICK

We should keep some cheese or protein in the frig in case you get an attack.

CATHERINE

(Opens refrigerator)
There's nothing in here but olives and tonic water.

(She stuffs a hand full of olives in her mouth.) I'm feeling a little better now.

NICK

That's good. We're newlyweds. We should be screwing all the time.

She sits on the couch and motions for him to sit by her. She places his head on her chest.

CATHERINE

There, there darling. We <u>are</u> screwing a lot. We're like little
rabbits.

NICK

If we're like rabbits where are the baby bunnies?

CATHERINE

Not now Nicky. I'm still on the pill.

NICK

When will you stop taking toxic drugs?

CATHERINE

We can focus on what you want after my show closes. We can
even go on a real honeymoon then.

NICK

When will that be?

CATHERINE

We're booked for six months, but we always hope for sellouts and
extensions.

NICK

We need time to learn each other's habits, foibles, mysteries.

CATHERINE

(She embraces him)
I know there is power in knowledge my love, but adults don't
change; they just get older.

NICK

Some get wiser. You will always get more beautiful in my eyes.

CATHERINE

And you are the kindest, sweetest, most amicable man I've ever
known.

NICK

(Kisses her)
My love, the actress. I find your flair for high drama amusing.

CATHERINE

Years of therapy haven't modified my behavior. Rude awareness is a necessary tool in theatre, but rusts in life.

NICK

(Kisses her as he speaks)
I love watching you. You have the body of a Botticelli maiden.

CATHERINE

(Stands, looks in mirror, horrified)
Is that your kind way of saying I'm putting on weight?

NICK

Like "The Three Graces" long...

CATHERINE

Long nothing! They are fleshy, have big breasts... Why didn't you just say Rubens? That would have made me feel even bigger.

NICK

You wouldn't be flattered if I said Bosch.

CATHERINE

At least his women are thin. I better go on a diet. No more olives.

NICK

I'm sorry, dear. I love your body. You don't need to lose weight. You might even be considered a little too thin. I thought I was paying you a compliment.

CATHERINE

Oh, I know you didn't mean it. I'm too sensitive and you're too academic.

NICK

You're heart and I'm mind; a good combination. You're the melody; I'm the lyrics.

CATHERINE

(Laughs)
I know, I know. We'll make beautiful music together.

NICK

We're more than a cliché.

CATHERINE

You're more. I don't deserve you.

NICK

You deserve more. What would you like me to do?

She hands him the phone.

CATHERINE

Dinner reservations?

He laughs and dials the phone.

Act 1. Scene 5. Living room of the Scott apartment which is similar in design to the Chase apartment except furnished differently. The Scott's are making love in the bedroom when a loud kitchen timer goes off. Anne, draped in a short robe, runs through the living room to the kitchen.

ANNE

My roast is done.

She runs back to the bedroom.

ANNE

That siren almost blew my head off.

PETER

It was startling... Now back to our earthquake.

ANNE

Back to us. (Loud kiss) I feel the earth shake and rumble when I'm with you.

PETER

I'm a doctor, the closest thing to a God.

ANNE

That must be why I kept saying 'Oh God. Oh God!"

PETER

And then you had an orgasm. Your prayers were answered.

ANNE

Did I find any of your hot spots?

PETER

My whole body is charged.

ANNE

Now we need to cool down before our dinner does. I'll run and set the table.

PETER

You don't need to run. Come back here and give me another wet kiss. (Loud kiss)

They enter the living room dressed in matching kimono style robes. He sits on the couch behind his slippers on the floor. Anne bends to the floor, massages and rubs his feet before putting his slippers on, as they talk.

ANNE

You have the most beautiful feet. (She kisses them)

PETER

That feels heavenly. I never knew a woman who would massage my feet before, though I have massaged many.

ANNE

I adore you.

PETER

I know. You are the best!

ANNE
When two people are in love all the world breathes possibility.

PETER
My breaths and visions transcend the imaginable.

ANNE
You're a poet. I can't believe after so many years of damaged men and confusion I've finally found my soul mate.

PETER
Soul mate? I'm not sure I have a soul. You're my mate!

ANNE
Remember our first date?

PETER
Yes, after you recovered from your surgery I took you dancing.

ANNE
I'll never forget that funky Cuban club.

PETER
We'll go back there for our first anniversary.

ANNE
You taught me how to mambo.

PETER
(He gets up and demonstrates.)
I can hear the music; a little mambo, salsa, son.

He tries to get her to dance. She doesn't respond.

ANNE
That was a magical night.

PETER
Two months later we were married.

ANNE
Now it's about time we discuss my biological clock

PETER
Keep winding it up. You have plenty of time.

ANNE
Not if we want more than one child.

PETER
We have plenty of time. It's our time to eat.

I'm starving.

ANNE
(Finishes putting on his slippers then gets up)
I'll get dinner. You can open the wine.

PETER
Great division of labor.

They scamper to get settled for dinner. Peter pours them wine, they toast and sit down to eat. The phone rings.

ANNE
I'll get it. (She picks up the phone.) Hello.

PETER
I hope it's not...

ANNE
It's the hospital.

She hands him the phone. He listens to the message then gets up.

PETER
(On phone)
I'll be there in twenty minutes.

He puts down the phone and heads to the bedroom to get dressed. She follows him.

> ANNE
>
> Can't you eat first?

> PETER
>
> Sorry honey, I have to leave.

> ANNE
>
> I thought you were on second call.

> PETER
>
> I am, but this is a patient of mine.

> ANNE
>
> When will you be home?

> PETER
>
> I have no idea. I'll finish up as soon as I can.

> ANNE
>
> I made a beautiful roast. Can you take some dinner with you?

> PETER
>
> Not enough time to pack it up. I'll enjoy it when I get home.
>
> I have to run.

Peter finishes dressing then heads through the living room to the coat closet by the apartment door. She helps him put his coat on. A pack of cigarettes fall out of his pocket. He picks them up and puts them back in his pocket.

> ANNE
>
> What are you doing with cigarettes?

> PETER
>
> I know I promised to stop. It's just at the hospital there's always so much stress. I won't smoke at home.

> ANNE
>
> You promised that if I married you you'd stop smoking period.
>
> *She puts out her hand and he gives her the cigarettes.*

PETER

I thought our love was unconditional.

ANNE

Unconditional love doesn't come with a license for pain and disappointment.

PETER

Unconditional love means I shouldn't always be faced with making apologies. I'm sorry I have to leave. I'm sorry if I hurt you. I'm just damned sorry about everything.

He leaves. She closes the door and leans on it in sorrow.

Act II. Scene I. A few weeks later at Catherine's New York City apartment. She is busy rearranging the furniture to block a scene she is rehearsing. The doorbell rings. She doesn't want to be disturbed, but the noise breaks her concentration. She checks through the door's peephole before opening. She opens the door to a huge bouquet of flowers. She signs for them, tips the delivery person and reads the card.

CATHERINE

I miss you sooo much. Love Nicky.

How sweet. Now I just need to find a vase, water and then back to work.

She places flowers on the table and ignores them as she tries to get back to her scene. The doorbell rings. She appears disturbed, checks the peephole and shakes her head and raises her arms with more frustration. She opens the door to a huge bouquet of red roses in a crystal vase blocking Peter's face.

PETER

(Charming)
Surprise!

CATHERINE

What do you want?

PETER

There's a conference in town and I thought I'd drop by to say Hi!

CATHERINE

You attend more conferences than any other doctor alive.

PETER

That's because I have more than one specialty.

CATHERINE

Look, I'm here to work. I have a preview in a couple of hours.
What do you want? How did you know I was here?

PETER

When I saw you leaving the building the other day with a suitcase
I remembered the Broadway opening your hubby bragged about.
Then I noticed Nicholas sulking around the building. But I didn't
follow you. I've been planning to attend this conference for
months.

CATHERINE

Sure. Then why aren't you there now?

PETER

Part of me is. I checked-in and went to the opening meeting.
Then while I was sitting through a boring video conference on
pulmonary cardio infarctions I thought of you.

CATHERINE

How romantic.

PETER

The heart is involved.

CATHERINE

I know. I know. I'm sick of organs.

She puts her hands to her ears and paces away from him.

PETER

Pulmonary as in designating the artery conveying blood from the right ventricle of the heart to the lungs or any of the veins conveying oxygenated blood from the lungs to the left atrium of the heart.

CATHERINE

(Interrupts him)
I heard all this before.

PETER

Yes, but you never listened.

CATHERINE

I was too busy working long hours in soaps and regional theaters to pay for your medical school loans. The theatre made you the success you are today.

PETER

I'm grateful. You're doing well. What's your problem?

CATHERINE

I worked very hard as an actress. You never appreciated my talent. Our whole relationship was about you. Now I'm a success in spite of you.

PETER

(Applauds)
Bravo! You were born to live in a Noel Coward play. I'm more Mel Brooks. Give me a straight jacket, not a smoking jacket.

He's still holding the vase of flowers.

PETER

Where should I put these?

CATHERINE

Do you have to ask? You studied proctology.

> PETER

Very funny. I bought you flowers in a vase because I know
you have trouble finding one, e.g. those wrapped flowers on the
cocktail table.

> CATHERINE

You are very thoughtful, as always.

> PETER

I know you.

*He puts down the vase of flowers and heads to the kitchen and continues talking to
her.*

> PETER

There has to be something we can use for your other flowers.

(Sounds of his opening and closing cabinets)

> CATHERINE

Why are you so obsessed with my fucking flowers?

> PETER

I don't like to see anything die.

> CATHERINE

Our marriage died. Remember?

*She sits next to the flowers. He returns with a large juice pitcher filled with water. He
arranges the flowers from the wrapped package as they talk.*

> CATHERINE

(Looks at the juice pitcher)
Not very elegant.

> PETER

We were given lovely vases as wedding gifts and you smashed
them all during your fits of rage. Remember?

CATHERINE

I couldn't smash you, so I shattered our memories. It was either them or you.

PETER

Why don't you get a punching bag?

CATHERINE

I don't need one. I have Nicky.

PETER

That dullard?

CATHERINE

He's kind and sweet and never provokes anger.

PETER

I doubt he could provoke anything. He's so dull, he'll bore you to death.

CATHERINE

(Refers to flowers)
This place is starting to look like a funeral parlor.

PETER

Aroma therapy. The scents should raise your spirits.

She shakes her head incredulously, but listens. He pulls a chair close to her and tries to take her hand. She pulls away. He takes cigarettes out of his pocket.

CATHERINE

Let me get back to my work. Why did you resent my acting?

PETER

I was jealous. You always seemed to be having so much fun.

CATHERINE

It takes a lot of work to make something look like <u>fun.</u>

PETER

Fine, fine, fine. You win. How did you feel when you saw me the other day?

CATHERINE

Pissed. Why did you buy a condo in my building?

PETER

First of all it is not "your" building.

He goes to light a cigarette and she stops him. He puts them back in his pocket. She refers to his cigarettes.

CATHERINE

I thought you gave those up.

PETER

I'm under too much stress right now. My new wife is very needy.

CATHERINE

Don't bring your stress and baggage here. Getting back to our building, my Nicky designed it.

PETER

Yes, but he doesn't own it. He, you, the both of you own one condo, not the complex, not the atrium.

CATHERINE

Point well taken. I guess it's just my rotten luck that you wound up there.

PETER

Or fate. When I saw you hiding behind the palms in the atrium my heart beat so fast I thought it would burst through my shirt.

CATHERINE

Is that why you went to the conference? Is there really a conference?

PETER

There's always some medical conference in New York.

CATHERINE

Probably why so many doctors get divorced.

PETER

Look, Kate. That's why I'm here.

CATHERINE

Stop talking in riddles and don't call me Kate.

PETER

All right Catherine. I'm sorry. I miss you.

CATHERINE

What do you miss?

PETER

I miss your heart, your voice, your scent…

CATHERINE

Stop talking in double entendres.

PETER

You have some time before your show.

Let's make love.

CATHERINE

So that's what this is about. Sex. Aren't you getting any with what's her name?

PETER

Anne. She's a wonderful woman.

CATHERINE

If Annie is so wonderful why are you here?

PETER

I'm ashamed of my behavior. She deserves better than me.

CATHERINE

Why don't you leave before you do something stupid?

                        PETER

Does that mean you are thinking about it? Thinking about doing
something stupid with me?

                        CATHERINE

It? It? As in sex?

                        PETER

It, as in making love.

                        CATHERINE

Now you're speaking in euphemisms. Why don't you just spell it
out. You want to f-u-c-k me.

                        PETER

Stop acting angry.

                        CATHERINE

I'm not acting.

                        PETER

Who can ever tell?

                        CATHERINE

Stop the repartee. You're the real actor. You never say what
you mean. You have fun distorting terms and confusing names.
You don't know anything about love. You bemuse love with
masturbation. That's why you're here; for mental masturbation.

                        PETER

Stop it. Don't destroy this moment.

                        CATHERINE

What moment?

                        PETER

Look at me. Tell me what went wrong with us.

                        CATHERINE

There's "no us." We've had this conversation before. You're
wearing me out. Get it through your penile brain that we can't
live together, that's why we divorced.

PETER

It's not that simple. I know you still feel something.

I can see it in your eyes.

CATHERINE

Did you have an optometry conference recently?

PETER

Stop making bad jokes. Take off your armor and hug me.

CATHERINE

What about Nicky and what's her name?

PETER

This isn't about them.

CATHERINE

I know. It's about the moment.

PETER

Yes, the moment.

They embrace and kiss. She suddenly jumps to her feet.

CATHERINE

Get out Peter! This won't work. When the moment is over
we'll be back in the ring trying to wrestle the other to the floor.
Moments are just that; temporary, ephemeral, illusionary.

PETER

I want you so badly.

She opens the door for him to leave.

PETER

You belong in a Noel Coward play; sophisticated sex, silk sheets
and a lot of martinis.

CATHERINE

I'll mail you a photo of my Tony. You can take that to bed.

For now, go home to whomever and do whatever makes you happy
for the moment.

PETER

Dinner at ten thirty at LaPapillion?

CATHERINE

Ten forty five.

She slams the door behind him, picks up her script.

CATHERINE

Why did I agree to that? I must be mad or (Pause)
in the moment.

*Act II. Scene 2. The same. Later that evening. The light is switched on to reveal
Catherine and Peter who appear intoxicated.*

PETER

I can't believe the maitre de thought I was dead.

CATHERINE

It was easier than explaining our divorce.

PETER

Brevity and wit, so much easier to handle than details.

CATHERINE

Thanks for the chaperone home, darling. Now you have to go
back to the sheltering palms.

PETER

I told Anne I was staying at the Marriott.

CATHERINE

Are you registered there? (He nods). Why not the Hilton?

PETER

I had to pay for the room. I didn't intend to spend much time there.

CATHERINE

Whatever. Now be gone!

PETER

Why can't I stay?

CATHERINE

Are you crazy?

PETER

Aren't you?

CATHERINE

What do you want?

PETER

(Tender, takes her hands)
I feel at home in you.

CATHERINE

(Breaks his grip)
How marvelously touching. What about your wife?

PETER

With her, I feel like a visitor.

CATHERINE

Stop it. Just go! Go back to the Marriott. Little Bo Peep has probably called you a dozen times.

PETER

What about Nicky?

CATHERINE

I'll return his calls after you leave.

PETER

Play your machine. Listen to his voice. You must miss his voice.

                    CATHERINE
Masochist.

She turns on her answering machine.

                    MACHINE
You have no messages.

                    CATHERINE
That can't be. Why didn't he call? It's after midnight.

                    PETER
Maybe he bored himself to sleep. Or maybe he has a date?

                    CATHERINE
Or maybe...

                CATHERINE/PETER
He's on his way here?

                    CATHERINE
You better leave.

                    PETER
Another time? Another place?

                    CATHERINE
Another lifetime? Another conference? A new disease? Forget it.
Good night.

She tries to rush him out the door. He pushes his way in.

                    PETER
I'd like to take a flower.

                    CATHERINE
To remember me by? (He nods sweetly) Go ahead. Take a whole
bouquet. Leave the juice pitcher.

He takes a rose.

PETER
I just want a rose to remember this evening.

CATHERINE
Fine. Why don't you take a dozen and create more memory moments.

He pricks himself on the rose stem, sucks on the blood from his wound and rubs the blood on her. He exits to the outside of the door, which she doesn't close as the phone rings. She goes to answer it, leaving the door ajar.

CATHERINE
Oh hello my darling. How are you? Sounds like you're on your cell; we have a fuzzy connection. Where are you? Oh you went out for dinner with John. How nice. I'll be back Sunday night in time for the awards dinner. Bye, Bye Love.

Peter re-enters then closes the door behind him.

Act II. Scene 3. The same living room, next morning. Catherine and Peter are in the bedroom. The alarm goes off. She screams.

CATHERINE
Oh my God, My God!

PETER
No. No! But, I'm the next best thing.

Catherine, naked under her flowing robe, runs to the living room. Peter, wrapped in a blanket follows her.

CATHERINE
You conceited fool! You have to leave.

PETER
Why are you always telling me to leave?

CATHERINE
What's wrong with you? Why don't you ever listen?

PETER
Because I know you only mean half of what you say. I've learned
to read between your lines.

CATHERINE
(Sarcastic)
And you read so well. You're such a bastard.

PETER
Sollocks!

CATHERINE
Sollocks? You remember sollocks from "Private Lives?"

PETER
Yes, whenever Amanda and Elyot got so angry that they were on
the verge of violence one said "sollocks." It was their peace treaty.

CATHERINE
I'm impressed that you know the play I'm working on.

PETER
Yes, I know the play. More importantly I know you.

CATHERINE
We do tend to complete each other's sentences.

PETER
I guess that means that we are each well connected or psychic.

CATHERINE
Probably psychotic. We're doomed.

PETER
It's destiny. Destiny is a worn card and we don't have a complete
deck.

I guess I should head back south to my office and the real world.

CATHERINE
Our world is certainly an illusion, but a pleasant one at times.

PETER
What should we tell Anne and Nicky?

CATHERINE
Let's bide our time. Both of us are great at courtship, lousy at marriage.

PETER
Nick has to wait to Sunday to get his award. I got mine last night.

CATHERINE
It was heavenly, but ephemeral. It will pass. I'm afraid someday we'll be horribly punished for our misdeeds.

PETER
You sound so noble. Shall I find you a nunnery?

CATHERINE
You know there isn't a nunnery with walls high enough to restrain me.

Let's not make any promises to each other. Let's just wait and see how we feel tomorrow.

PETER
Indeed. Tomorrow is another day. Nick seems like such a pleasant guy. Does he play golf?

CATHERINE
You don't play golf.

PETER
Anne was suggesting I take it up.

CATHERINE
You always looked good in caps.

PETER
Maybe the four of us could play.

CATHERINE
Unlikely. One of the big things Nicky and I have in common is our dislike of organized sports. I also don't like a lot of sunshine. The sun does wretched things to one's skin.

PETER
Yes, it...

CATHERINE
No medical reports darling. It is time to leave. Get dressed.

She directs him to the bedroom to get dressed.

PETER
How about breakfast?

CATHERINE
Breakfast? You know I don't do breakfast.. (Pause) I suppose I could make coffee.

PETER
Not your coffee. It's probably been in an open can for years.

CATHERINE
Probably.

PETER
You'll never change.

CATHERINE
I never promised to. With your help I'll age well.

He's almost out the door.

PETER
When will I see you again?

                    CATHERINE
I can't promise anything.

                       PETER
You never could. That's why we got divorced.

                    CATHERINE
That's not why.

                       PETER
Then why?

                    CATHERINE
It's too early to have this tiresome discussion, again.

                       PETER
I'll come back again.

                    CATHERINE
No.

                       PETER
I still have keys.

                    CATHERINE
You gave me back the keys.

                       PETER
After I had copies made.

                    CATHERINE
I'll change the locks.

                       PETER
No you won't, you're too lazy. You promised not to ever change
anything, remember?

He leaves and she goes back to bed.

*Act II Scene 4. Sunday morning. .Laundry room of the condo building. Anne is doing
her wash and reading a paperback book. Nick enters with a small bag of wash, Tide
and his copy of "The Fountainhead."*

                    NICK
Hi Anne, remember me?

                    ANNE
Sure, you were reading that the other day.

                    NICK
I'm a slow reader. Catherine recommended it. It's about
architecture.

                    ANNE
Yes I know it was made into a movie.

                    NICK
Maybe I should rent the video. I can't get into this. It's too dreary.

What are you reading?

                    ANNE
A new volume of Alice Munro's short stories.

                    NICK
Short stories. A good idea. Can you suggest something for me?

                    ANNE
I think you might like Richard Ford. I have a book of his short
stories upstairs that I could lend you.

                    NICK
I remember Peter said you were a teacher. What do you teach?

                    ANNE
English.

                    NICK
I should have figured. High School?

                    ANNE
College.

                    NICK
(Surprised)
Wow!

ANNE

I'm smarter than I look.

NICK

You look great so you must be <u>really</u> smart. PhD?

ANNE

Two.

Her washer stops.

ANNE

Excuse me while I put my clothes in the dryer.

NICK

I better get started with my wash. I have a lot to do. This is a big day for me.

ANNE

Is it your birthday?

NICK

No. I'm getting an architectural award tonight.

ANNE

How exciting! I knew you were brilliant. It's in your eyes.

NICK

Really? Are you psychic?

ANNE

No. I study faces. I like to paint portraits. I also do landscapes. Painting is my hobby.

NICK

Are you working on anything now?

ANNE

Yes, I'm doing a watercolor of the view from my porch. I'm really only an amateur.

NICK

Don't apologize. I sense you are very good at whatever you do.
You're not bold, but ingenious like a fox.

ANNE

(She laughs)
I've never been called a fox before. I'm flattered. You know,
Sunday is my free day. Let me do your wash. I can leave it with
the doorman when I'm done.

NICK

That's very kind of you, but I couldn't ask you…

ANNE

I'm asking you. My pleasure. Our secret.

NICK

All right. But I will owe you a favor. I could use this time to do a
little shopping. Catherine is coming down after her matinee.

ANNE

Oh that's right, she's in previews and will be opening soon.

NICK

Oh yes. The splendor of opening night. (Pause) Thank you for
helping me out.

*He hands her his bag. She touches his hand during the transaction. Their eyes meet.
They laugh. He leaves, turning around to glance at her again before exiting. They
wave as she separates his wash, drops one of his briefs, holds it up and laughs.*

*Act II. Scene 5. Chase condo apartment, late evening. Catherine and Nick enter, both
dressed beautifully. She is holding his plaque/award.*

CATHERINE

Where shall we hang your award?

NICK

We don't have to hang it. I'm not sure it goes with the décor.

She takes down a picture from the wall and replaces it with Nick's plaque.

CATHERINE

Now, like you your award is well hung.

NICK

I guess I'll have to rise to the occasion.

CATHERINE

I am so proud of you. You are the most talented man I have ever
known, in and out of bed. (She kisses him as she speaks)
And your speech was brilliant. What did I do to deserve you?

NICK

Being with you is my prize. Wait until you get your Tony.

CATHERINE

I don't want to think about my show tonight. I'm so worried about
the opening. I need a success. It's been so long.

NICK

Your anxiety doesn't show.

CATHERINE

I'm an actress. I try to wear a happy face and a glowing smile.

NICK

Would you like me to mix a batch of vodka martinis? I
bought a new bottle of Sky today.

CATHERINE

Let me do it, darling. You relax, take your shoes off,
savor this glorious evening.

He obeys. She fixes the drinks as they speak.

CATHERINE

I'm a terrible cook, but a "fantastico" bartender.

NICK
Please go easy on the vodka, darling.

CATHERINE
Don't worry. They'll be smooth. Relax.

NICK
I forgot to tell you that I had a little chat with Anne this morning.

CATHERINE
Anne? Who's that?

NICK
Your ex's wife.

CATHERINE
What's she like?

NICK
Very smart. Two Phd's.

CATHERINE
How could you get past her "butch" haircut and lack of make up.
That woman needs to get a degree at a local beauty school.

NICK
You hardly ever talk about Peter.

CATHERINE
It's poison to talk about former relationships.

NICK
Sorry, I thought maybe people could learn from discussing
problems or issues from old relationships. You're my first wife. I
don't have that
much experience.

CATHERINE
One of the things I adore about you is your innocence.

She pours their martinis. They raise their glasses in a toast.

NICK

Here's to the most beautiful girl in the world.

CATHERINE

Now who could that be? Is she married to the most handsome man?

They kiss. She sips her drink. He practically chokes on his.

NICK

Whow! Too strong!

CATHERINE

Sorry. I can get a little heavy handed.

NICK

I don't think I can manage this. I'll get myself some ginger ale.

CATHERINE

Put it in a martini glass so I don't feel like I'm drinking alone.

He puts down his drink then gets himself some soda that he puts in a martini glass as he speaks.

NICK

Let's plan on staying in New York together on your opening night.

CATHERINE

Absolutely! Then we can go to the opening night party, drink bottles of champagne and not worry about getting a DWI.

NICK

Ever think of joining AA?

CATHERINE

Don't be silly. I'm troublesome in support groups.

She goes to the desk drawer, takes out a small blue box and hands it to him.

NICK
You bought me something from Tiffany's?

CATHERINE
To celebrate tonight... architect of the year!

He opens the box. It is a gold engraved tie clip. He reads the inscription.

NICK
"I thank you God for this amazing day..."
It's from what you read at our wedding.

CATHERINE
E.E.Cummings.

NICK
I'll treasure it always.

CATHERINE
As I'll treasure you my love. To bed!

NICK
Reminds me of how you read that line when I saw you play Lady
Macbeth.

CATHERINE
It was after the Macbeths killed the king.
(She performs)
"To bed. To bed. There's knocking at the gate.
What's done cannot be undone. To bed!"

They run dramatically to the bedroom.

Act 2.Scene 6. Scott apartment, a few days later, dinner time. Anne and Peter are seated at a candle lit dinner table, eating. Anne plays with her food and stares at the phone.

PETER

Why are you staring at the phone?

ANNE

It's one of the time bombs in our life. Any minute now the phone, your cell or pager will go off and there goes our evening.

PETER

I'm a very popular doctor. What do you expect? If I'm not on call, I have my rounds, office, emergencies.

ANNE

Was Catherine jealous of your work?

PETER

I was more jealous of hers. You haven't stopped talking about her since she left us our comps for her show and opening night party.

ANNE

I'm sure she will be excellent in "Private Lives." From what you told me she was born to play an alcoholic sex maniac.

PETER

Catherine probably had her first martini in her mother's womb. Her mother was a lush who read Shakespeare aloud in the nude to sober herself and get her young daughter to sleep. When Catherine was in first grade she told her teacher that she was afraid of the merchant of Venice and was worried she would never find true love because Romeo is dead.

ANNE

Was Catherine ever unfaithful?

PETER

Why don't you ask her? I don't want to discuss Catherine. I want to enjoy this lovely dinner you prepared.

ANNE

I spoke with Nick the other day?

PETER

Nick?

ANNE

Nicholas Chase. Catherine's husband.

PETER

Oh yes, Nicholas, another one of Kate's wind up toys.

ANNE

He's an architect. He designed this building. Remember?

PETER

If she married him he must be good at playing dead.

ANNE

Nick is a very lively and intelligent man. Actually we did more than talk.

Peter seems more concerned than amused.

PETER

What are you trying to tell me?

ANNE

I did his wash. You can learn a lot about a man from his wash.

PETER

You did his wash? I find that absolutely emasculating. How dare you do another man's wash? I don't even want you doing my wash. Send it out like any normal woman.

ANNE

I like doing laundry. It relaxes me.

PETER

Fine. If wash makes you happy, wash away! Did you do Kate's wash too?

ANNE

No. She was in New York working on her show. You certainly know about that.

PETER

Kate's life doesn't concern me. Laundry doesn't concern me. I
need to go.

He puts on his jacket and starts gathering his things.

ANNE

Where are you going? What about dessert?

PETER

I'll get coffee at the hospital. I need to make rounds-see patients.

ANNE

But, I thought you were free tonight. I thought we could talk, have
some wine, watch a movie, relax.

PETER

Another time, dear. (He kisses her forehead) There's a patient I'm
worried about.

ANNE

(Points to herself)
What about me, your old patient? I'm worried about us. What
about the needs of our relationship; our love life?

PETER

I'm no expert in the field of love. I get buried in the manure and
the flowers don't grow.

ANNE

It seems like all our flowers are dying before they see the light.

PETER

I'm too busy for riddles tonight.

ANNE

You said you'd be free tonight.

PETER

I'm never free.

He exits. She takes an umbrella resting by the door and throws it into the room knocking over a vase of flowers. She falls to the floor by the flowers and sobs.

Act 2. Scene 7. The next morning. Chase apartment. Catherine sits on the couch in the living room and picks up her script. Nick enters from the shower wrapped in a towel.

CATHERINE
God, you're in great shape.   What a stud!

NICK
I have a lot of time to work out. (He pulls off her robe) You look pretty great yourself.

CATHERINE
Can I interest you in sharing a shower?

NICK

Love to, darling, but I'm already running late for work.

He heads back to the bedroom to dress. She watches him through the open door.

CATHERINE
I saw how neatly your clean clothes were folded in the dresser.
Did you send your wash out as I suggested?

NICK
I never send anything out. Actually a neighbor in this building did it for me.

CATHERINE
What kind of neighbor would do such a thing? Has our building started some sort of support group in the laundry room?

NICK

Actually, it was Anne.

CATHERINE

Anne as in Peter's hobby?

NICK

Anne, as in Peter's wife. She is a very charming and well
educated lady.

CATHERINE

Does she sit up and beg? Oh, so that little chat you mentioned
yesterday was actually a bonding laundry moment.

NICK

Anne's a kind lady. She had a lot of wash to do and
sensed I was rushed, so she offered to do me a favor.

CATHERINE

Now I guess you owe her a favor. Maybe she needs her plumbing
checked.

NICK

I don't think she expects anything. She's not like that.

CATHERINE

How did you discover she was so well educated? Do you use the
same kind of soap?

NICK

We were chatting after she noticed I was carrying the same Ayn
Rand book I was reading when we met. Did you know that she has
two PhD's?
(She shakes her head) One from Columbia and another from Yale.

CATHERINE

You mentioned her Phd's yesterday. I guess that kind of thing
really impresses you. My tenure at RADA didn't put a glow in
your eye. So Anne is Ms. Ivy league. I'm very impressed. And
now she takes in laundry.

NICK

I'm sorry. I didn't think it would upset you.

CATHERINE

Maybe she can do my wash sometime. (She laughs)
I wonder what Peter would say if he knew his pristine bride was
fondling your dirty underwear?

NICK

(Shrugs his shoulders)
You'd know his response better than I. (Pause) When are you
going up to New York?

CATHERINE

Before noon.

NICK

You don't need to be at the theater until 6 PM.

CATHERINE

Monday is my only day off for previews. When I get back to the
City I'd like to take a little nap before I go to the theater.

He enters the living room dressed.

NICK

Are you going to tell Peter?

CATHERINE

Why? This is all so stupid; a waste of energy.

NICK

I'm sorry I mentioned Anne. I was in a hurry. Maybe a little
lonely.
She was being neighborly, friendly.

CATHERINE

Enough of Anne and your laundry! I need to focus on doing my
best during the previews and knocking out the critics on opening
night.

NICK

Stop worrying. It's less than a week to your opening night. You'll be wonderful. You are wonderful.

CATHERINE

You are my best man. For now, I'm off to the shower. I'll call you tonight when I get home from the theater.

NICK

(To himself)
Best man? I'm the groom. (To her) I'll miss you!

She picks up her robe and throws him a kiss as she heads towards the bedroom's bath. He looks sad, as if the kiss flew by him. He leaves.

Act 3. Scene 1. The laundry room of the condo building, a little over a week later. Anne is knitting. Catherine enters with two small bags of wash. Anne looks surprised.

ANNE

Hi Catherine. I never thought I'd run into you down here.

CATHERINE

I need a few clean things to take back to the City and I have no time to send out.

ANNE

It's a comfortable place.

CATHERINE

Did you move in down here?

ANNE

No. I just have a lot of wash. Peter changes his clothes three times a day.

CATHERINE

(Looks at Anne's knitting)
Nice tight stitches. There's no end to your talents.

ANNE

Or yours. You were great in the play.

CATHERINE

Thank you. Did you and Peter enjoy the opening night party?

ANNE

Oh, yes. Thank you so much. I loved meeting so many celebrities and press people.

CATHERINE

I find so many of those people tiring, but I guess I'm one of them now.

ANNE

Oh, definitely. I bet you'll get a Tony for your performance.

CATHERINE

Stranger things have happened.

ANNE

I guess Nick told you about his wash.

CATHERINE

My husband can afford to send his wash out. I always sent your husband's wash out.

ANNE

I guess I'm more frugal than you. I prefer doing it myself.

CATHERINE

And you do it so well.

ANNE

I guess you're heading back to New York? (Catherine nods) I'm sorry about Nick's wash. I didn't mean to cause trouble. He just seemed hassled, eager to get to work.

CATHERINE

Oh! I thought nothing of it! (Pause) You seem to spend a lot of time down here. I thought you worked at being a teacher or something.

ANNE

Or something. I'm a college professor. My schedule varies day to
day.
I don't have any early classes.

CATHERINE

Well I need to get back to New York this afternoon. I have a
performance tonight.

ANNE

I'd be happy to… Oh no, no. I better not offer.

CATHERINE

(Laughs. Then extends her hand.)
I forgive you. (Pause) Look, I'm sorry Anne. I guess it makes me
jealous to hear of some other woman washing my husband's briefs.

ANNE

I understand. Peter wasn't happy either.

CATHERINE

You told Peter? (Laughs) I can't believe that.

ANNE

I won't do it again.

CATHERINE

Thank you. I'm not the domestic type, but I'm not immune to hard
work.
I've worked since I was sixteen. Some people think theatre is fun
and games. It's not; it's very demanding. As Stanislavski said,
"Talent is hard work."

ANNE

I guess I was more fortunate. I didn't work until I finished my first PhD.

CATHERINE

So you had a privileged childhood.

ANNE

I guess so. I was an only spoiled child. Peter told me that you worked to help put him through medical school.

CATHERINE

It's an old story that has been played out many times. Wife puts husband through school, then once he makes it he puts her through hell.

ANNE

I'm sorry.

CATHERINE

So am I.

ANNE

If you need to do anything now you can leave your wash in the machine and I'll watch it.

CATHERINE

Actually I do have some things to take care of upstairs, if you don't mind. This is my first trip down here. Do I need to give you coins?

ANNE

No, it's free. It should be done in about twenty minutes. If you're not back I'll throw it in the dryer. It should all be done in less than an hour.

CATHERINE

Thank you. I do appreciate your help and apologize for snapping at you. (Anne shrugs it off)
I'll be back within the hour.

Catherine exits. Anne checks the machines and goes back to her knitting.

Act 3. Scene 2. Chase apartment, that evening. Nick is watching "Jeopardy." The doorbell rings. He answers it, but tries to stay focused on the show. Anne is at the door carrying two covered bowls.

NICK

Anne. What a surprise.

ANNE

Peter got called to the hospital tonight and I know
Catherine is in New York, so I thought I'd take a chance and bring
over dinner for two lonely hearts.

NICK

How thoughtful. I love home cooking.

He shuts off the TV, switches on the stereo, and puts in a Mozart CD while she heads to the kitchen and puts one of the bowls in the microwave and the salad on the dining table.

ANNE

I love to cook. I especially like to cook for others.
Actually I made my famous shrimp scampi over angel
hair pasta.

NICK

I love scampi. What a treat! I have Chardonnay and Rose wine.

ANNE

Chardonnay is perfect. Do you have balsamic vinegar?

NICK

I'm afraid all we have in terms of condiments relate to
mixed drinks or canapes.

He looks at the salad on the table.

> NICK-CONT.

What a beautiful salad. Arugala too.

> ANNE

I guess you don't have extra virgin olive oil.

> NICK

Catherine abhors virgin anything.

> ANNE

I'll run down the hall and get the oil and vinegar. Do we need
anything else? Sea salt and peppercorn mill?

Nick nods.

> NICK

So sorry. If you don't mind fetching those things I'll be
happy to set the table and open the wine.

*Anne smiles and scoots out the door. Nick starts setting the table and takes the wine
out of the fridge. Then he has a thought, sets down the wine and dials the phone.*

> NICK

Yes, I'd like a dozen yellow roses. Could they be delivered ASAP?
Great.

He takes a credit card out of his wallet.

> NICK

100 Ocean Avenue penthouse 1. Thank you. My credit card is
Visa, account number 111-234-7788. Expires eight zero eight.
Thank you so much.

*He opens the wine and puts finishing touches on the table as Anne rings doorbell
with her shopping bag filled with necessities. They quickly complete preparations. He
heads to his entertainment center and shows her his CD collection.*

NICK

What kind of music do you like?

ANNE

I like Mozart, on a lower volume would be nice.

He adjusts the stereo then sits next to her.

NICK

I'm sorry I didn't ask if you wanted a cocktail. I just thought
scampi-wine.

ANNE

I'm not crazy about hard liquor cocktails. I prefer wine.
These are beautiful glasses. Mikasa?

NICK

Baccarat. Catherine loves beautiful things-the best.

ANNE

I appreciate beauty, but I also have a sense of economy. I found
wonderful red and white wine glasses at Pottery Barn on sale.

NICK

You sound like a sensible lady. Does Peter also prefer wine?

ANNE

Peter will drink anything. Sometimes he mixes red and white
wine at dinner. I couldn't do that. That would give me a terrible
headache. I get migraines.

NICK

Really? Me too. Sounds like we have a lot in common.

ANNE

How do you feel about pets?

She serves him as they speak.

NICK

I always had a dog growing up. I had a cat while I was living alone. A black Persian named Midnight. The cat and Catherine didn't get along.

ANNE

Ah. What did you do?

NICK

We put an ad in the paper. Found him a home in one day.

ANNE

Oh, I'm so sorry. (Pause) Do you have any children?

NICK

No. This is my first marriage. Do you have any?

ANNE

No, but I really want a baby. My biological clock is ticking like a metronome in double time.

NICK

Maybe you'll have twins.

ANNE

I would love that. Peter's not crazy about kids.

NICK

Neither is Catherine. She's into her career and takes the pill. She knows I want a child someday, someone to carry on my name and inherit all my architectural tools.

ANNE

I was an only child. My parents are gone. I hardly have any family.

NICK

I understand. What are you going to do?

ANNE

I stopped the pill. Peter doesn't know. He hasn't asked and we are married after all.

NICK

Of course. Most people get married to start a family.

The doorbell rings. Nick runs to the door. It's the flowers. He tips the delivery man and hands the flowers to Anne.

ANNE

I don't know what to say.

NICK

Yellow roses mean friendship.

She gets teary eyed, kisses him on the cheek.

ANNE

They are so beautiful. I'll have to get a vase.

NICK

I have something you can use then switch to a vase when you get home.

He goes to the kitchen and takes a plastic water bottle from the recycling container. He takes a knife, cuts the top to make the opening wider, fills the bottle with water then sets it on the table.

ANNE

Stunning! You are so inventive and creative. I can understand why you became an architect. Look how even you cut the top of the bottle. You have a good eye.

NICK
I was an Art History major in College. I'd appreciate seeing your paintings sometime.

ANNE
I'd be honored. Most of them are sort of dark, not beautiful.

NICK
You have a beautiful smile. May I propose a toast?

ANNE
Please. Propose.

They lift their wineglasses, entwine their arms and toast.

NICK
Here's to friends!

Their crystal glasses chime.

ANNE
Friends!

He moves his chair closer to her. He accidently spills wine on her shoulder. They giggle. He dries her shoulder with his napkin. Their eyes meet. They kiss.

Act 3. Scene 3. NYC apartment. Catherine has furniture arranged for her scene and is working on her lines.

CATHERINE
"It was my fault. I'm terribly sorry, darling."

Knock at the door. It's a Chinese food delivery. She tips the person, puts bag on the table and gets back to her lines.

CATHERINE

(Louder than before)

"It was my fault. I'm terribly sorry, darling."

Knock at door. She opens it and it's Peter.

PETER

(Dramatic)

I forgive you my darling.

CATHERINE

I'm reviewing my script, not my life.

PETER

Your apology sounded so sincere and clear through that locked door.

CATHERINE

Everything sounds better behind a locked door. What are you doing here?

PETER

I know you want to see me.

CATHERINE

Why? Why can't you leave me alone?

PETER

Let's play! Let's pretend!

CATHERINE

Let's not. (She opens door) I'm working and you need to leave. You can listen to me rehearse from the other side of this door.

PETER

Why can't we work together? I can read opposite you while you rehearse.

You can work off of me.

CATHERINE

You never wanted to rehearse with me when we were married.

Why now?

PETER

We both love the lure of the forbidden, the magic when wills are free and passion soars.

CATHERINE

If I can't get rid of you, take the script and read Elyot. (She hands him the script and points to the starting point.) I have my lines down, but I like to refresh them everyday, like watering flowers.

PETER

(Some confusion)
"Sollocks!" (Pause) Then there's all this stage direction.

CATHERINE

Just read the dialogue. You should know better. Let's start again.

PETER

'Sollocks!" That's such a stupid word.

CATHERINE

Who cares what you think? Just read the lines.

PETER

Sorry. I do know the play. I just wanted to find the right emotional subtext.

CATHERINE

Think surrender. You want to stop quarreling.

PETER

I see.

CATHERINE

Don't see. Read!

PETER

(Gets back to the script)
"Sollocks!"

(He sits next to her in silence. They both sigh.)
"That was a near thing."

CATHERINE
"It was my fault. I'm terribly sorry, darling."

PETER
"I was very irritating. I know I was. I'm sure Victor was awfully nice, and you're perfectly right to be sweet about him."

CATHERINE
"That's downright handsome of you. Sweetheart!" (She kisses him.)

PETER
"I think I love you more than ever before. Isn't it ridiculous?"

She takes script out of his hands and stands up.

CATHERINE
This isn't working.

PETER
Maybe it's working too well. Coward's lines mirror our lives.

We're getting intimate and you're scared.

CATHERINE
That's ridiculous. You have no grasp of the character, which is curbing my motivation in the scene.

PETER
Are you saying I'm a bad actor?

CATHERINE
You're like a robot. Words pour out of your mouth like motor oil.

PETER
I'm just trying to help.

CATHERINE
It's good you went to medical school. You're a terrible actor.

PETER

I never promised you a role model. Let's go back to our private lives.

CATHERINE

Mine and yours, not ours.

PETER

Why won't you let me help?

CATHERINE

You can help me by leaving.

PETER

Why are you always telling me to leave? We know you don't mean it.

CATHERINE

Go home! (She tries leading him to the door. He heads to the table.)

PETER

Actually I'm hungry and this Chinese food smells so good. (He opens the bag and takes out the cartons.)

CATHERINE

All right, I'll feed you then you go home. (She goes to the kitchen and brings back plates, spoons and chopsticks.)

PETER

You know I can't use chopsticks. Where are the forks?

CATHERINE

In the dishwasher.

PETER

How long?

CATHERINE

(Shrugs her shoulders)
No idea. I can't remember the last time I turned it on.

PETER

You are such a slob.

CATHERINE

(Angered)
Coming from you that's a compliment. You're a pig!

PETER

Is that why you're serving slop?

CATHERINE

I'm not serving anything. Help yourself. You can either wash a fork or use a spoon.

PETER

You were always a lousy hostess. At our parties you held court, hired waiters and never moved from your throne.

CATHERINE

I'm an actress. I need a spotlight.

PETER

I wouldn't face too bright a light, your audience may focus on your wrinkles more than your lines.

CATHERINE

(Takes a spoon of egg foo young and throws it in his face)
Look who has egg on his face.

PETER

(He takes a hand full of rice and rubs it on her face)
This will help your complexion.

CATHERINE

You're lucky I didn't order soup.

They continue to fling food at each other. When they exhaust each other they stop and stare at each other like looking in a mirror.

PETER

I can't go home like this.

CATHERINE

Tell your wife you were so eager for take out food that you decided to wear it.

PETER

Life with you was one big food orgy.

CATHERINE

And I got food poisoning.

PETER

I'm so confused. You're like chocolate. I can't resist it. Then it rots my teeth and makes me constipated.

CATHERINE

You're like white bread. You rise well, but no substance.

PETER

Sollocks! Sollocks!

CATHERINE

Now you grasp the word. By the time you know your lines the audience would have left the theater.

PETER

Fine, you want to win. Win! I'm rotten, shallow, selfish, arrogant and jaded.

CATHERINE

Don't forget sloppy.

PETER

No, sloppy is you.

CATHERINE

Fine. Now leave.

PETER

How can I face my wife like this?

CATHERINE

Love is blind. She won't notice your menu. Now leave.

PETER

You sure you don't want to decorate me with more food? How about chocolate syrup? Then you can lick it off me.

CATHERINE

Stop it! You know we can't be together. I can't live with you.

PETER

I can't live without you.

CATHERINE

You are living without me. Remember our past?

PETER

You need to project yourself into the future, not let the future impose the past on you.

CATHERINE

I'm tired of your double-talk, double entendres and double life. You can't come here anymore.

PETER

I can, but I won't, if that's what you really want.

CATHERINE

Yes, that's what I really want.
(She opens door for him to leave.)

PETER

Good night. This is the end!

CATHERINE

Good riddance. The END!

(She slams the door behind him.)

Act 3. Scene 4. Scott apartment, a few days later. Anne is dressed in a suit, ready to leave for work. Peter is still in his pajamas.

PETER

I never know what to do on my day off.

ANNE

You can always find a medical conference to attend.

PETER

Actually there is another one in New York today.

ANNE

Do New York hotels cater to anything but medical conferences?

PETER

They're important to my education and career.

ANNE

You could go to the gym. You're getting a gut.

PETER

What's wrong? You're not yourself today. Why don't you call in
sick then we can play. I could write you a note.

ANNE

I have an important meeting this morning. You should notice that
I never go to work this early. And then there's my Chaucer class.
We always talk about your work. We never discuss mine.

He follows her around the room as she gets ready to leave. She avoids eye contact.

PETER

I'm sorry... Anything you'd like me to pick up for dinner?

ANNE

I hate take out.

She notices that the yellow roses on the coffee table are wilted.

PETER

I'm just trying to make life a little easier for you.

ANNE
(Picks up vase and heads to the kitchen)
I better throw these away.

PETER
(Sarcastic)
You could dry them and make an arrangement for the laundry room.

ANNE

Maybe.

She goes to the kitchen with flowers and brings back a travel mug with coffee, then organizes her briefcase. He's disappointed that she didn't get him coffee. He gets himself coffee and returns.

PETER
What's wrong? You seem hostile.

ANNE
I'm not hostile, just worried. I never see you. I didn't get married to feel lonely.

PETER
What does that mean? You feel lonely, so you take in wash for company?

ANNE
I know I'm not the most exciting woman in the world, but I do have feelings.

PETER
What do you want from me?

ANNE

Monogamy.

PETER
What's on your mind?

ANNE

You know that night a few weeks ago when you said you had a cardiology conference in New York?

PETER

Yes, I stayed at the Marriott.

ANNE

Really? I called there several times. I also called your cell phone, which was off.

PETER

I always turn my phone off when I'm at a meeting or asleep.

ANNE

I asked someone from the hotel to check your room; see if you were all right. I was afraid you could have had a heart attack or something.

PETER

Are you trying to say that you don't trust me?

ANNE

What I'm trying to say is when the clerk checked your room at 11 PM, you weren't there and your bed wasn't slept in.

PETER

I can't believe you called the hotel. I can't believe the hotel clerk would go check my room. Aren't they supposed to respect the privacy of their paying customers. What did you say?

ANNE

I said you were prone to heart failure.

PETER

Very funny. What are you getting at?

ANNE

Were you with Catherine?

PETER

Why would I be with Catherine?

ANNE

Why not?

PETER

I don't know what to say. You obviously don't trust me.

ANNE

You've referred to trust a lot today. Guilty conscience?

PETER

The grand inquisition. Is this what our marriage will be like?

ANNE

No. More like a civil war.

PETER

What do you want me to say?

ANNE

How about the truth; it will surface someday.

PETER

Like the body of someone who has drowned.

ANNE

Did you drown?

PETER

No. I've just gone in over my head. I'm sorry.

ANNE

Does that mean you slept with her?

PETER

Maybe once?

ANNE

Maybe. Once. Don't you know? You were probably there other
times, like the night you came home smelling like expensive
perfume and soy sauce.

PETER

It doesn't matter. It has nothing to do with us.

ANNE

You were unfaithful to me. That's about us.

PETER

All right. I'm caught. I'm sorry.

ANNE

Sorry? You're sorry? We're not even married a year. This shouldn't happen to us.

PETER

It's my problem. I don't want to hurt you. I can't help myself.

ANNE

(Tries to look him in the face)
Why?

PETER

(Resists her)
Time is so precious. I see death around me all the time. I see people who have lost loved ones clasp the hand of their lover for the last time. I try to see into the eyes of the one left living and all I witness is the blank stare of grief. Their future lives in the stolen memories of the past.

ANNE

Why do you want to steal precious memories from me?

PETER

I don't want to hurt you. If I stay with you I will hurt you. I can't be faithful. You deserve better.

ANNE

Why can't you be happy with just me? I put my life in your hands.

PETER

Don't do that. Don't say things like that. Keep your life in your hands and find someone worthy to hold hands with. I really wanted to change for you. I just couldn't.

ANNE

You're telling me you refuse to be faithful.

PETER

I tried. Believe it or not in our short marriage I tried, but I can't help myself. Every time I see an attractive interesting woman I want to get to know her. I want to get to her soul through her body.

ANNE

On the way you might do a nose job or a tummy tuck.

PETER

Sometimes. Sometimes it's just an afternoon.

ANNE

Can you imagine how this makes me feel?

PETER

I can't. I'm sorry.

ANNE

We got married too fast. We didn't really know each other.

PETER

I knew you would be good for me. You're a nurturer. I'm a child emotionally.

ANNE

I want a real child, not a man/child.

PETER

Believe me, I really wanted this to work. I thought you would bring order and constancy to my life.

ANNE

I have, but you don't want it. I give; you take. Our foundation is crumbling and we're falling apart.

PETER

(He goes to embrace her. She withdraws.)
Look, why don't we give us another try, erase the past, settle my debt.

ANNE

You can't erase emotional debt. I need you to pack up and leave.

PETER

I have nowhere to go. (Beat) I do care about you. (Beat) I'm confused.

ANNE

You can't keep promises. What about our wedding vows?

PETER

Keys to the kingdom. I'll work on trying to change. You are such a nice sensible woman. I need you. No one ever took care of me before. I told you how my mother was a space case who lived on tranquilizers and scotch. We've never had a lucid conversation let alone tenderness and affection.

ANNE

I'm sorry about your childhood. I can't fix that. Have you thought of therapy?

PETER

I don't have time for that.

ANNE

Maybe you should make time.

PETER

I did try therapy once. It didn't work for me. I tend to manipulate the conversation away from my issues and feelings and the shrink couldn't bring me back. It's sort of like being lost in space without retro- rockets.

ANNE

Now you're sinking. Maybe you should rent a submarine. I can't solve your problems and you don't want to. I can't live without trust.

PETER

I can't believe you're throwing me out.

ANNE

Believe it! I don't care where you park your baggage as long as it's not here. I can afford this place on my own.

PETER

What about the deposit I gave you from my house in Rumson?

ANNE

I'll sell some stock and send you a check.

PETER

Seems like your MBA came in handy.

ANNE

Yes, that with my PhD in English should provide me with enough poetic allusions to cope with my pain.

PETER

I am sorry. I do care about you.

ANNE

Care? What does that mean to you? How do you show it? Do you love me?

PETER

I thought I loved you. I believed I made you happy. I just don't know. We had good sex, didn't we?

ANNE

Sex and love are the heart valves of true intimacy. You still need a brain, muscle, vision and a soul. Partners must put the needs of the other first. It's like your BMW needs more than an engine to run properly. (Beat) Well, I have to go to work now. I'll be back around eight tonight. I hope you'll be all out by then.

PETER

I really don't have much.

ANNE

Good, then you'll be out sooner.

She exits. He seems lost, starts gathering his things.

Act 3 Scene 5. Chase apartment, moments later. Catherine enters the front door as Nick is about to leave. They almost collide. She is taking off her coat as he puts his on.

CATHERINE
I was hoping we could spend the day together.

NICK
Why didn't you call?

CATHERINE
I thought you'd be happy to see me.

NICK
I have a job in Rumson to check on.

CATHERINE
Do you have to leave this minute?

NICK
I guess not. I don't have an appointment.

CATHERINE
I used to live in Rumson.

NICK
I know. This isn't about you.

CATHERINE
Can I go with you? It's Monday; I have the whole day free.

NICK
No. This is important. I need to focus and write up some plans.

She leads him to take off his coat and sit on the couch.

CATHERINE
Do you want me to spend the day all alone?

NICK
I spend a lot of days and nights alone while you work.

CATHERINE
Maybe I should just get a few of my things and go back to New York?

NICK

Maybe. Whatever you want.

CATHERINE

What's wrong?

NICK

What's right? We're never together. Now that your show's opened
and running strong I hardly see you and when I call you at night
when you're finally home from the theatre you're either too tired
to talk or have your machine on which I guess means you went to
bed.

CATHERINE

What are you trying to say?

NICK

For one thing I can understand why Peter married Anne.

CATHERINE

What?

She stands and upstages him. She paces as she talks.

NICK

Anne came over here the other night. She's a very compassionate
woman. We had a nice dinner.

CATHERINE

Why?

NICK

Why not?

CATHERINE

You're married.

NICK

That never stopped you.

CATHERINE
What are you getting at?

NICK
Did you meet Peter in New York?

CATHERINE
What are you talking about?

NICK
Did you spend time with Peter while you were "working" in New York?

CATHERINE
Maybe once, but it was nothing.

He stands as they confront each other.

NICK
What is something to you? What about our marriage? What about me?

What about us? Everything's a game with you. Play.

CATHERINE
You know that I love you.

NICK
How do I know that?

She tries to embrace him. He retreats.

CATHERINE
I'm here.

NICK
For five minutes? A marriage isn't five minutes a couple of times a week. A marriage is a lifetime commitment. Whenever you're not on stage you should be with me.

CATHERINE

Are you saying you resent my career, my New York apartment?

NICK

Your career! You're apartment! What about our lives?

CATHERINE

What do you want from me?

NICK

I don't know. Maybe a trial separation. Though I guess we've been having that instead of a honeymoon.

CATHERINE

You knew I'd be working on a show.

NICK

I trusted you and you disappointed me.

CATHERINE

What about you? How do you know so much about Anne? Have you done more than laundry together?

NICK

We've done more than that.

CATHERINE

Really? What? Bingo?

NICK

She made me dinner while you were in New York and Peter was at the hospital.

CATHERINE

How cozy.

NICK

Yes it was. She's a real woman.

CATHERINE

What am I "goosey" liver?

>   NICK
You can do better than that.

>   CATHERINE
I can do better than you.

She notices he's wearing the tie- pin she gave him. She rips it off of him and throws it out the glass balcony doors. He's startled, shocked.

>   NICK
Perhaps I should move out.

>   CATHERINE
No. I'll go back to New York. I'll give you more time to think, see if we miss each other.

>   NICK
Maybe we will miss each other.

>   CATHERINE
And maybe we won't. I guess I should leave.

He looks out the window, away from her.

>   NICK
I knew your dramatic life came first. I just didn't want to believe it.

>   CATHERINE
I don't know what to say.

>   NICK
Do you need a script to express your feelings?

>   CATHERINE
I do have feelings for you. My work always interferes with my relationships. I try to keep the two separate, but my roles get confused with my life. Right now I'm consumed by the play.

NICK
Our play or "Private Lives."

CATHERINE
I don't know. Please give me some time to think.

NICK
I do admire your work, but I want a wife.

CATHERINE
I want to be your wife. I just don't know how. I'm sorry.

NICK
I know you are. Let's see what time brings or takes away.

CATHERINE
So, this is our first fight and a trial separation?

He turns to look at her. She reaches out. He doesn't move.

NICK
Yes. Maybe we'll get back together. Maybe we'll miss each other.

CATHERINE
I hope we miss each other. I do.

She picks up the bag she brought and heads to the door. She tries to hold back tears. He stares at her, frozen.

CATHERINE
I'm going downstairs. Could you call me a cab?

He doesn't answer. Catherine opens the door. There is a moment of silence between them. He turns back to look out the window.

CATHERINE
"Good night sweet prince..."

He doesn't respond. Another moment of silence.

                CATHERINE

Enjoy the view.

She leaves. A moment later there is a knock at the door. He answers it. It is Anne in tears. She falls into his arms.

Act 3. Scene 6. Lobby, moments later. Catherine, looking forlorn, is waiting with her bags as Peter passes her with his suitcase. She kicks one of her bags in his way. He trips and their eyes meet.

                PETER

Going my way?

                CATHERINE

Another conference?

                PETER

Another casualty. I just don't know how to behave.

                CATHERINE

You don't know how to be married.

                PETER

Neither do you.

She nods agreement. He sits opposite her.

                CATHERINE

So you and what's her name couldn't make it?

                PETER

Anne is disappointed in me. She wants a man capable of honoring a commitment.

CATHERINE

That's what most women want. You and I are weapons of mass destruction. Nick is devastated. Somehow he knew you and I met in New York.

PETER

Big deal. Our whims don't impact world peace. In the big scope of things our behavior doesn't matter. What matters to me is us. Why did our marriage end?

CATHERINE

You keep asking me the same question.

PETER

I need an answer. Why did our marriage end?

CATHERINE

Because you could never be faithful. That's why I married Nick. I knew I could trust him. I really wanted him. I need his stability to balance.

PETER

But he doesn't need you. He's learned he can't trust you.

CATHERINE

Big problem. I may have to change.

PETER

But you know you can't.

CATHERINE

I'll work to change. I will. I will change.

PETER

What if you can't? What will you do?

CATHERINE

I'll just keep working. I'll work until they carry me off stage in a body bag.

PETER

Then I'll perform the autopsy.

CATHERINE
What makes you think I'll die before you?

PETER
Don't worry, our spirits will live on until we get "it" right.

CATHERINE
That will give us a lot of time. I wonder if you can ever really
settle down. I wonder if your womanizing will fade as you get
older and can't run as fast or dodge a bullet...

PETER
Or a vase. (They both laugh.) We had some wild fights.

CATHERINE
I really don't want to grow old alone.

PETER
We're aging and wasting time just standing here. How about a lift
to the train?

CATHERINE
I told Nicky to call me a cab.

PETER
Maybe he didn't hear you.

CATHERINE
Poor Nicky. He's such a sweet man. Why can't I appreciate a
kind, normal guy like him? Why do I always get sucked-in to
neurotic, selfish fools like you?

PETER
Simple, because you are a neurotic selfish fool yourself.

CATHERINE
We're not the same.

PETER
Oh heavens no, but we complement each other so well.

CATHERINE
Like Bonnie and Clyde.

PETER

Or Amanda and Elyot?

CATHERINE

Back to "Private Lives."

PETER

I know you need to get back to that bloody play. Our drama has bursting stars rather than Coward's mere fireworks.

CATHERINE

Now we're both burned out; buried in the ashes of our private lives.

PETER

Destiny.

CATHERINE

My cab is coming.

PETER

I need to get going too.

CATHERINE

Funny how tonight you'll really be staying in the doctor's lounge or a hotel.

PETER

Real funny, except right now I feel stranded, lonely... and older.

He picks up his suitcase and heads out the door.

PETER

Have a long run of your play, more roles to conquer; a wonderful life..

CATHERINE

You too. Take care. Peter?

PETER

Yes?

                    CATHERINE
Will you come back to see my show again?

                    PETER
Sure, I'm one of your biggest fans. I always love the closing night
party.

Will you invite me?

The cab arrives and Catherine heads out the door behind Peter.

                    CATHERINE
Sure. (Beat) Here's my ride. Ciao!

                    PETER
You know if you give me a minute I can put our bags in my car
and take you to New York.

                    CATHERINE
You are not taking refuge with me.

                    PETER
I wouldn't think of it. Actually I just remembered a conference I
could go to today at the Hilton.

*He gives the cab driver some money and tells him to go. He picks up their bags. She
follows him.*

                    CATHERINE
Another day, another conference.

                    PETER
Live for today, tomorrow we'll compromise.

                    CATHERINE
Compromise? Peter, do you miss me?

                    PETER
Not at this moment. You're here!

CATHERINE
We're both here because we've been tossed out on our private lives.

PETER
I must confess, I did miss you. (He moves closer to her.)

CATHERINE
What did you miss? The fighting, sparing, cocktails, sex?

PETER
Yes. (He kisses her.)

CATHERINE
Seriously. What do you miss about me?

PETER
Mystery. There's a certain mystery about you I just can't solve.

CATHERINE
And you never will.

PETER
You're like the Sphinx, masked with riddles.

CATHERINE
Do you love the actress or the woman?

PETER
Okay. You win. I love the actress and the woman. (Pause) What do you want?

CATHERINE
What does anybody want?

PETER
A happy ending?

CATHERINE
A love story with an intermission?

PETER

Our final curtain?

CATHERINE

Want to give it another try?

PETER

We never stop trying. It might be fun growing old together.

CATHERINE

Are you up to the challenge?

PETER

Do you think this time we can get it right?

CATHERINE

Can we keep promises to each other?

PETER

I promise to love, honor and obey you.

CATHERINE

I can love you, but cut the honor and obey part.

PETER

I'll cut whatever makes you unhappy. Would you like some blood?

CATHERINE

I have your blood. I want your heart.

PETER

(He exposes his chest.)
Rip it out.

CATHERINE

I love you. I wish I didn't, but I can't help myself.

PETER

Let's help each other.

She kisses him.

CATHERINE

Can you see our names in lights?

PETER

Like you, I love bright lights, applause and rave reviews.

CATHERINE

First we need to rehearse.

PETER

Savor our lines, perfect our blocking, live in the moment.

CATHERINE

Until... the end.

He puts his arm around her and they slowly dance away.

End

www.ingramcontent.com/pod-product-compliance
Lightning Source LLC
Chambersburg PA
CBHW020720180526
45163CB00001B/42